Small States and Segmented Societies

edited by
Stephanie G. Neuman

The Praeger Special Studies program—
utilizing the most modern and efficient book
production techniques and a selective
worldwide distribution network—makes
available to the academic, government, and
business communities significant, timely
research in U.S. and international economic, social, and political development.

Small States and Segmented Societies
National Political Integration in a Global Environment

PRAEGER SPECIAL STUDIES IN INTERNATIONAL POLITICS AND GOVERNMENT

Praeger Publishers New York Washington London

Library of Congress Cataloging in Publication Data
Main entry under title:

Small states and segmented societies.

   (Praeger special studies in international politics and
government)
   Includes bibliographical references and index.
   1. States, Small. 2. Allegiance. 3. Ethnic
groups. 4. International relations. I. Neuman,
Stephanie Glicksberg.
JC365.S57   327   75-23986
ISBN 0-275-55730-8

PRAEGER PUBLISHERS
111 Fourth Avenue, New York, N.Y. 10003, U.S.A.

Published in the United States of America in 1976
by Praeger Publishers, Inc.

Printed in the United States of America

To my mother and father

PREFACE

    The essays included in this volume passed through several stages of development. Five were originally delivered on a panel sponsored by the Divided Nations Internet of the Comparative International Studies Association, which was held February 19-22, 1975, in Washington, D.C. The theme of the panel was "The Impact of Systemic Factors on National Political Integration." After the conference the editor asked a few additional people to contribute to the symposium. Sections of two essays appeared in periodicals prior to publication here and a third—on Bangladesh—was, at the request of the editor, prepared especially for this collection. However, either by incorporating suggestions and criticisms received in Washington, D.C., or by adhering to an outline distributed by the editor after the conference, all the writers substantially revised, and in most instances entirely rewrote, their essays for publication in this volume.

    The editor is grateful to Fred Riggs for his part in making this project possible. The formation of the Comparative Interdisciplinary Studies Section under his leadership was instrumental in bringing together an interdisciplinary group such as ours—we are composed of political scientists, a sociologist, a historian, an anthropologist, and an international development administration expert—with a common interest in a given subject so that a fruitful exchange of ideas could take place. Fred Riggs also warmly encouraged the idea of bringing these essays together in published form. The editor and the authors, however, accept full responsibility for the contents of this volume.

    The editor would also like to thank her husband, Herbert Neuman, for his patience and support throughout the project.

CONTENTS

Chapter

Chapter

INTRODUCTION

The traditional ideal model of the nation-state is a political unit that is homogeneous—one in which the members share a common culture, language, and history. Although such polities are commonly referred to in social science textbooks as "integrated" states, they are rare in the real world. As Walker Conner has pointed out, "of a total of 132 contemporary states, only 12 (9.1 percent) can be described as essentially homogeneous from an ethnic viewpoint."[1] Yet until very recently integration theorists held that heterogeneous states were unnatural and inherently unstable. States characterized by social and political cleavages would eventually move toward greater homogeneity and consensus or cease to exist as viable political units. Assimilation was not only the desired and natural outcome of inter-group relations but the sine qua non of political stability.

But today, as parochial consciousness is increasing throughout the world and divisions are reappearing in new guises, assimilation and social homogeneity do not appear to be the dominant trend. The assimilationist model has proven inadequate to the task of explaining and predicting not only the dynamics of group relations but also the significance of those relations for the structure and functioning of the state. Theorists are unable to tell us how and why parochial identity becomes important at different historical periods. Why do groups begin to feel separate from each other at one point of time and united at another? What determines when large segments of a population are no longer satisfied with the existing sociopolitical arrangement? Furthermore, the traditional theory does not indicate when these dissatisfactions imperil the viability of the state. Why in some countries are divisions highly politicized to a degree that threatens the survival of the political unit or the groups themselves, while in others political tension and conflict between groups do not seem to arise?

In response to this lack of theoretical progress, a number of social scientists are beginning to question the validity of some of the earlier assumptions and approaches. They are questioning whether the condition of social homogeneity or fragmentation is in fact an independent variable determining the way a polity operates. Perhaps it is a dependent variable—the product of other internal or international political, economic, and social forces.

The studies in this volume are representative of the spirit of revaluation that is growing steadily today in the fields of comparative and international politics. Although it is not our purpose here to

offer an analytical model or to provide a set of propositic
national political integration, this collection does repre.
attempt to break out of the traditionally accepted paradigm tha.
dominated integration research in the past, in order to search for
new approaches to the study of integration.

First, because the evidence indicates that division of one
sort or another is characteristic of a majority of human societies,
the line of inquiry is not to question the extent of homogeneity existing
in any political unit, but rather to ask how and why societies succeed
(or fail) in regulating their affairs effectively. As a guideline, and
for purposes of discussion, integration is defined as a measure not
of social homogeneity but of the ability of a political unit to conduct
its important and necessary business without disaffecting large
bodies of its constituents (so they are no longer willing to have their
affairs regulated by or to participate in the particular system). The
focus, then is upon (1) the role various internal institutions, such as
the government, the economy, the educational system, and religion
play in alienating or accommodating important parts of the population
and (2) the impact international events and forces have upon these
processes.

Second, the essays in this volume set out to examine a group
of variables generally overlooked in the field of integration studies
in general and in national political integration literature in particular,
namely, the effect of international environmental factors upon the
process of consolidation and accommodation within national political
units. The authors describe and analyze the extent to which external
forces—over which the political unit has little or no control—can
affect the social organization, performance, and stability of a state.
The studies in this volume argue that the extent of internal cohesion
or division may be directly related to pressures from the environment
rather than to existing ethnocultural or political cleavages within the
society itself.

Third, as indicated above, this volume self-consciously eschews
developing still another approach to the study of integration. Rather,
its purpose is simply to investigate and illustrate in various contexts
the influence the international environment has had upon integration.
By bringing an intensive and focused case study method to bear on
seven states (Cyprus, the Philippines, Zaire, Yugoslavia, East
Germany, Bangladesh, and Guyana), this symposium will, the editor
hopes, contribute a new perspective for the study of integration and
at least provide some empirical justification for going ahead with
the search for more productive research designs and theoretical
models.

In the first chapter the editor presents a critical overview
of some of the integration literature. She concludes that the concept
of integration as it has been used in the social sciences is an example

of jargon that has not proven to be a useful tool for social science research. The essay discusses some of the biases implicit in national political integration theory that have, in the author's opinion, hindered progress in the field, and explores the role the international system plays in internal integrative processes. Developing the hypothesis that enthnocultural or political divisions within a society may not be causally related to the extent of cohesion within the political unit, the editor argues that internal divisions may themselves be a product either of domestic institutional arrangements within the boundaries of the state or of international forces beyond them, or the result of a complex, symbiotic relationship between both external and internal influences. The essay concludes by urging the inclusion of international environmental factors in models of integration and suggests several new directions integration research might take.

The chapters that follow investigate the integration experiences of several small states, many of which have suffered insurgency movements or are attempting to cope with sectarian demands on the part of dissatisfied groups.

Adamantia Pollis presents a historical analysis of the relations between Greeks and Turks on the island of Cyprus, indicating how relations between these two ethnic groups have been determined by the British, the Turks, the Greeks, and now the Americans, rather than by the indigenous peoples themselves. She maintains that the institutional devices the Crypriots have adopted in order to govern themselves have been influenced by powers external to Cyprus. The result has been a historical inability of the Cypriots to regulate their own affairs for any length of time and the pending division of the island into two separate autonomous units.

The progressive alienation of a regional elite is analyzed by Inayatalluh in his description of the relationship between West and East Pakistan before partition. Due to a combination of geographical factors, scarce resources, and the inability (or unwillingness) of existing political, economic, and social institutions to satisfy the demands of the Bengalis, the separatist tendencies of the Eastern wing of Pakistan grew more insistent. The author relates how these internal conditions were aggravated by shifts in international power relations and regional political alliances, culminating in the disintegration of Pakistan into separate political entities, Pakistan and Bangladesh.

Wyatt MacGaffey studies the development of Zaire in terms of the effect various external forces such as colonialism and Pan-African nationism had upon political relations among the indigenous peoples. Using M. G. Smith's framework, MacGaffey indicates the crucial impact external and internal factors have had upon Zaire's structural development and its ability to govern itself.

One international environmental variable, a messianic foreign ideology, is considered by Lyman Legters in connection with its impact upon internal integrative processes. Describing the role Soviet ideology has played in Yugoslavia's attempts to unify and govern itself, the author indicates how inventive the Yugoslav governing elite has been in adapting the ideology of a dominant power to its integrative needs.

Arthur Hanhardt, Jr. and William Sharp analyze East Germany's attempts at political, social, and economic consolidation. They describe how the domination of the Soviet Union and the example of West Germany's economic development influence the functioning of its major institutions and the progress the GDR is making toward socializing its citizenry and fulfilling their social and economic needs. East Germany provides a contrast with the other more classically plural societies discussed in this book. Since the GDR is not an ethnically divided state, it furnishes a control study on the importance of ethnocultural homogeneity in determining the ability of a state to govern. It is interesting to compare the adaptive devices the GDR develops, in response to external pressures and its need to direct and unify the GDR population into a new socialist identity, with those adopted by elites in ethnically plural societies.

The Muslim insurgency movement in the Philippines is discussed by Lela Noble in terms of the complex and reciprocal relationship that exists between internal integration efforts and external relations among states in the region and beyond. She depicts the attempts of the Philippine government to satisfy the demands of the Muslims, and the reasons for its failure thus far to do so. Focusing in particular on Malaysian-Philippine relations, Noble shows how internal dissension within one political unit can affect the delicate political balance and policies of the second. She also explains how divisions within the rebellious ethnic group itself have influenced the course of the insurgency and suggests the possible consequences these divisions may have for the successful accommodation of insurgent demands by the existing regime.

Finally, Raymond T. Smith, in a study of the development of Guyanese social and political institutions, concludes that it has been American and British interference, the structure of the internal system, and a complex of other historical and developmental factors that have contributed to the divisiveness and instability of Guyanese affairs rather than the plural nature of that society in and of itself. This study maintains that the extent to which such small, divided states as Guyana are penetrated by environmental forces is perhaps generally underestimated.

It is the hope of the editor that these studies offer enough evidence to suggest the importance of external factors to the highly complex and thus far perplexing process of integration. It is also the editor's hope that as a result of this exploratory venture, other students of integration will be encouraged to search for more elegant research designs and relevant theoretical models. That is the primary purpose of this volume.

NOTE

1. "Nation-Building or Nation-Destroying?" World Politics 24 (April 1972): 320.

INTEGRATION: CONCEPTUAL TOOL OR ACADEMIC JARGON?

Stephanie G. Neuman

Jargon: language vague in meaning and full of
circumlocutions and long, high-sounding words.

Webster's Third New International Dictionary

The concept of integration has been widely discussed in the
social sciences. Unfortunately, there still is little agreement about
the meaning of the concept, and the ramifications of that lack of
agreement are reflected in the kind of research produced and in the
widely differing conclusions scholars reach regarding the present
state of integration theory.

The purpose of this chapter is twofold: to examine the progress
made by the social sciences, particularly comparative politics, in
the direction of theory building (that is, the formulation of a set of
logically clear general statements capable of being tested) and to
evaluate the utility of the concept of integration for empirical
research. Is the term a helpful conceptual tool, or is it one more
example of academic jargon?

The discussion is divided into four parts. The first part
assesses the progress social scientists have made in formulating
logically clear definitions of integration. It analyzes the extent to
which major theorists have been able to describe integration in
terms that sharply distinguish it from other social phenomena. The
second section is concerned with the utility of the various concepts
of integration for empirical research. In what way, for example,
do theorists explain how integration does or does not come about?
Is there a set of logical hypotheses that relate integration to explanatory
variables—that is, the processes or institutions that cause it? If
so, what are they? Can we measure them?

The third section discusses some of the normative biases
that have influenced the work of integration theorists and examines
a few conceptual blinders that have resulted from them. The fourth
and final part points out a singular omission in integrationist writings:
the influence of the external environment. An attempt is made to show
how adding this factor to the models in many cases helps explain
developments we are observing today.

LACK OF DEFINITIONAL CLARITY

Historically there has been general agreement among social
scientists on the definition of the integration problem. From the early
sociological thinkers to the modern nation-building* theorists, the
main question has been how and why social units cohere. What is it
that holds a unit together?[1]

But after achieving agreement on the problem, theorists
part company on the definitional issue of what exactly an integrated
social unit is. Is an integrated social unit the same as an integrated
political unit? If not, how does it differ? There also has been little
agreement on how to determine whether the political or social unit
under analysis is in fact holding together and on how to identify
an integrated unit in the real world. The result is that social
scientists either pay little attention to the description of the

---

* Walker Conner has pointed out the imprecise way in which
social scientists use the terms "nation" and "state": "Thus a
dictionary designed for the student of global politics defines the state
as a 'legal concept describing a social group that occupies a
defined territory and is organized under common political institutions and an effective government.' By contrast a nation is defined
as a 'social group which shares a common ideology, common
institutions and customs, and a sense of homogeneity. . . . A nation
may comprise part of a state, be coterminous with a state, or
extend beyond the borders of a single state.'" Unfortunately, social
scientists are prone to indiscriminate interutilization of the two
terms. The present author is aware of the justice of Conner's
criticism. However, terms such as "national identity," "nationalism,"
and "nation building" have taken on fixed meanings in the vocabulary
of the social sciences. To be precise, these terms should be referred
to as "state identity," "statism," or "state building," but the
resultant semantic confusion would make such usage counterproductive.
This essay therefore distinguishes wherever possible between the
two terms "nation" and "state" but reverts to imprecise usage in
instances where not to do so would further confuse the meaning.
See Walker Conner, "Nation-Building or Nation-Destroying?"
World Politics 24 (April 1972): p. 333.

dependent variable (integration) or present divergent conceptions
of what integration means.

For example, some scholars define integration as a process.
Donald G. Morrison et al. state:

> Integration is a process by which members of a social
> system [citizens for our purposes] develop linkages
> and cohesion so that the boundaries of the system per-
> sist over time and the boundaries of subsystems
> become less consequential in affecting behavior. In
> this process, members of the social system develop
> an escalating sequence of contact, cooperation, con-
> sensus, and community.[2]

Claude Ake also implies a process in his definition of an integrated
political system:

> to the extent that the minimal units [individual
> political actors] develop in the course of political
> interaction a pool of commonly accepted norms
> regarding political behavior and commitment to
> the political behavior patterns legitimized by
> these norms.[3]

However, these conceptualizations of integration give no clear
indication of what the end product would look like and how one
would recognize it.[4] How much cohesion and which commonly
accepted norms denote an integrated political or social unit?
How would the observer identify integration, or is he dependent upon
some other manifestation (such as conflict) to demonstrate a lack of
integration? And what institutional form will an integrated unit
take? Will it be democratic or authoritarian? Would it be a
centralized organizational entity with full sovereignty, or would
it be a loosely federated unit? Or are institutional forms irrelevant
to integration?

Some scholars seem to envision integration in terms of
a condition that either exists or does not exist. For example, Karl
Deutsch et al. have defined integration as "the attainment, within a
territory, of a 'sense of community' and of institutions and practices
strong enough and widespread enough to assure, for a long time ,
dependable expectations of peaceful change among its population."[5]
This is called a "security community"; put another way, a security
community is a group of people who are integrated. According to
Deutsch et al. , a "sense of community" is "a belief on the part
of individuals in a group that they have come to agreement on at
least one point: that common social problems must and can be

resolved by processes of 'peaceful change.'" Peaceful change means
the resolution of social problems without resort to large-scale
physical force.[6]

As an indicator of this state of community, Deutsch postulates
that increasing social contact (transactions) between peoples indicate
increasing integration (or causes increasing integration—the relationship is not clear; this is discussed further below).[7] But how many
kinds of transactions must be carried out and to what degree of
intensity before a unit can be considered finally integrated? What
proportion of the population must participate in these transactions?
All? A majority? Particular segments of the population?
Are all transactions of equal importance? If one measures the flow
of mail as an example of transactions in one society, does it have
the same meaning in another? Are all socioeconomic transactions
of equal importance, or are some more significant for integration
than others? Thus, upon closer examination, even where integration
is rather precisely defined in operational terms, problems of
identification and measurement remain to be solved.

The obvious disparities between definitions of integration
illustrates the state of conceptual confusion in the field. Although,
as Fred Hayward observes, the term "integration" may be defined in
an endless number of ways without violating the standards for
scientific investigation,[8] failure to agree on common concepts of
what integration is makes useful comparison and theory building
very difficult. It is not a question of the rightness or wrongness
of a definition, but rather a matter of agreeing on a set of sharply
defined concepts and submitting them to rigorous testing.[9]

However, in spite of a general inability of integration theorists
to clearly define dependent variables, most writers concerned with
nation building in developing countries continue to use the term as
though it were a generally understood concept.[10] But despite wish-
ful thinking on the part of many researchers, the term remains vague
in meaning. What the field has are various definitions that are
incomplete or inapplicable and for the most part are at variance with
each other.

CAUSE AND EFFECT OR CONFUSION AND MALAISE?

Lack of conceptual clarity in definition has retarded theoretical
development in integration studies in another respect. In order to
relate what is to be explained (the dependent variable) to what is
thought to have caused it (the explanatory, independent, or causal
variable), a cogent definition of the concept that separates it from
social phenomena is necessary. Because of the ambiguity of the

dependent variable, it is hardly surprising to find that students integration have difficulty in establishing a clear relationship between cause and effect factors. In other words, there is as much confusion about what causes integration to take place, as there is about the definition of "integration."

One problem has been that of logically relating causal variables to the integration process. For example, integration in comparative studies is variously associated with any one of the following factors: stability (defined as persistence or lack of conflict), common experiences, common values, types of political structures (parties, extent of centralization, existence of institutionalized bargaining), ideology, degree of compliance with governmental directives, or size of units. But it is rarely made clear in the literature what role these variables play in the process.

Upon close examination of the literature, it becomes plain that there is a general, if often unarticulated, agreement about the importance of consensual attitudes and values to the integration process.[11] (Implicit in this assumption is the belief that when people identify with the national state their attitudes are consensual, and when they identify primarily with particularistic groups their attitudes are not. This assumption will be discussed further below.) But there has not been clarification of the relationships between consensus and other variables and how they, either together or individually, determine the degree of integration.

The work of Deutsch and other transactionalist theorists illustrates this difficulty. Their hypothesis holds that cohesiveness— a sense of "we-feeling" or "community"—can be measured or is caused by the amount and extent of interaction among people. However, connection is never established between this kind of social interaction and the political institutions and practices that assure peaceful change:

> The populations of different territories might easily
> profess verbal attachment to the same set of values
> without having a sense of community that leads to
> political integration. The kind of sense of commu-
> nity that is relevant to integration, and therefore
> for our study, turned out to be rather a matter of
> mutual sympathy and loyalties; of "we-feeling,"
> trust, and mutual consideration; of partial iden-
> tification in terms of self-images and interests;
> of mutually successful predictions of behavior,
> and of cooperative action in accordance with
> it. . . . "Peaceful change" could not be assured
> without this kind of relationship.[12]

If we translate this proposition into hypothetical figures (as in the two-by-two matrix below) the difficulty of establishing a relationship becomes apparent. The authors are proposing that increasing communication means or will mean mutual liking:

		Frequency of Interaction	
		Rare	Frequent
Mutual Liking	Low	(1) 85%	(2) 15%
	High	(3) 15%	(4) 85%

Using the following percentages for illustrative purposes only, Deutsch and his collaborators are saying that in units where there is frequent interaction between people, 85 percent of the population, or most of the people, like each other (right-hand column, boxes 2 and 4) and, therefore, that unit is considered integrated. The left-hand column (boxes 1 and 3) represents for them a state of nonintegration.

But this proposition assumes that social learning takes place in one direction only, and leaves out other possible intervening variables that may determine whether or not people share a "we-feeling." Increased communication, for example, in a situation of economic scarcity, may provoke antagonistic rather than cooperative attitudes among the majority. Increased communication may also reflect conflict rather than peaceful exchange. [13] It is difficult, therefore, to use transition analysis as either a descriptor or predictor of political integration in Deutsch's sense, unless the logical steps between the two processes are more definitely described.

A second and closely related problem for theorists has been that of drawing a fine line of distinction between the factor chosen to explain how integration occurs and the definition of integration itself. In the Deutschian model, does a high positive pattern of transaction flow in some way facilitate integration or does it indicate that integration has to some extent already taken place? [14]

Deutsch holds that both propositions are true. [15] Bruce Russett has made a similar statement. [16] But if this is so, then Deutsch's definition of integration is empirically tautological, since variables used to indicate the state of integration also serve to explain the process. The reasoning is circular and the causal process has still not been explained. Transactions are caused by a preexisting consensus, and transactions cause consensus that leads to integration.

This confusion between explanatory and definitional variables are used to explain why integration does or does not exist. Jacob and Teune, for example, define integration as follows:

> Political integration generally implies a relationship
> of community among people within the same political

entity. That is, they are held together by mutual ties of one kind or another which give the group a feeling of identity and self-awareness. Integration, therefore, is based on strong cohesiveness within a social group; and political integration is present when a political-governmental unit of some sort is cohesive.[17]

However, in their listing of ten factors explaining the presence or absence of integration one, "homogeneity," is apparently tautological:

The hypothesis is that social homogeneity will contribute strongly to the feasibility of political integration and, conversely, that communities whose members are very different from one another will have a very hard time achieving or maintaining political integration.[18]

Indicators for social homogeneity, along with race, religion, language, and ethnic identification, are attitudes and values. "Similarity in people's expressions of social distance toward one another and toward persons and groups outside their community is taken as evidence of a feeling of social homogeneity."[19] Feelings of identity indicate integration—and a "feeling of social homogeneity" causes integration.

MEASURING INTEGRATION

Compounding the confusion in definition and conceptualization has been the problem of operationalization—or how and by what means to measure integration. The difficulties of measuring concepts as broadly and ill-defined as those associated with integration are staggering. Judging from the nonadditive nature of empirical research and the lack of theoretical progress in the field, one can only conclude that the absence of terminological specificity and conceptual clarity has left potential researchers without empirical guidelines. The concepts are so vague as to prevent the logical deduction of empirical measures.

For example, comparative politics, as we have seen, has emphasized statewide value consensus as essential to integration. But which values must be nationalized in order to achieve integration has never been satisfactorily answered. What values does the researcher measure? What sorts of parochial identities and how many are relevant (or irrelevant) to the process? Are there various types or degrees of consensus? Do they vary over time? Are all subnational loyalties inimical to the integration process?

And even if these questions were answerable, how does one measure the extent of internalization of societal norms without making intuitive leaps from the indicators one has chosen to the conclusion that units are or are not integrated? The problem here is best illustrated by the operational methods followed by Donald Morrison and his collaborators in Black Africa. They define integration as a process whereby citizens develop linkages and cohesion that strengthen the boundaries of the system and weaken those of subsystems. States may vary in four different types of integration. One is value integration: the congruency between values held by individuals in the system under consideration.[20] The indicators of value integration—the way the authors measure whether values are system or subsystem-oriented—"relate to differences in language, religion, and ethnicity in populations of black African nations."[21] But choosing that particular set of variables to represent value integration forces the researcher and the reader to make the assumption that ipso facto the existence of cultural differences in society means a lack of loyalty to the central political system. Not only has this assumption never been empirically tested, it implies a second corollary assumption. It presupposes that language, religious, or ethnic groups are homogeneous in values and orientation and that these orientations are unchanging. But existing research shows that differential value orientations exist within communal groups and that at certain times system-wide loyalties are mobilized and at others parochial loyalties are predominant. It also suggests that even the content of these identities changes over time.

Stephen Morris, in "Indians in East Africa: A Study in a Plural Society," asserts that class and cultural divisions among Indians are more significant to individual Indians than the broader Indian ethnic identification and these crosscutting allegiances lead to alliances of interests across racial lines.[22] But this research was done in the 1950s, before the independence of the countries in East Africa, and circumstances have changed since then. For a variety of reasons, ethnic identities have taken on paramount importance in the area.

In the Western world as well, states considered models of various forms of integration—such as Britain, Canada, Belgium, and Lebanon—suddenly are faced with communal conflicts that threaten the political stability of the state. Are these old parochial loyalties come to life, or are they new identities, a response to changing conditions in the environment? Or are they perhaps a complex combination of old and new loyalties?

The Smocks in their research on Ghana argue that "many of the most significant communal entities now vying for men's loyalties are not traditional in origin."[23] Cited as an example of a new parochial loyalty is the Akan identity, born of the fusing of the once antagonistic Fanti and Ashanti ethnic groups in Ghana. The Smocks point out that in traditional societies modernization has expanded the traditional communal identification beyond the village to include members of other, but similar communities. "Thus, with the expansion in scope of communal identities, individuals and groups retain their original primary ties but new bloc identities are superimposed over layers of more traditional orientations."[24] But this is true in other countries as well—witness the changing identities of the black community and women in the United States, to cite only two of the most obvious examples.

The problem, then, in integration theory, has been the "fallacy of the misplaced level."[*] Social scientists have been inferring

---

[*]The term "fallacy of the misplaced level" was coined by Frederick W. Frey in "Cross-Cultural Research in Political Science," in Robert T. Holt and John E. Turner, eds., The Methodology of Comparative Research (New York: The Free Press, 1970), p. 290. David Singer first wrote about the level of analysis problem in international relations in 1961. He pointed out that in general systems theory the researcher is confronted with "a system, its sub-systems, and their respective environments, and while he may choose as his system any cluster of phenomena from the most minute organism to the universe itself, such choice cannot be merely a function of whim or caprice, habit or familiarity. The responsible scholar must be prepared to evaluate the relative utility—conceptual and methodological—of the various alternatives open to him, and to appraise the manifold implications of the level of analysis finally selected." From "The Level of Analysis Problem in International Relations," in Klaus Knorr and Sidney Verba, eds., The International System: Theoretical Essays (Princeton, N.J.: Princeton University Press, 1961), pp. 77-92, reprinted in James N. Rosenau, ed., International Politics and Foreign Policy: A Reader in Research and Theory (New York: The Free Press, 1969), p. 21.

For international relations specialists, the unit of analysis is the nation-state. Comparative politics scholars generally concentrate on the institutions and processes within the state; for political psychologists the unit is the individual or group. Conceptual and methodological problems arise when scholars either ignore the linkages between these levels or make improper inferences from them. Often social scientists draw inferences from units observed and measured at one level to unobserved and/or unmeasured units at another. These have been variously referred to as the "ecological fallacy" or the "individualistic fallacy." The former occurs when the characteristics of individuals are inferred from data observed or measured

characteristics of the total system from the assumed identities of
individuals within groups. In other words, they have been deducing
that a system's integration is related to the existence (or nonexistence)
of particularistic groups and in turn (on the basis of this information)
have been attributing permanent attitude and behavioral characteristics
to individuals. In so doing, integration theorists are making inferences
(which may or may not be correct) about units of analysis that are
lower and higher than the observed groups, without establishing logical linkages between them. They are, so to speak, committing the
"ecological" and "individualistic" fallacies at the same time. Where
there are strong parochial groups, a system will be less integrated.
Where there are strong parochial groups, individuals will have a
weak sense of national identity.

But it is an error in logic to infer from the observed fact that
disparate groups exist in a society either that a political system is
not integrated or that all the individuals in those groups share the
same political attitude. Persons from the same group occupy different
positions within society and within the group. They find themselves
living within different contexts, which may have a stronger influence
over their attitudes and behavior than membership in a primordial
group. As an illustration, a rural Malay may hold entirely different
attitudes toward the central Malaysian government than an urban
Malay. And a Malay whose business contacts are primarily with
Indonesians or with other Malays may exhibit different political attitudes and behavior than one whose commerce is with non-Malay
peoples. In times of war, economic distress, or government crisis,
identities may undergo change. The possible contextual and environmental influences on attitudes and behavior are innumerable.[*]

---

only at a higher level of analysis (such as the region); see William S.
Robinson's seminal article, "Ecological Correlations and the Behavior of Individuals," American Sociological Review 15 (June 1950):
351-57. The latter error occurs when the reverse misplaced inference is made; see Erwin K. Scheuch, "Social Context and Individual
Behavior," in Mattei Dogan and Stein Rokkan, eds., Quantitative
Ecological Analysis in the Social Sciences (Cambridge, Mass.:
MIT Press, 1969), pp. 138-41. The last two references are concerned with quantitative rather than qualitative research, but the
errors in logical inference apply to both kinds of research.

[*]The term "context" is here used to mean the milieu created
by units at the same level of interaction. For example, individuals

To determine the relationship between systemic and individual behavior requires not only knowing that primordial identities exist but also knowing the conditions under which they are relevant to the effective functioning of the state. It is evident from the new data being presented and the daily events reported in the newspapers that primordial ties should be viewed as fluid rather than static identities. It may even be that these identities are as much a response to the realities of the larger political system as they are to the demands of primary group allegiances. As the context in which interaction between people and the political regime takes place changes, so do the perceptions of individuals about themselves in relation to others and the state. Parochial identities may be dysfunctional to the operation of the larger political system in one context and not in another. Moreover, parochial identities also may be stronger in one political situation than in another. As Aristede Zolberg has stated, perhaps the term integration should be used in an open-ended way to refer to "a shifting relationship between changing identities within the framework of a variety of possible political arrangements capable of coping with a specifiable range of stresses."[25]

It is clear that the inability of integration theorists to agree upon a general concept of integration has precluded their agreement on which variables in the real world represent what it is they want to describe and explain and how to measure them. Each theorist, with his collaborators, is proceeding along separate lines of investigation and there has been little communication between them. Progress in the field is equated with the progress of each school's own particular approach, and the tendency is to dismiss the work of others who base their research on different premises and definitions. The result is a theoretical and methodological confusion that has produced integration research that, despite claims of empirical rigor, is nonadditive, noncomparative, and is supported by a scanty, unsystematically organized data base.

---

constitute a context for other individuals, groups for groups, states for states. It is a horizontal concept.

"Environment" refers to vertical relationships between units. For example, a higher-level unit, such as the international system, constitutes an environment for a lower-level unit such as the nation-state. The distinction between the two terms was drawn by Heinz Eulau in "Some Aspects of Analysis, Measurement and Sampling in the Transformation of Micro- and Macro-Level Unit Properties," a paper presented at the conference on Design and Measurement Standards for Research in Political Science, Delevan, Wisconsin, May 13-15, 1974.

NORMATIVE BIASES: IMPLICIT AND UNPRODUCTIVE

The difficulty in establishing definitional guidelines, causal relationships, and methodological procedures has been compounded by two other theoretical problems. The first, discussed here, involves the normative assumptions upon which much of integration theory rests. The second, discussed in a later section, is the critical omission from existing theoretical frameworks of the international environment.

Upon close examination of integration literature, two related normative assumptions implicitly thread their way through the labyrinth of approaches and conceptual frameworks. First, as briefly pointed out above, there is the predisposition toward consensus and shared values, which are equated with a form of national identity or national political consensus. Second, there is a bias against force and coercion as integrative measures. With few exceptions, integration researchers have assumed that the condition of integration can exist only in the absence of violent conflict, where there is an inner coherence or equilibrium of values on a statewide scale that makes the use of force unnecessary. Leonard Binder's definition of national integration is a good example of social scientists' thinking on this question: "National integration requires the creation of a cultural-ideological consensus of a degree of comprehensiveness that has not yet been seen in these [developing] countries."[26]

This conception goes hand in hand with the assumption that, in order to achieve consensus, social cleavages must be eliminated or neutralized. It is assumed that a common core of values requires either an ethnically homogeneous unit or one in which cleavages are numerous and crosscutting so as to reduce the possibility of serious conflict between groups. James S. Coleman and Carl G. Rosberg's conception of territorial integration illustrates this line of reasoning. It is "the progressive reduction of cultural and regional tensions and discontinuities on the horizontal plane in the process of creating a homogeneous territorial political community."[27]

The association of integration with national political consensus, it will be argued, is in reality an association of integration with democracy. Common to these conceptions is the association of integration not with just the nation-state (as Cynthia Enloe has observed[28]) but with the stable democratic nation-state. The question integrationists are implicitly asking is not the purely empirical one of what makes social or political units cohere, but the normative one of what makes democratic units cohere and how they can be established in the non-Western world. It is democratic theory that holds that attitudinal consensus is a prerequisite to the functioning of a stable

democratic system. Particularistic loyalties indicate a high probability of intergroup conflict and unity can be achieved only through
coercion and/or force. Force and coercion are undemocratic means
of attaining unity.*

---

*The two strands in American democratic theory, often called
the conflict and consensus models, are here illustrated in the writings
of John Stuart Mill and James Madison (see note, pp. 14-15, for modern
versions of their arguments). In Considerations on Representative
Government, Mill sets forth his theory of the relationship between
nationality and representative government. He argues that as a general principle the boundaries of a government should coincide with
nationality. A nationality is composed of people "united by common
sympathies which do not exist between them and any others." This
"harmony of feeling" among people can be caused by identity of
language, religion, race, and geography, "but the strongest of all
is identity of political antecedents." He concludes that in a country
composed of different nationalities, popular government is not possible. (The book was first published in April 1861 in London; the
modern edition was published in New York by the Liberal Arts Press,
1958, pp. 229-37.)

Although Mill stressed a preexisting harmony among people as
a prerequisite for democracy, Madison, in The Federalist Papers,
no. 10, saw territorial expanse and governmental institutions as
necessary and sufficient harmonizing influences. He emphasized that
the proposed form of representative government to be inaugurated
in the United States would provide the necessary equilibrium for the
crosscutting interests that exist in the country. Noting that factions
are a threat to the stability of "popular" government, but that force
is an unacceptable means of dealing with them, he maintained that
the proposed form of federal government is the best way of controlling
conflicting parochial interests and molding them into a national political consensus. Through elected representatives "whose wisdom may
best discern the true interest of their country and whose patriotism
and love of justice will be least likely to sacrifice it to temporary or
partial considerations," a common good is arrived at that the central
government can legislate and administer without recourse to coercion.
(New York: New American Library of World Literature, 1961, pp. 77-
84; first published in the so-called "McLean edition" of 1788.) In
Mill's theory, national consensus is the independent variable. In
Madison's, it is the dependent variable. However, in both theories,
some form of national political consensus is essential for the stability
of a democratic political system.

The democratic bias of integration theory is best illustrated by the two-by-two matrix below. In spite of other intervening variables that students of integration consider important to the integration process, their theories assume one kind of identity consensus or another as a precondition for the kind of political system that evolves.

| | | Identity with Central Regime | |
		High	Low
Identity with Parochial Groups	High	(1) Elite cooperation Normative consensus Consociational democracy	(3) Pluralism or fragmentation Rule by force Colonialism or authoritarian regimes
	Low	(2) Homogeneous population or cross-cutting cleavages Normative consensus Centralized democratic state	(4) Apathy or alienation Mass society Totalitarianism

Until recently, only the model in box 2, based on an idealization of the Anglo-American experience, represented political scientists' conception of an integrated state. Political science has tended to reflect two variations of one model of national integration only: a democratic assimilationist version and a democratic pluralist version.[*]

---

[*] The definitions of integration by Binder, Coleman and Rosberg, and Deutsch, above, follow the assimilationist model. Integration is seen as a process of assimilation of diverse groups. The end-state is envisioned, by either definition or implication, as a unified homogeneous political and social unit with authority securely and democratically centralized.

The pluralist model (sometimes referred to as the "conflict model" or the "equilibrium model") is based on a romanticized version of the American experience. It postulates that multiple group affiliations and crosscutting social cleavages reduce the importance of parochial identities within society and thus produce a basically homogeneous (national) political culture—or normative consensus. "The multiple groups of individuals make for a multiplicity of conflicts crisscrossing society. Such segmental participation, then, can result in a kind of balancing mechanism preventing deep cleavages along one axis." Lewis A. Coser, The Functions of Social Conflict (Glencoe,

INTEGRATION: CONCEPTUAL TOOL OR JARGON?

The primary concern has been to determine not "whether cultural unity is a necessary and/or sufficient condition for political unity, as Rabushka and Shepsle aver,[29] but whether it is a necessary and/or sufficient condition for <u>democratic</u> political stability. By omission, nondemocratic polities are implied to be both less integrated and less stable.

Lijphart added a third national integration model with his consociational democracy (box 1). He takes exception to other integration theories, not because of their concern with stability and democracy but because he believes a society segmented by strong particularistic loyalties can also be democratically ruled. He contends that not only box 2 but box 1 as well can produce a stable democratic system:

> Political stability can be maintained in culturally fragmented systems if the leaders of subcultures engage in cooperative efforts to counteract the centrifugal tendencies of cultural fragmentation.[30]

Lijphart introduces an intervening political variable—conscious cooperation among elites drawn from all major social groups willing to control ethnic competition and to accept the principle of the right of political autonomy for other subcultures. This kind of system gives legitimacy to parochial loyalties, but it also requires an overlay of ideological national consensus. Particularistic groups are incorporated into the larger political system by giving each a stake in the perpetuation of the system, thus producing a national political culture in the form of what Lijphart calls "moderate nationalism."[31]

Even with Lijphart's amendment, then, the mere presence of factional groups is still linked with lack of loyalty to a central regime, a condition that can be ameliorated by a particular form of consensual behavior on the part of elites and citizens. The term integration remains firmly associated with states presumed to contain populations with some sense of national identity, which in turn is still considered a prerequisite of stability and democracy. Basically, integration is conceived as a covariant process of gradually increasing national political consensus along with the growth of democratic institutions and stability.

Dismissed from the lexicon of integrated states are those in the second vertical column (boxes 3 and 4). Presumed to harbor groups with little sense of national identity, these states are

---

Ill.: The Free Press, 1956), pp. 78-79. See also Seymour Martin Lipset, <u>Political Man: The Social Bases of Politics</u> (Garden City, N.Y.: Anchor Books, 1963), pp. 70-78.

associated with force, lack of consensus, authoritarianism, and
instability. A plural society (box 3), for example, as described
in Furnivall, is one in which primary individual loyalties remain
with the communal group. [32] Various groups may reside side by
side within the same political system but, as Leo Kuper has stated:

> Integration rests on common values and common moti-
> vations at the individual level. . . . It presupposes
> cultural homogeneity. . . . Cultural diversity or plural-
> ism automatically imposes the structural necessity for
> domination by one of the cultural sections. It excludes
> the possibility of consensus . . . and necessitates non-
> democratic regulation of group relationships. This
> implies a distinction between two basic types of society,
> integrated societies characterized by consensus and
> cultural homogeneity . . . and regulated societies char-
> acterized by dissensus and cultural pluralism. [33]

Evidently the assumptions upon which the plural society model rests
are the same as those of the two integration models. A society with
high subgroup identity and low central identity can be neither democratic nor integrated since it is force rather than consensus that
maintains the system. [34]

The absence of loyalty to either subnational groups or the
central state is characterized by other theorists as a mass society
(box 4). Hannah Arendt describes it as an atomized society with an
alienated population that is particularly vulnerable to totalitarian
movements and regimes. The term "masses" refers to people who
no longer are identified with either parochial interest groups or the
prevailing regime—to people "who cannot be integrated into any
organization based on common interest, into political parties or
municipal government or professional organizations or trade unions."[35]

Thus, subnational loyalties and atomization are associated with
a lack of national consensus, nondemocratic forms of government,
coercion, and instability. It is also assumed that societies so cate-
gorized represent various forms of mal- or disintegration.

Seen from this perspective, it appears that integration theory
as developed thus far has been little more than a restatement of
democratic political theory. It is represented by a series of descriptive hypotheses setting forth what seemed, to its proponents, at the
time of writing, to be the bases of stable, functioning political systems, which happened to be democracies. But recent events indicate
that these hypotheses have little explanatory power today, nor will
they probably have much predictive power for tomorrow for other
democratic or nondemocratic societies.

"Democratic" states classified as "amalgamated security communities" and considered well past the threshold of national integration, such as the United States and Britain, have experienced the rebirth of conflicting parochial identities. Scotland's claims for greater local autonomy and the Welsh demand for improvement in the status of the Welsh language have forced the central government of Great Britain to agree to some form of devolution of power.[36] Northern Ireland's religious factions are warring. In Europe, old animosities between the Flemish and French-speaking Walloons have surfaced again. In Spain, the Basques and Catalans are demanding autonomy. And suddenly the 46,000 inhabitants of Greenland are threatening secession from Denmark.

Even more puzzling is the extent of communalism today. Discriminating against no particular type of political system and respecting no geographic boundaries, particularistic demands have taken on a worldwide dimension. Like their democratic counterparts, communist states such as the Soviet Union and Yugoslavia are attempting to deal with recently articulated (whether old or new) regional and cultural claims, and China periodically must cope with outbreaks of regional restiveness.

Lebanon, declared a model of consociational democracy prior to 1975, is being torn apart by religious strife. Using a model similar to Lijphart's, called "national accommodation," the Smocks in 1974 predicted increasing stability for Lebanon.[37] Evidence of Lebanon's progress was found in the fact that Lebanon had maintained the same basic constitutional order and democratic political process for thirty years[38] and in an observed increasing consensus between Muslim and Christian Lebanese:

> Data from our adult survey of Lebanon show a clear trend toward convergence of political opinion between Christians and Muslims on a wide variety of issues which have divided these groups in the past. Discrepancies still remain, but a comparison of the responses of younger with those of the older and more educated with the less educated indicates that within the foreseeable future many of the Christian-Muslim differences may decrease in magnitude or even disappear.[39]

How can researchers as sensitive as the Smocks have been deceived by their data? Were their data wrong or has something changed? Why is the world witnessing severe political crises and the rebirth of parochial identities among peoples in countries long since declared "integrated"? What relationship does the political unrest in authoritarian regimes have to these events? Why have

integration theories been unable to predict or explain these occur-
rences? Is bias in favor of democratic systems obscuring some fundamental intervening variable that affects the functioning of political
systems regardless of type? If the sights of theorists interested in
integration were directed toward nonnormative formulations, would
the potential explanatory power of integration theory be increased?
If social scientists are interested in discovering the factors that
encourage all social units to cohere, need integration theory continue
to be constrained by biases that lead to the rejection of force and
dictatorial repression as legitimate means of establishing a cohesive
political system?

In other words, perhaps it is time to discard the Western concept
of integration as a unilinear, universal, democratic process. It may
have as little relevance for the Western world of tomorrow as it does
for the non-Western world of today. Integration can be diagnosed as
stable or unstable, democratic or nondemocratic, static or dynamic,
but whatever the descriptive condition, the theorist should not be led
by an unarticulated normative bias to ignore any phenomenon that may
be an important determinant of the dependent variable.

Experience has shown that the frameworks, paradigms, and
models provided by the comparativists in the 1960s, who were devoted
to the principle of deriving theoretically relevant generalizations from
crosscultural comparative research, have produced a body of integration theory so abstract as to have little connection with either
democratic or nondemocratic reality. As Sidney Verba has commented:

> If the monographic literature provides us with few gener-
> alizations, the second kind of literature provides us with
> many generalizations that do not seem to fit many or any
> of the relevant cases. . . . Generalizations fade when we
> look at particular cases. We add intervening variable after
> intervening variable. Since the cases are few in number
> we end with an explanation tailored to each case. The result
> begins to sound quite idiographic or configurative.[40]

Certainly, recent events suggest that integration may be a more
complex, multilinear process than existing integration models reveal.
Taking place on different sociopolitical levels, proceeding at different
rates of intensity, integration appears to be a fluctuating process
responding at different times to as yet unknown contextual and environmental conditions. Perhaps, because of the complexity of the
process, the first order of business at this stage of theory building
should be an attempt to explain what it is in specific societies that
makes them cohere. Although admittedly this is a more configurative,
inductive approach, perhaps for the time being it is all social science

methods allow. However, if area specialists follow a "disciplined configurative approach"[41] by making explicit their implicit assumptions, then the factors that they are testing in one sociopolitical setting can be measured in others and may in the long run lead to a general theory. Thus the absence or presence of parochial identities found to be important to societal cohesion in one context may or may not be significant in another. Explaining the absence or presence of these factors may lead to a logically coherent series of hypotheses that relate many variables and arrange them into various configurational patterns. Consequently, by diligently enumerating all the dependent and independent variables investigated in specific social settings, social scientists may eventually be able to explain which factors under what conditions foster cohesion and which inhibit the process. "A disciplined configurative approach is, thus, based on general rules, but on complicated combinations of them. Explanations may be tailored to the specific case, but they must be made of the same material and follow the same rules of tailoring."[42]

At this stage of theory development, integration need not refer to a known end-state but to a process of changing relationships and identities within a framework of a variety of possible political arrangements,[43] conceivably extending beyond the nation-state as we know it today. Integration, as a multilinear phenomenon, implies there can be degrees of cohesion at many different levels. At certain times in a people's history, a significant proportion of the members may on some issues identify with groups beyond the boundaries of the nation-state and at other times, perhaps on other issues, with citizens of the political unit within which they reside.

Broadly speaking, integration and disintegration can be defined in terms of the process that determines whether group members regard the sociopolitical arrangements regulating the group's affairs as worth preserving or not. Commitment to these arrangements can be high or low, more or less. Group cohesion can expand and contract. It can rise and fall. It can include members of many different interest groups, or individuals with similar backgrounds and interests. Differences over ethnocultural, political, or ideological issues can become of paramount political importance at one time and dissipate as political issues at another.*

---

*Most research on integration deals with ethnocultural differences within various states. However, as Douglas W. Rae and Michael Taylor point out, cleavages can be any criteria that divide the members of a community or subcommunity into groups with important political differences. They divide cleavages into three general categories: (1) ascriptive such as race or caste; (2) attitud-

Also, at some point in a group's history substantial segments may be willing to delegate authority over most social, economic, political, and military matters to a central government and at other times only some or none. In some circumstances certain institutional arrangements will be acceptable and in other circumstances they will not. The measure of integration, then, is the ability of a political unit to conduct its important and necessary business without disaffecting large bodies of its constituents so they will no longer accept regulation by or participate in that particular system. The sociopolitical arrangements of the unit may change in response to challenges to its structure, and the stabilizing devices used at various times may differ, but the political unit that can regulate its affairs effectively is, by definition, considered integrated. The task for social scientists, then, is to investigate all the possible conditions that determine how committed (or uncommitted) groups are to what sets of sociopolitical arrangements over a long period of time.

If it is seen as a changing process, many factors may conceivably influence the dynamics of integration, not the least of them the use or threat of coercion. Force or the threat of punishment may at times determine whether groups accept rule by one administration or another. At other times, perceived economic or political self-interest may influence individuals' allegiance to a particular form of government. In fact, the use of force at one stage of organizational development may establish a habit of loyalty to a particular administrative center that is perpetuated for reasons unrelated to the use of coercion. In thinking about the unthinkable, it may even turn out, upon examination of the past and present histories of many societies, that a strong army and/or police force have been important determinants of the size, type, and durability of most political systems. It was, after all, the successful use of force by the North against the South in the nineteenth century that perpetuated the political structure of the prototypic democratic state as we know it today—the United States.

Although the democratic nation-state has been the integration model to date, as the future unfolds the very concept of the nation-state (and for that matter, democracy) may change so radically that the old definition will have little meaning.[44] If social scientists can divest themselves of the Western referents with which they have measured and judged events occurring in other parts of the world,

---

inal such as ideology or "preference"; and (3) behavioral such as those elicited through voting or organizational membership. See The Analysis of Political Cleavages (New Haven, Conn.: Yale University Press, 1970), p. 1.

and attempt a more inductive comparative procedure, it may be that our perspective, although initially idiographic, will broaden through comparison to distinguish several variant patterns (or models) of integration. For the time being, this may seem a throwback to the prebehavioral days of nonadditive, idiographic studies. But although it may be empirically necessary now to conceive of integration as a culturally specific process, disciplined research in a large number of societies in time may produce several logically refined and relevant typologies of the integration process. In the long run, it may well prove to be that it is not the type of method used by the intuitive intelligence of scholars that will determine whether social science can explain the dynamics of human behavior.

THE GLOBAL ENVIRONMENT: CAUSAL OR IRRELEVANT FACTORS?

A second theoretical problem, and one that also may account for the lack of explanatory power of integration models is the disregard with which the global environment is treated as a possible causal factor.* In general, regardless of approach or method, international systemic factors have not been considered important independent or intervening variables in the integration process. For the most part the external environment has been treated as either neutral or benign. In the few instances where external factors have been judged to be positive factors—that is, increasing the extent of integration— the thesis propounded is the long-standing but never empirically verified belief, common among social scientists, that because of a perceived potential danger to society's survival, an external threat tends to increase identification with the nation-state. Lijphart, for example, states:

---

*The terms global environment, international environment, international system, external environment, and environment are used interchangeably in this discussion. They are conceived in James Rosenau's terminology to consist of all "the human and non-human phenomena that are located external to the geographic space of the society of which the polity is a part." See James N. Rosenau, "Toward the Study of National-International Linkages," in James N. Rosenau, ed., Linkage Politics, Essays on the Convergence of National and International Systems (New York: The Free Press, 1969), p. 45n.

My comparative analysis of five consociational
democracies shows that a strikingly favourable
factor in the establishment of strengthening of
consociationalism is the existence of a foreign
threat. In all five countries, over-arching
cooperation among the subcultural elites was
either initiated or significantly extended during
periods of international crisis, especially during
the First and Second World Wars. And in most
cases these changes proved quite durable. [45]

However. Lijphart himself takes note of the disparity between
his findings and those of Deutsch. [46] In Political Community and the
North Atlantic Area, Deutsch et al. specifically exclude external
factors as important to the integration process, dismissing the
effects of foreign military threats as neither strong nor positive.
Even when they were positive, Deutsch finds "their effects were
transitory." [47]

But even if this interest in the positive effects of outside
threats on integration is interpreted as a sign of modest progress in
conceptualization, theorists still evidence little consideration of either
outside states or other factors in the international environment as a
possible negative influence on integration.

The neglect of these factors in integration theory is puzzling,
given the large amount of attention students of international relations
are devoting to models of dependency, global interdependence, the
increasing penetration of states, and the linkages between their
domestic and foreign affairs. * Moreover the growing number of

----

*Dependency has been defined as a situation in which the
economic development of one or a group of countries is conditioned
by the development and expansion of another country's economy. The
relationship of interdependency between two or more economies, and
between them and world commerce, assumes a dependent nature when
one state's economy can act only as a reflection of the expansion of
the other; see Theotonio Dos Santos, "The Structure of Dependence,"
in K. T. Fann and Donald C. Hodges, ed. Readings in U.S. Imperialism (Boston: Porter Sargent, 1971), p. 226. Other theorists
concerned with dependency are: Osvaldo Sunkel, "The Crisis of the
Nation-State in Latin America: Challenge and Response," in
Yale H. Ferguson and Walter F. Weiker, eds., Continuing Issues
in International Politics (Pacific Palisades, Calif.: 1973); Ronald
H. Chilcote, "Dependency: A Critical Synthesis of the Literature,"
Latin American Perspectives 1, no. 1 (Spring 1974); Patricia Weiss

examples of penetration and interdependence appearing daily in
newspapers side by side with reports of the worldwide rash of ethnic
conflicts and particularistic demands would seem to suggest a possible
relationship between integration and the international environment
that is worth investigating. Unquestionably, the similarity of these
examples of communal unrest as well as their temporal proximity
implies that, in addition to the internal sociopolitical process, some

---

Fagen, "Chilean Universities: Problems of Antonomy and Dependence,"
Sage Professional Papers in Comparative Politics 4 (1973).
    Although there is little agreement on a definition of the
term "interdependency," Richard Rosecrance and Arthur Stein have
noted that "In its most general sense, interdependence suggests
a relationship of interests such that if one nation's position changes,
other states will be affected by that change"; see "Inderdependence:
Myth or Reality?" World Politics 26, no. 1 (October 1973):1.
Other scholars who have written on interdependence are: Kenneth
Waltz, "The Myth of Interdependence," in Charles P. Kindleberger,
ed., The International Corporation (Cambridge, Mass.: Harvard
University Press, 1 9 7 0); Edward L. Morse, "The Politics of
Interdependence," International Organization 23 (Spring 1969);
Oran R. Young, "Interdependencies in World Politics," International
Journal 24 (Autumn 1969).
    "A penetrated political system is one in which nonmembers of
a national society participate directly and authoritatively, through
actions taken jointly with the society's members, in either the allocation of its values or the mobilization of support on behalf of its
goals." See James N. Rosenau, "Pre-theories and Theories of
Foreign Policy," in R. Barry Farrell, ed., Approaches to Comparative
and International Politics (Evanston, Ill.: Northwestern University
Press, 1966), p. 65.
    Linkage politics is concerned with: (1) establishing "propo-
sitions that link the stability, functioning, institutions, and goals
of national political systems to variables in their external environment";
(2) formulating "hypotheses linking the stability, functioning, and
organizations of international systems to variables within their
national subsystems"; and (3) discovering "linkages in which national
and international systems function in such a way as to continuously
reinforce each other ('fused' linkages)." See James N. Rosenau,
"Introduction: Political Science in a Shrinking World," in James N.
Rosenau, ed. Linkage Politics: Essays on the Convergence of National
and International Systems (New York: The Free Press, 1969), p.7.
See also Rosenau, "Theorizing Across Systems: Linkage Politics
Revisited," in Jonathan Wilkenfeld, ed., Conflict Behavior and Linkage
Politics (New York: David McKay, 1973).

external factors are causally operative, and that in this respect
the analytical tools presently available to students of integration
need amendment.

Two factors explain in part the curious omission of environmental
variables from integration theory. First, systems theory, which has
dominated social scientific thinking since the late 1950s, has created
a bias in this direction. Second, the sheet complexity of the subject
matter challenges the information-processing ability of social scientists
encouraging them to narrow rather than to enlarge the field of
investigation.

The Parsonian interpretation of systems theory and several
key concepts employed by Parsons, Gabriel Almond, and others
have influenced most of social scientific thinking about society in
general and integration in particular. Parsons defined integration
as a process coordinating the interdependent specialized roles and
structures of a social system, which, as Fred Riggs points out, is not
very different from Almond's definition of the "conversion" function. [48]
This formulation interprets integration in terms of a "whole-system
framework." "Its focus is on how the various parts of a given system
interact with each other," [49] at the expense of "ecological" analysis
(analysis of the relationship between systems and their environment).
Riggs argues effectively that this omission is not intrinsic to systems
theory itself but arises from errors in application. [50]   Nevertheless,
whether because of theory or practice, the result has been that much
of social science research treats the international environment as
irrelevant to internal sociopolitical processes, and integration theory
is a product of that bias.

A second and related contributing factor is the complexity
of the process itself. Social scientists are committed to analyzing
the most complicated set of units known: total societies. The number
of variables at different levels of analysis makes for formidable
research problems and any attempt to relate these variables in a logical
theoretical framework is a supremely difficult task. As Rosenau has
observed:

> few among us ever feel that our comprehension at
> one level is sufficient and thorough enough to identify
> the master variables that account for varying
> phenomena at that level. A lifetime of concentrated
> inquiry often seems necessary to the acquisition of
> parsimonious theory at a single level, so that to
> achieve such competence at two levels looms as a
> fine but unobtainable aspiration. [51]

Complexity and human limitations, therefore, have conspired, along
with the conceptual bias of systems theory, to eliminate a whole

range of variables that may be crucial to understanding what is, admittedly, a very complicated process.

The following examples in this chapter were chosen to demonstrate the important part played by the external environment in the integration process, and the necessity of including it in any serious study of the subject. Randomly selected and culled from newspapers and secondary source materials, these illustrations are meant to be only suggestive of the kinds of linkages that might be sought in any primary research on the integration process in specific societies

Environmental phenomena that intrude into national and subnational group relations can be the product of events and actions originating in many different networks in the global system. They may issue from other political units in the regional or international environment, or from nonstate transnational actors such as political parties, religious societies, ethnic groups, and economic organizations. The imput may be the result of direct covert or overt actions by foreign actors, or the result of indirect outputs from the international system, the spread of technology or ideas. In this context, writers speak of the "demonstration effect, "coup contagion," and "reactive" or "emulative" processes.*

The consequences for internal group relations may be intended or unintended by forces operating in the environment. Many events taking place in the international system have unintended and unexpected consequences that may not become apparent until long after they have taken place. Other events may have an immediate and more obvious

---

* Rosenau defines the latter two processes in the following way: A reactive process is one where "the actors who initiate the output do not participate in the allocative activities of those who experience the input, but the behavior of the latter is nevertheless a response to behavior undertaken by the former. . . . An emulative process is established when the input is only a response to the output but takes essentially the same form as the output. It corresponds to the so-called "diffusion" or "demonstration" effect whereby political activities in one country are perceived and emulated in another." (James N. Rosenau, "Toward the Study of National-International Linkages," in James N. Rosenau, ed., Linkage Politics [New York: The Free Press, 1969], p. 46.)

The "coup contagion" hypothesis postulates that military coups in one country influence in some fashion the military coups in other countries; see Richard P. Y. Li and William R. Thompson, "The 'Coup Contagion' Hypothesis," Journal of Conflict Resolution 19, no. 1 (March 1975): 64.

effect. Thus, in thinking about the external environment, it is necessary to conceive of inputs as coming from many different networks (or systems) operating transnationally at diverse levels, which may at various times affect social and political relations in specific societies in a variety of ways. The following examples, although configurative and unsystematically selected, are intended to demonstrate the complexity of the relationship between the international system and the integrative processes and the variety of forms this relationship can take.

　　　　Lebanon is a case in point. Lijphart, in discussing the important integrative effect of external threats, gave Labanon as an example:

> Consociational democracy is primarily a response to the national emergency created by internal divisions, but external threats may also contribute significantly to its establishment or reinforcement. . . . The Lebanese National Pact of 1943—the country's unwritten consociational constitution—was concluded during the Second World War; it followed an insurrection which united the religious communities against the external control of the French under the Mandate. [52]

However, although external factors may well have provided the proper climate for integration in 1943, it is apparent that by 1976 many factors in the international environment conspired to produce the opposite effect.

　　　　The same conditions Lijphart postulated for integration in 1943 hold for disintegration in 1976. Armed conflict in Lebanon may be a response to internal divisions, but if so, external conditions have contributed significantly to its development. The National Pact, based on a national census taken in 1932, was spelled out in a careful system of checks and balances between Christians and Muslims. Reflecting the slight preponderance of Christians, the president of Lebanon would be a Maronite Christian and the premier would be a Muslim of the Sunni sect—the next most populous group. The speaker of the house would be a Shiite Muslim, and elective offices were to be shared on a 6 : 5 Christian-to-Muslim ratio. [53]

　　　　By the 1960s and 1970s, however, the situation had changed. Although no census has been taken since 1932 because of the rami- fications the differential birth rates have for the delicate Lebanese balance of power, it is generally known that the ratio has been more than reversed. [54] The Christian preponderance has given way to a Muslim majority, and the Shiites who comprised the third largest community in 1932 are probably the most numerous. Furthermore, the Christian community and some Sunni Muslims have over the years amassed great wealth out of all proportion to their numbers, while the Shiites remain the poorest, least educated, and least powerful class.[55]

Although these disparities existed for a number of years prior to the outbreak of violence, it can be argued that it was the increasing momentum of events beyond Lebanon's boundaries, not the economic or political disparities themselves, that inflamed and altered the relationship between the various groups within Lebanon from peaceful coexistence to armed conflict.[56]

Since the seventh century when Islamic tribes drove the Christians to the mountains, Maronites have feared being submerged in the Arab sea. But during and after the French mandate, the Christians derived some sense of security from the fact that Lebanon had come to symbolize a refuge for Christian sects in the Middle East and the National Pact became their guarantee that Christian culture would not be absorbed into the surrounding Islamic world.[57]

After independence the question of Lebanon's relations with its Arab neighbors remained a sensitive issue. The Sunni Muslims were sympathetic to some sort of Arab federation since it meant transforming their minority status to that of a majority community. But the Christians, firmly in power, declared the sovereignty of Lebanon to be indivisible (understandably, equating it with their own survival, since Arab federation would transform them into a tiny minority in a predominately Sunni Muslim state[58]) and conducted a moderately pro-Western foreign policy based on that principle, which included nonalignment in dissensions among other Arab states. The Shiites remained politically passive.

Ironically, it was the establishment of Israel in 1948—a non-Islamic state—that indirectly was responsible for regenerating Christian fears. After 1948 the Arab world surrounding Lebanon violently erupted, threatening to envelop Lebanon in its wake. By late 1968 Lebanon's position in the Middle East had become acutely difficult. The presence of displaced Palestinian refugees within Lebanon's borders,[59] the provocative activities of the Palestinian fedayeen operating from Lebanon toward Israel, and the pressure exerted by other Islamic states upon Lebanese leaders to take a more active role in the struggle against Israel all conspired to transform the question of Lebanon's role in the Arab world to one of immediate urgency.

As the Palestinian guerrillas increased their activities along the Lebanese-Israeli border, Israeli retaliatory raids became fiercer and more numerous. Greater sympathy among Muslims for the Arab cause made them more willing to suffer the consequences of allowing the commandos to carry out operations on and from Lebanese soil. But the Christians favored stricter control of the commandos by

asserting Lebanese authority over the camps, in order to avoid
or minimize Israeli reprisals.[60] They voiced their fear that the
activities of the fedayeen would compromise Lebanon's nonprovocative
position in the Arab-Israeli dispute and Lebanon's sovereignty,
ultimately pulling it into the tide of regional Arab politics and armed
confrontation with Israel. The Christians also suspected the Palestinians
of being a potentially divisive and disruptive element in the internal
balance of Lebanese political forces. These fears and suspicions were
not unfounded.

In 1969, as a result of Israeli reprisals for Arab commando
activities mounted from Lebanon, Lebanon suffered a series of
severe political crises. Torn apart by dissension over how to
handle the guerrilla problem, cabinets collapsed while public
opinion tended to polarize along the Christian-Muslim divide. In
April clashes between the Palestinian guerrillas and the Christian-
dominated Lebanese army occurred and antigovernment riots flared
throughout the country. On October 20 the Lebanese armed forces
initiated another crackdown on guerrillas that came close to involving
the country in civil war. In both instances third parties contributed
to the escalation and resolution of the conflict: Syria provoked some
of the fighting and Egypt intervened as mediator. On November 3
a compromise settlement was reached that involved government
concessions to the guerrillas and an agreement by the commandos
to respect Lebanese sovereignty.[61] Essentially unresolved, the
problem continued to fester with violent confrontations between
Palestinian fedayeen and the Lebanese army occuring in 1973 and
again in 1974, while guerrilla raids and Israeli reprisals continued
unabated.

But the injection of the Palestinians into Lebanese society had
other internal political repercussions as well. Beginning in 1970,[62]
as Israeli raids became more destructive, thousands of poor Shiites
in southern Lebanon were driven off the land. Gravitating toward
Beirut and settling in or near Palestinian refugee camps and shanty-
towns there, they found themselves in close proximity to an activist,
proselytizing group espousing Pan-Arab solidarity and greater social
justice. To the embittered Lebanese Muslims, the Palestinians must
have appeared to be natural allies and their political mobilization, seen
in retrospect, became inevitable. In 1975 it was reported that Shiite
Muslims were demanding an end to the National Pact , greater involvement in Pan-Arab causes (in these two demands they were joined by
other Muslims), and a more equitable distribution of the economic
pie.[63]

In addition, reverberations of the October 1973 war could not
but be felt inside Lebanon as well. If, as the Smocks report, the
1967 defeat of Egypt and Syria by Israel undermined the movement
for Arab unity and reconciled many Arab nationalists in Lebanon to the

permanence of the Lebanese state, [64] then it is not farfetched to
assume that the October 1973 war, joyously hailed by the Arab world
as a military and diplomatic victory, served to reinvigorate Arab
nationalism among the various Lebanese Muslim sects, uniting them
on this issue and further separating them from the Christians. [65]

A shooting incident in spring 1975 between Palestinians and
Christians[66] was merely the spark that set off the conflagration. It
was to involve all the various political and religious factions in
Lebanese society in a conflict that grew in intensity and threatened
the partition of the country. [67] Clearly, as the war between the
factions grew in intensity, the international environment intruded to
an even greater extent, exacerbating tensions, prolonging and
escalating the conflict. States within and outside the region lent
diplomatic and material support to the warring sects.* Some
threatened to intervene, others warned of counterintervention. [68]
As the internal war continued, factions within factions formed, each
with its own private army. Arms and financial assistance poured into
the country as Lebanon sank closer to anarchy. [69]

It would seem, on the basis of even this cursory review of
Lebanon's recent history, that since 1969 hardly a political event
occurs within Lebanon that is not influenced by the international

---

*According to U.S. government sources, the Libyan government
sent $30 to $40 million to Lebanon between April and September 1975
to support leftist Muslim groups battling Christian forces, and the
funding continues. The State Department stated that as of September
13, 1975, Libya had become the principal source of outside funds
for six or more Lebanese Muslim fighting bands. It also reported
that Libya seemed to be spending twice as much in support of
Lebanese as in support of the Palestinian guerrillas. "In the
estimate of American analysts, the Libyan spending and the activities
of Libyan agents. . . could prolong or renew the fighting to the point
where a full-scale civil war would be inevitable. A civil war in
Lebanon could easily draw in the Palestinians, Syrians and Israelis..."
Furthermore, the flow of weapons and ammunition to opposing
sides in Lebanon reached such large proportions that U. S. officials
predicted that a continuation of the conflict seemed inevitable. Libyan
money was buying vast quantities of Soviet arms and arms dealers in
Western Germany, Belgium, France, Italy, and Portugal were
selling weapons and ammunitions to the rightwing Phalangist groups
for cash. Occasionally, Phalangists also purchased arms from
Palestinian guerrilla groups in Lebanon (for further details, see
below). The Maronite Christian church and wealthy Lebanese
Christian businessmen and perhaps some conservative Arab
governments financed the rightest arms traffic. (New York Times,
November 18, 1975, p. 3.)

environment.[70] Foreign meddling as well as the outside support
solicited by Lebanon's communal leaders has created a political
and social system so penetrated that any solution will have to be a
product of actions by and agreement among foreign powers.

In general, it is difficult to assess the role the global
environment plays in determining the degree of cohesion within a
political unit. The question smacks of the chicken and egg dilemma.
Does the existence of distinct communal groups make penetration more
probable and intervention more attractive to external actors? Or are
there factors in the international environment itself that are responsible
for igniting and feeding the flames of separatism? The extent to
which exogenous factors have intruded into the political life of
Lebanon indicates the importance of investigating and answering the
question.

Other examples abound. Although information on linkages
derived from the daily newspapers is often by its nature sporadic
and unreliable, the sheet volume of reports indicating the involvement
of foreign powers and other external forces in internal communal
relations suggests that the situation in Lebanon is far from unique.

In the Philippines a constellation of external circumstances
made both internal conflict and its peaceful resolution possible. In
August 1975 a ceasefire agreement was reached through the mediation
efforts of the World Conference of Islamic Nations. The conference,
it was reported, held out the possibility of loans for the economic
development of Mindanao—one of the issues in dispute between the
insurgents and the government—if the settlement was reached.
During the period of conflict, however, the Middle Eastern oil
states—also members of the conference—supplied 70 percent
of Philippine oil needs, while other members are reputed to have
given financial and military aid to the insurgents,[71] thus prolonging
and escalating the conflict.

The situation in Portugal furnishes another example of direct
inputs from the international environment affecting the internal
political balance between dissident groups. Wracked by political
dissension after 40 years of rightwing dictatorship, it seemed in
June 1975 that the disciplined Communist Party under the leadership
of Alvaro Cunhal was about to take over the government. The
socialists charged that the communists were generously funded from
Moscow, which enabled them to employ over 2,000 full-time paid
workers and purchase arms abroad.

But the intervention of other foreign actors apparently turned
the tide. According to James Reston, the Vatican "intervened" to
defend the Catholic community from anticlerical demonstrators of
the Portuguese extreme left. Tourist trade dropped and foreign
investment and the flow of foreign exchange from outside diminished,

threatening the economic viability of the country. But, in Reston's
opinion, it was the pressure the Western powers brought to bear on
the Soviet union to uphold its commitment to détente that probably
turned the political tide. He reports that the United States and other
European governments informed the USSR that if the basis of "détente"
is that the status quo between East and West not be upset, then by
meddling in Portuguese affairs, the Soviet Union risks similar manipulation in Eastern Europe on the part of West. The Soviet Union, they
argued, was risking the end of détente. If the strategic status quo is
to be maintained, there must be nonintervention both ways:

> It is not clear that Moscow is entirely responsible for
> the uprising here. . . . Nor is it clear that these outside
> forces are responsible for the moderate tone of the
> Portuguese military council in recent days. But some-
> thing is changing their tune—some combination of outside
> economic, political, and religious pressure.[72]

By November 1975 the political balance had shifted.[73] For the time
being future political arrangements within Portugal will depend upon
the extent to which forces in the international environment refrain
from or persist in intervening.

A final illustration of the crucial role direct external inputs can
play in determining the willingness of a group to accept some form of
central political control and/or its ability to resist it, can be found
in Iraq. On March 23, 1975, General Mustafa Barzani, leader of the
Iraqi Kurdish rebellion, complained that because he no longer had
foreign support his revolt was over. As a result of a political agreement between Iraq and Iran, Iran withdrew weaponry deployed in the
rebel enclave in mountainous northeast Iraq and stopped all financial
aid and shipments of arms and ammunition. In exchange, Iraq ceded
Shatt-al-Arab Riverain rights to Iran. The termination of Iranian
aid to Barzani eliminated a rebellion by a large ethnic minority that
had festered on and off for years.[74]

The examples thus far have demonstrated the effects direct
outputs from the environment can have upon internal political dissension and cohesion. However, indirect or unintentional environmental
inputs into societies can have a similar impact. Although the relationship between these factors and internal integration is less clearly
established in daily news reports, it is possible to reconstruct
scenarios that may have taken place or perhaps will take place in
the future.

For example, the effect the world economic system can have
upon internal political cohesion may be inferred from events in
Malaysia. The primary problem the government in Malaysia faces

is closing the communal gap between the Malays on the one hand and
the Chinese and Indians on the other, so that political and economic
development can proceed smoothly and ethnic conflict can be avoided.
The issue revolves around the Malay population (55 percent), which
has remained for the most part rural in residence, agricultural in
occupation, and poor. The modern sector of the economy is controlled by the non-Malays out of all proportion to their numbers.
The dilemma for Malaysian leaders has been how to give the Malays
a bigger slice of the economic pie without disrupting the economy or
precipitating communal violence. From the time of independence the
Alliance Government has chosen to deal with the problem by pouring
a disproportionate amount of its revenues into educational and development programs designed to uplift the economically backward
Malays, while at the same time expanding the modern sector of the
economy. However, Malaysia's dependence on the world prices of
tin, rubber, and palm oil for its foreign exchange has meant that
fluctuations in the world market have caused fluctuations in the
progress of the development programs and the rate of economic
expansion.

In 1967 and 1968 sharp declines in the world prices of tin and
rubber so affected government revenue sources that a number of
social welfare and development projects were curtailed and unemployment increased. Communal rioting followed in 1969, hundreds were
killed, and on May 14 the constitution was suspended. Although a
unicausal relationship between world market prices and internal
unrest cannot be established, the widespread discontent of unemployed
Malay youth, according to one report, was a major reason for the
riots,[75] and the year before the minister of finance had publicly
worried about the possibility of communal conflict on those grounds.[76]
Communal discontent in Malaysia may have been a response to
internal factors, but it can be argued that the international economic
environment contributed indirectly but significantly.[77]

The Malaysian example raises certain questions about the
general relationship between integration and the global economic
system. It has been suggested by Deutsch et al. that economic prosperity or decline is an important factor determining national political
integration.[78] But if economic prosperity operates as a kind of
internal social cement, then in a shrinking world economy, will the
external environment determine the degree of social cohesion within
political units? And are certain types of societies—perhaps small
states, or plural societies—more vulnerable to the ups and downs of
world business cycles? In the future will it be the unintended consequences of external economic events rather than internal developments that determine whether group members regard preservation

of the social-political unit as worthwhile or not? And will this be so in all societies or only in some?

Other possible indirect sources of influence on internal integration processes can be derived from news reports. The arms trade system, for example, appears to be taking on a life of its own, bringing about results unanticipated by the donors or the sellers. For instance, the arms sent to Palestinian guerrillas in Lebanon from radical Arab governments to be used in the cause of Pan-Arabism have found their way into the hands of the rightwing Phalangists fighting against the Lebanese Muslims. "It's all very venal," one official is reported as saying, "but there are some Palestinian Fadayeen who will sell to the highest bidder."[79] Prior to spring 1975 Eastern European manufacturers also were selling arms to the rightwing Christians for cash, until the matter became potentially politically embarrassing. Now arms are flowing into Lebanon from private arms dealers all over Western Europe. The New York Times reported: "United States officials . . . believe the flow of weapons and ammunition to the opposing sides there is so large and varied that even despite the current calm, continuation of the civil conflict seems all but inevitable."[80]

Apparently, arms dealers throughout the world are supplying weapons indiscriminately to all sides in various internal wars spanning four continents, from Northern Ireland to the Philippines. In thousands of guerrilla actions hordes of people have been killed or maimed by weapons illicitly and sometimes overtly purchased in the world market. As an illustration, from 1971 to 1975 the Irish Republican Army acquired 50 Soviet-manufactured rocket-launchers from Libya, 175 Armalite hunting rifles from the United States, Chinese-modeled Kalashnikov rifles from Belgium, and German submachine guns from Czechoslovakia. The Basque Homeland and Liberty organization (ETA) purchased from a dealer in Hamburg a stock of Israeli-made Uzi submachine guns.[81]

Although some kind of relationship between the arms trade and integration exists, the nature of that relationship is unclear and needs further exploration. What, for example, is the connection between changes in social structure and the importation of arms? Are countries with communal divisions more prone to escalating arms races? Do the increasing arms imports by a central government induce dissident groups to seek weapons from other governments or private sources? Or are the arms imports themselves catalysts in creating divisions within society? Is a new military class created that strives to replace civilian regimes and does this initiate internal discontent and an arms race? In states where communal divisions in society spill over into the army, as in the case of Lebanon and Malaysia, does military assistance to one or another branch of the military have a differential impact on the development of one particular community? Does it place one group in an advantageous position in terms of technical skills and/or power?

And what role does the structure of the international system play in the relationship between society and arms? Does the international system's structure itself determine the availability of arms to government and dissident groups? For instance, does a bipolar system encourage foreign meddling in the internal affairs of political units and increased arms traffic to a greater extent than does a multipolar system? Would a global international system, characterized by crosscutting networks of thousands of interest groups, reduce the sales of arms? Would the unavailability of weapons increase internal political integration in societies throughout the world?

Questions such as these can be asked in connection with a variety of other variables operating in the international environment. Similar queries might be raised in relation to the transfer of technology and economic assistance. Does the transfer of technology from developed to less developed areas create divisions in either society? On the one hand, in the recipient country, does it create social differences that matter between those with technical training and those without? On the other hand, does technical assistance engender antagonisms between the government and have-not groups in the donor society over whether resources should be distributed within state boundaries and not beyond them? Does foreign technical assistance create elites who by their exposure to travel and study abroad acquire orientations that separate them from other groups in society, thereby creating friction and dissension? Does it introduce regional inequalities?

The number of possible influences originating in the international environment boggles the mind at this pretheoretic stage of conceptualization. Everyday news reports imply new lines of interdependency between internal sociopolitical processes and the environment. But perhaps these examples (and the questions prompted by them) will suffice to give support to the argument presented here that the international system is causally related to the integration process and that an integration model that excludes external factors is of questionable utility.

What is more, the issues raised here lead to other challenging levels of inquiry. Because the observed linkages suggest some kind of relationship between internal integrative processes and the present and future structure of the international system, they call forth additional research questions of immediate concern to many international affairs specialists and policy makers today. For instance, what does the increased penetration reported here mean in the long run for the nation-state and other traditional organizing political units? Is the world witnessing the emergence of a new global system as interdependence theorists have predicted? Have scientific and technical inventions created a global environment where whatever happens anywhere on earth can be known almost instantly everywhere else? Has a shrinking of the universe occurred so that the world has become more alike and the habitats of men at the far reaches of the globe become more and more similar? Has the world reached the stage where disasters in one region, such as crop failures or war, have important economic and political consequences in another? Are the forces in the international system so penetrative that individuals and groups have begun to perceive their self-interest in terms of ever larger agglomerations of groups, stretching beyond subnational and national boundaries on one or many or all issue levels?

Or is the increased particularism reported here evidence of a turning-in, a reversion to a kind of preindustrial feudal communalism? Or perhaps it is a combination of both—"a polarchy in which nation-states, subnational groups, and transnational special interests and communities would all be vying for the support and loyalty of individuals, and conflicts would have to be resolved primarily on the basis of ad hoc bargaining in a shifting context of power relationships."[82]

It is probable, therefore, that the play of international factors described above signifies changes taking place not only within the boundaries of states but in the structure and functioning of the international system as well. However, it is apparent that integration theory has not thus far developed an analytic model capable of dealing with the effects of these international forces. Until it does so, integration theory will remain a crude tool for social scientific investigation. Perhaps the combined efforts of social scientists interested in subsystem levels of analysis and international relations specialists will in the future produce some order out of the conceptual chaos.

CONCLUSIONS AND FUTURE PROSPECTS

The discussion in this essay has admittedly raised many more questions than it was able to answer. But raising questions is a necessary first step toward restructuring the analytical models available to students in the field. Evidently, in its present state of conceptualization, the term integration is not a useful tool for empirical analysis. On the basis of this limited survey, the conclusion, unfortunately, must be that the concept of integration as developed

·thus far is indeed a fitting example of jargon: "Language vague in meaning and full of circumlocutions and long high-sounding words."

First, there is confusion regarding what it is integration theorists are trying to explain. Second, there is no general theory or even logically related conceptual framework, there are no guidelines for research that distinguish between dependent and explanatory variables and link them in some hypothetical framework. Third, implicit biases and overt omissions have made what research findings we do have inapplicable to present-day reality. Integration is a term that remains central in the minds of social scientists in many disciplines, but it has borne little theoretical fruit thus far.

There are, it appears, two possible strategies open to the prospective student in the field: one, to abandon integration as a focus of research because it is too broad and general as a conceptual tool to be of any empirical value; two, to begin to think of new approaches and methods for its analysis.

The latter solution is the more likely one since it is improbable that scholars will willingly give up after years of fascination with the concept of integration, and at a time when parochial uprisings throughout the world make understanding the integrative process ever more urgent.

But the time has come to change the field's methodological and conceptual perspective. In order to overcome the difficulties associated with high-level generalization, it may be necessary for students of integration to use a disciplined but largely configurational method. Asking the right questions and observing a wide variety of political and social units may eventually lead to identifying patterns and constructing typologies on the basis of these queries and observations. For insightful case studies may be all we can hope to achieve in the immediate future.

Factors overlooked by theorists in the past, because of inadvertent conceptual bias, may guide researchers toward important new insights into the process and should be included in future research designs. The interrelationship between the international environment and integration remains an unexplored field of investigation, as does the role force and coercion as integrative (or disintegrative) mechanisms have played in the past and are playing in the present.

It has been suggested by Clifford Geertz that by watching the integrative process at work we shall come to understand it. "This may seem like a mere wait-and-see policy, inappropriate to the predictive ambitions of science. But such a policy is at least preferable, and more scientific, to waiting and not seeing, which has been largely the case to date."[83]

NOTES

1. Myron Weiner, "Political Integration and Political Development," Annals 358 (1965): 54.

2. Donald G. Morrison et al., Black Africa: A Comparative Handbook (New York: The Free Press, 1972), p. 385.

3. Claude Ake, A Theory of Political Integration (Homewood, Ill.: Dorsey Press, 1967), p. 3.

4. See also James S. Coleman and Carl G. Rosberg, eds., Political Parties and National Integration in Africa (Berkeley: University of California Press, 1964).

5. Karl Deutsch et al., "Political Community and the North Atlantic Area," International Political Communities: An Anthology (Garden City, N.Y.: Doubleday, 1966), p. 2.

6. Ibid.

7. Karl W. Deutsch, "Communication Theory and Political Integration," and "Transaction Flows as Indicators of Political Cohesion," in Philip E. Jacob and James V. Toscano, eds., The Integration of Political Communities (Philadelphia: J. B. Lippincott, 1964), pp. 46-97.

8. Fred M. Hayward, "Continuities and Discontinuities between Studies of National and Internation Political Integration," in Leon N. Lindberg and Stuart A. Scheingold, eds., Regional Integration: Theory and Research (Cambridge, Mass.: Harvard University Press, 1971), p. 316.

9. "Concepts are judged not by their truth or falsity, but by their theoretical utility." This is a maxim underscored by Holt and Richardson in their discussion of the nature and function of paradigms. Robert T. Holt and John M. Richardson, Jr., "Competing Paradigms in Comparative Politics," in Robert T. Holt and John E. Turner, eds., The Methodology of Comparative Research (New York: The Free Press, 1970), p. 24.

10. For example, David S. Smock and Audrey C. Smock, The Politics of Pluralism: A Comparative Study of Lebanon and Ghana (New York: Elsevier, 1975). Although the Smocks make fifteen references to the problem associated with "national integration" or the prospects of Ghana or Lebanon achieving it, the term is never defined.

See also Joseph LaPalombara's study of Italy, "Italy: Fragmentation, Isolation, Alienation," in Lucien W. Pye and Sidney Verba, eds., Political Culture and Political Development (Princeton, N.J.: Princeton University Press, 1965), pp. 282-329. LaPalombara devotes over five pages to a discussion of "imperfect integration"

without defining what he means by it. The examples are so numerous
in the comparative politics literature that one can almost pick out a
study at random and find similar treatment of the term.

11. See Arend Lijphart, "Cultural Diversity and Theories of
Political Integration," Canadian Journal of Political Science 12
(March 1971): 1–14.

12. Deutsch et al., "Political Community," p. 17.

13. Louis J. Cantori and Stephen L. Spiegel, "Analysis of
Regional International Politics: The Integration Versus the Empirical
Systems Approach," International Organization 27 (1973): 480–81.

14. Hedley Bull, "International Theory: The Case for a Classical
Approach," World Politics 18 (April 1966): 373–75.

15. Philip E. Jacob and Henry Teune, "The Integrative Process:
Guidelines for Analysis of the Bases of Political Community," in Jacob
and Toscano, eds., Integration, p. 23; Ernst B. Haas, Beyond the
Nation-State: Functionalism and International Organization (Stanford,
Calif.: Stanford University Press, 1964), p. 27.

16. Bruce M. Russett, Community and Contention: Britain and
America in the Twentieth Century (Cambridge, Mass.: MIT Press,
1963), p. 33.

17. Jacob and Teune, "The Integrative Process," p. 4.

18. Ibid., p. 18.

19. Ibid., p. 19.

20. Morrison et al., Black Africa, p. 385.

21. Ibid., p. 386.

22. British Journal of Sociology 7, no. 3 (October 1956): 194–
211.

23. Smock and Smock, The Politics of Pluralism, p. 12.

24. Ibid., p. 13.

25. Aristede R. Zolberg, "Patterns of National Integration,"
Journal of Modern African Studies 5, no. 4 (1967): 451–52.

26. "National Integration and Political Development," American
Political Science Review 58, no. 3 (September 1964): 630.

27. Coleman and Rosberg, eds., Political Parties, p. 9. They
define the integration process in two senses: territorial integration
quoted above in the text and "political integration which refers to the
progressive bridging of the elite-mass gap on the vertical plane."

28. Cynthia H. Enloe, Ethnic Conflict and Political Development (Boston: Little, Brown, 1973), pp. 261–74.

29. Alvin Rabushka and Kenneth A. Shepsle, Politics in Plural
Societies: A Theory of Democratic Instability (Columbus, Ohio:
Charles E. Merrill, 1972), p. 18.

30. Lijphart, "Cultural Diversity," p. 11.

31. Arend Lijphart, "Typologies of Democratic Systems,"
Comparative Political Studies 1 (1968): 29–30.

32. J. S. Furnivall, Netherlands India: A Study in Indirect Rule (Cambridge: Cambridge University Press, 1939); and Colonial Policy and Practice: A Comparative Study of Burma and Netherlands India (New York: New York University Press, 1956).

33. Leo Kuper, "Plural Societies: Perspectives and Problems," in Leo Kuper and M. G. Smith, eds., Pluralism in Africa (Berkeley: University of California Press, 1971), p. 11.

34. M. G. Smith expands Furnivall's definition of the plural society in The Plural Society in the British West Indies (Berkeley: University of California Pres, 1974): "Given the fundamental differences of belief, value and organization that connote pluralism, the monopoly of power by one cultural section is the essential precondition for the maintenance of the total society in its current form" (p. 86).

35. Hannah Arendt, The Origins of Totalitarianism (New York: Harcourt, Brace, 1951), p. 305. See also William Kornhauser, The Politics of Mass Society (Glencoe, Ill.: The Free Press, 1959).

36. On November 19, 1975, Prime Minister Harold Wilson's Labor Party government announced its intention to provide Scotland and Wales with some form of home rule, a move that represents a profound constitutional change for Great Britain. (New York Times, November 20, 1975.) Scotland, Wales, and Britain were constitutionally joined in 1707 by the Act of Union that formed the Kingdom of Great Britain.

37. In the Smocks' framework, movement toward national accommodation is characterized by "decreasing strife and political instability arising from communal confrontation; increasing attachment to the political system; more accommodative behavior on a personal level; greater acceptance of a national frame of reference; and convergence in basic values pertaining to the major goals of the political system. Although it is not possible to measure precisely the degree to which either the Lebanese or the Ghanaian political system has moved in these directions . . . the Lebanese system exhibits decreasing strife and instability." Smock and Smock, The Politics of Pluralism, p. 322.

38. Ibid.

39. Ibid., p. 325.

40. Sidney Verba, "Some Dilemmas in Comparative Research," World Politics 20 (October 1967): 113.

41. Ibid., p. 115.

42. Ibid.

43. Zolberg, "Patterns of National Integration," p. 452.

44. "When and if the word [nation-state] becomes flesh, it may differ so much from any previously existing political entities that we shall have to stretch the referents of our own definition of the nation

as a set of political arrangements, or invent a new word altogether."
Ibid., p. 467.

45. Lijphart, "Cultural Diversity," p. 12.

46. Ibid., p. 16.

47. Karl Deutsch et al., Political Community and the North
Atlantic Area (Princeton, N.J.: Princeton University Press, 1957),
pp. 44-45.

48. Fred W. Riggs, "The Dialectics of Developmental Conflict,"
Comparative Political Studies 1, no. 2 (July 1968): 201.

49. Ibid., p. 202.

50. Fred W. Riggs, "Systems Theory: Structural Analysis,"
in Michael Haas and Henry S. Kariel, eds., Approaches to the Study
of Political Science (Scranton, Pa.: Chandler, 1970), pp. 208ff.

51. James N. Rosenau, "Theorizing Across Systems: Linkage
Politics Revisited," in Jonathan Wilkenfeld, ed., Conflict Behavior
and Linkage Politics (New York: David McKay, 1973), p. 29.

52. Lijphart, "Typologies of Democratic Systems," pp. 28-29.

53. James M. Markham, "Cry, Lebanon," New York Times
Magazine, November 9, 1975, p. 22.

54. Ibid. See also Smock and Smock, The Politics of Pluralism,
p. 328.

55. Smock and Smock, The Politics of Pluralism, p. 327.

56. Writing before the outbreak of communal violence in 1975,
the Smocks noted that "although economic disparities between communal groups exacerbate communal conflict in both Lebanon and Ghana,
in neither country does the sharpest intergroup conflict arise between
the most deprived group and the more advantaged. The deepest cleavage in Lebanon comes between the Maronites and the Sunnis, although
the Shiites are the most disadvantaged group and seemingly would
have the most legitimate grounds for complaint." Ibid., p. 310.

57. Markham, "Cry, Lebanon," p. 30.

58. Smock and Smock, The Politics of Pluralism, p. 312.

59. The number of Palestinians residing in Lebanon in 1975 is
estimated to be about 400,000. See Markham, "Cry, Lebanon," p. 30.

60. Smock and Smock, The Politics of Pluralism, p. 312.

61. Paul L. Hanna, "Lebanon," Encyclopedia Americana
Annual, 1970, p. 415.

62. The Palestinian commando movement shifted its headquarters to Lebanon after King Hussein drove it from Jordan beginning
in "Black September" of 1970. Markham, "Cry, Lebanon," p. 30.

63. On July 7, 1975, the New York Times reported that an
explosion at a training camp disclosed links between Palestinian
guerrillas and Shiite leftist Muslims. Apparently, a Palestinian in-
structor had been demonstrating the use of explosives to a group of
130 followers of Imam Musa al-Sadr, the religious leader of the

Shiite Muslim sect. Imam Musa, the article states, advocates sending the Lebanese army and other military units to join the guerrillas along the border with Israel. He also stands for political and social changes in Lebanon that would give Muslims a stronger voice in government and channel more funds into development of the poorest regions. "During the fighting in this capital, Shiite militiamen were in the thick of combat in the Chiah district, where they were joined by Palestinians and other Lebanese leftists in fighting against the Phalangist [Christian] groups."

64. Smock and Smock, The Politics of Pluralism, pp. 156-57.

65. The Smocks commented on the unity of Muslim opinion on this issue in 1974: "During 1974 the continuing confrontations between Lebanon and Israel and between Lebanon and Palestinian commandos led to somewhat divergent reactions between Christians and Muslims. Muslim leaders charged that the two leading Christian political parties, the Kataeb and the Liberal National Party, were strengthening their paramilitary units in preparation for a showdown with Palestinian commandos, and one armed skirmish did occur. Regarding Israel, many Muslim leaders wanted Lebanon to strengthen its defenses in the face of Israeli incursions and to achieve closer military coordination with other Arab states." Ibid., p. 155.

66. On April 13 a busload of Palestinian militants was fired on by machine guns; 27 Palestinians were killed. The Palestinians accused the Phalangists; although the accusation was denied, sporadic street fighting began. Markham, "Cry, Lebanon," p. 30.

67. Reporting from Beirut, James M. Markham writes that although the Maronites accuse the leftists of wanting to divide the country, some Maronites privately favor the idea themselves. Pierre Gemayel, the Phalangist leader, has implied that the Lebanese situation might be resolved in that way. New York Times, September 24, 1975, p. 3.

68. On November 16, 1975, Syria's foreign minister hinted that Syria might intervene militarily to prevent any partition of Lebanon. (New York Times, November 17, 1975.) The following day Israel warned of dire consequences if Syria intervened militarily. By November 29 Saudi Arabia had joined the admonishing chorus. Crown Prince Fahd was quoted as saying that if a Christian state was established "on the debris of the present coexistence among the Lebanese communities, this will have the most serious consequences" on Lebanese-Saudi relations. "We will deal only with the Arab Lebanon that we have known for many years." New York Times, November 29, 1975.

69. See New York Times, November 22, 1975, for a description of life in Beirut during the period of communal fighting. Teen-age armed gangs ruled the streets and "every householder keeps a pistol

if not an automatic rifle" because of the increase in robbery. Shakedowns and protection were a part of everyday life. One man commented: "People say now a man's life is worth two piasters."

70. As of this writing, for example, Syria has taken an overtly dominant role in Lebanese internal affairs. On January 22, 1976, a cease-fire negotiated under the auspices of Syria was agreed to by the various Lebanese factions. On March 12, however, a military coup took place, apparently with the knowledge and consent of the Syrian government. Fifty Syrian military officers stationed in Lebanon under the terms of the cease-fire agreement were withdrawn and fighting among various Lebanese factions began again (New York Times, March 19, 1976).

71. New York Times, August 18, 1975.

72. James Reston, "Portugal and Detente," New York Times, June 6, 1975.

73. It was reported in the New York Times, November 29, 1975, that Portugal's military leaders had started a wide-ranging purge of the leftwing elements among the press, politicians, and the armed forces.

74. C. L. Sulzberger, "His Kurds, and Why," New York Times, March 29, 1975, p. 23.

75. C. Paul Bradley, "Malaysia," The Americana Annual, 1970, p. 427.

76. "The real basic problem, however, which we face in the coming years is the problem of growing unemployment. It is not only an economic problem, it could well become an explosive social and political problem unless we tackle it in time and overcome it, and the realistic way of dealing with this problem is to achieve an adequate rate of economic growth." Text of speech by Minister of Finance Tan Siew Sin, introducing the Supply (1968) Bill to the House of Representatives, January 18, 1968, p. 51.

77. For another example of the interrelationship between the world economy and communal disparities in Malaysia, see the description in the New York Times, September 4, 1975, p. 2, on the effect of plummeting palm oil prices on the fortunes of Malay settlers participating in the Federal Land Development Authority's jungle-clearing program.

78. Deutsch et al., Political Community and the North Atlantic Area, p. 63.

79. New York Times, November 18, 1975, p. 3.

80. Ibid.

81. Robert Fisk, "The World's Terrorists Sometimes Are United," New York Times, August 17, 1975, section 4, p. 3.

82. Seyom Brown, New Forces in World Politics (Washington, D.C.: Brookings Institution, 1974), p. 186.

83. Clifford Geertz, "The Integrative Revolution: Primordial Sentiments and Civil Politics in the New States," in Clifford Geertz, ed., Old Societies and New States: The Quest for Modernity in Asia and Africa (Glencoe, Ill.: The Free Press, 1963), p. 157.

2

INTERNATIONAL FACTORS AND THE FAILURE OF POLITICAL INTEGRATION IN CYPRUS
Adamantia Pollis

Current literature on political integration by and large reveals considerable conceptual and analytic confusion. There is little concern with or agreement on what it is that is being investigated, and little distinction is made among descriptive statements regarding an integrated state, the requisites for the integration of nation-states, and the general processes of integration. The question of "integration into what?" is frequently sidestepped, so that international integration, regional integration, community integration, and national integration are all lumped together.

Yet the content of political integration, the specifics that characterize it, vary depending on the legitimating principle of the particular ideology underlying different social orders. Thus, political integration in the Chinese dynasties, in the Austro-Hungarian empire, and in the Ottoman empire has a different meaning and a different content than political integration in nation-states. The ideological underpinnings and the legitimacy principle of each of these political regimes were distinctive. Hence the requisite behavior, attitudinal, and institutional patterns for political integration similarly differ.

Analytically there are at least three distinct issues posed: (1) the question of the requisites for political integration in varying "systems" with differing legitimating principles; (2) the question of what variables bring about integration in particular "systems"; and (3) the question of the processes of integration that may be similar regardless of the differing requisites for different political systems.

This chapter addresses the processes of integration (or disintegration) with reference to a particular social order—a nation-state. Legitimate political authority in the modern world is predicated on the principle of nationality. It is this principle that justifies a world order composed of nation-states. Therefore, discussion of political integration must specify the parameters of political integration within the context of a nation-state. Given the world view and value presuppositions of a nation-state system, the requisites for the integration of such political regimes would seem to include: acceptance by its members of the legitimacy of the state; primary loyalty to the nation-state; some form of participation in the political system; a belief in shared commonalities; and national political and economic institutional structures. Therefore, an analysis of political integration must consist of an investigation into the variables relevant for bringing about the aforementioned set of conditions.

Theorists of political integration share an assumption that the processes of integration can be looked for or analyzed within the confines of the boundaries of the sovereign state—of the state being investigated. The problems of national integration, the persistence of cleavages, and the absence of consensus are invariably attributed to factors internal to the system. One group of theorists tends to focus on the need to eradicate ethnic, religious, and cultural differences and to develop common loyalties and shared symbols as a way of creating integration, thereby emphasizing the psychological and cultural aspects of integration. Another group of theorists concern themselves with instituting function interdependence that is visible and measurable, as a means of creating integration. But all theories of integration look for the relevant variables within the unit being studied; systemic factors (those impinging upon the state from outside its boundaries) by and large are neglected. This study intends to investigate the extent to which—at least in one particular case, Cyprus—political integration may have been precluded, not primarily because of internal factors but because of the policies and actions of foreign powers.

A study of Cyprus is in essence a study of political disintegration. As such it provides significant insights into the crucial variables that transformed a society that was integrated within the context of the political system of the Ottoman empire into a sovereign state devoid of political integration. The historical investigation that follows, by pointing to systemic factors as significant determinants of developments in Cyprus, thus challenges prevailing theories of political integration.

During the nineteenth century Cyprus manifested the requisite conditions for the transformation of a prenationalist society into a politically integrated nation-state. Within the context of the parameters of the Ottoman empire, Cyprus was integrated. There were religious differences, but the population was characterized by a high degree of cultural homogeneity and economic integration. But the potential for the formation of a modern nation-state did not materialize. In fact, during the first half of the twentieth century, Cyprus became increasingly polarized between Greeks and Turks, eventuating in nearly complete segregation of the two communities and, albeit within the legal framework of a sovereign state, the formation of two nations. How a people within the boundaries of a clearly defined geographic area, an island, who had shared a culture and a history, evolved into two separate nationalities, may be understood in terms of the historical processes of social change. Several relevant factors require investigation: first, the fabric of Cypriot society and culture prior to British rule which began in 1878, including the spheres of integration and cleavage; second, the impact of British colonial policies on Cypriot culture, society, and politics; third, the impact of Greek and Turkish mainland nationalisms on the Cypriot people; and fourth, the impact of the policies of foreign powers—Greece, Turkey, Great Britain, and the United States—on developments within Cyprus.

As is evident, the focus of the discussion will be on the role of foreign powers, both as the crucial decision makers for Cyprus and as crucial determinants of internal Cypriot realities. It will be contended that the policies and actions of foreign powers, in pursuit of their own national interests, thwarted the evolution of a unified nationalist movement and a shared national consciousness in Cyprus. The structuring of a Cypriot reality by foreign powers, through control over areas of Cypriot policy making through penetration of Cypriot institutions and the very imposition of new parallel institutions for the "Greek" and "Turkish" communities, deflected a potential nationalist movement into two distinct and antagonistic nationalisms. Concomitantly, institutions (both governmental and nongovernmental) that might have enabled Cyprus to function effectively were "prohibited" from developing.

By and large, theoretical analyses of integration, particularly as applied to developing areas, have ignored the role of foreign powers as crucial factors in the integration process both in terms of the colonial legacy and in terms of their continuing policies. With the exception of countries in which political division was a consequence of international conflict rooted in the cold war—Germany, Korea, Vietnam—the role of foreign powers in dividing potentially integrated states where there has been no great power ideological conflict has been ignored. Cyprus has not been an East-West ideological battleground. Yet its experience seems to indicate that "foreign powers" still are largely responsible for creating the requisite conditions and the structural and psychological framework for the emergence of two nationalisms and for eventual political division.

DIVISION AND DISUNITY

Political scientists have been rightly accused of being a-historical both in terms of the static nature of their models and in terms of ignoring historical developments. A view of Cyprus, and many other countries such as Northern Ireland, from a contemporary perspective would tend to provide some confirmation of the integrationist theories regarding the causes of internal division and conflict. Thus a static analysis of Cyprus, ignoring the developmental processes and restricting itself to internal factors, would attribute the divisiveness in Cyprus to the existence on the island of two hostile ethnic groups, Greek and Turk, a situation that will lead irrevocably to the establishment of two separate states. The current conflict between the Cypriot communities, precipitated by the Turkish invasion of Cyprus in July 1974 (ostensibly to protect the Turkish Cypriot minority threatened by developments in the Greek Cypriot community) has presaged a probable end of the 15-year-old sovereign state of Cyprus. Whatever the solution to the current stalemate regarding the future of the island—two autonomous geographic areas, one Turkish, one Greek, joined in some kind of federation, or a canton system "united" in some form of federation, or partition*—the outcome from the perspective of the political integration theorists must appear to be an inevitable consequence of the "traditional" enmity between two conflicting ethnic groups.

The history of postindependence Cyprus from 1960 to date has in reality been one of continual conflict and at times violence between the Greek and Turkish communities. The London and Zurich agreements of 1959 provided for Cyprus's independence but saddled the country with an inoperative constitution. The partnership notion, incorporated in the constitution and extolled by the British when they relinquished control in 1960, lasted less than four years. December 1963 marked the first outbreak of violence between the Greek and Turkish Cypriot communities—first in the capital, Nicosia, and then in the countryside. The violence was precipitated in part by President Makarios's proposals for constitutional revision, which incorporated provisions for a unitary state.[1] The violence subsided, threats of a Turkish air invasion in 1964 were dropped, and a United Nations Peacekeeping Force (UNFICYP) was sent to Cyprus in 1964.

---

*Another possibility that became evident during the fall of 1975 is that Turkey's policy may be the eventual annexation of the entire island.

Another major conflict arose in 1967, and another threatened air invasion by Turkey was deterred by U.S. and Soviet pressure. Then, with the aid of UNFICYP, peace was maintained on the island until July 1974, except for minor incidents. On July 15 the Greek military junta, in conjunction with Cypriot National Guard officers (the only legal armed forces in the country), executed a coup in Cyprus, overthrowing President Makarios and replacing him with Nicos Sampson, a member of EOKA B, a fanatical rightwing terrorist organization advocating union of Cyprus with Greece. Turkey understandably viewed these developments as a threat and danger to the Turkish Cypriot community and invaded the island.

From 1964 to 1974 numerous proposals for a solution to the problem of the political relations between the Greek and Turkish Cypriot communities had been made and intermittent negotiations had taken place. Intercommunal talks between the Greek and Turkish Cypriot leadership initiated in January 1968 were held off and on. In November 1971 the Greek and Turkish Cypriot representatives at the talks were augmented by one Greek and one Turkish government representative, ostensibly sitting as "constitutional experts," and by a representative of the secretary-general of the United Nations, sitting as a mediator. The respective proposals of the two sides stemmed from such divergent and antagonistic premises that reconciliation and compromise were hardly possible. With the Turkish invasion of July 1974, a de facto situation of partition was created with the potential of becoming de jure.

Even before the Turkish army occupation of 40 percent of the island in the summer of 1974, segregation had become thorough. The separate institutions for the two communities required by the imposed constitution of 1960 had been extended to cover voluntary associations; after the violence of 1964 social segregation, if not economic and territorial segregation, had become almost total.[*] The Turkish invasion of July 1974 imposed in addition nearly complete geographic division through forced population movement. Greek Cypriots from the Turkish army-controlled northern area have fled south, and it is estimated that there are approximately 183,000 refugees. Approximately 12,000 Turkish refugees, predominantly on British bases on the island, were airlifted to Turkey and then moved to northern Cyprus and settled on land owned by Greek

---

[*] Significantly, even with this segregation some trading between the Greek and Turkish sectors persists. See M. A. Ramady, "The Role of Turkey in Greek-Turkish Cypriot Relations," paper presented at the Middle East Studies Association, Louisville, Ky., November 22, 1975.

Cypriots.[2] Concurrently, many Greek Cypriots are attempting to
flee the island. On February 13, 1975, Turkish Cypriot leader
Rauf F. Denktash announced the formation of a Turkish Federated
State of Cyprus consisting of the northern 40 percent of the island
occupied and controlled by the Turkish army from mainland Turkey.
Administratively, the northern area has been incorporated into the
Turkish district of Mersin, a port on mainland Turkey approximately
40 miles from the island, while the Turkish postal service is used
and Turkish currency circulates in this area. Renewed Greek and
Turkish Cypriot talks broke down with the formation of the Turkish
Federated State of Cyprus but resumed in the summer of 1975 while
the Greek Cypriots brought the issue before the Security Council of
the United Nations.*

The recent political developments discussed above are under-
pinned by the existence in Cyprus today of two competing and conflicting politically relevant reference groups—Greek and Turkish. In
the past decade it would have been difficult to find a Cypriot nationality with a common history, a common culture, shared symbols, and
so forth. On one level the history of the Greek Cypriots has become
the history of Greece, and the history of the Turkish Cypriots, the
history of Turkey. The Turkish Cypriots cannot be viewed as a
minority within an alien nation-state since the majority, the Greeks,
themselves have related to another country and nation-state, Greece.
As a Turkish information officer stated during the summer of 1972,
"In Cyprus you are not dealing with the question of minority rights.
You are dealing with two national groups."[3] Or as Rauf R. Denktash,
leader of the Turkish Cypriot community, has stated, "Cypriots are
the extension of Turkey through Turkish Cypriots and the extension
of Greece through Greek Cypriots."[4] The Greek Cypriots concur in
large measure, although arguing that most nation-states have minority
ethnic, tribal, or religious groups within their boundaries.

---

*The Cyprus issue has been before the United Nations several
times since the Cyprus coup in July 1974 and the subsequent Turkish
invasion. The first discussion in the Security Council in August 1974
provided for a ceasefire, while in November the General Assembly
adopted a resolution that, among other provisions, asked for the
withdrawal of foreign troops and the return of the refugees to their
homes. The Security Council considered Cyprus again in February
1975 after the proclamation of the Turkish Federated State of Cyprus
and provided for intercommunal talks under the auspices of the
secretary-general. These talks broke down in July 1975 and the
General Assembly considered Cyprus again in November 1975,
reaffirming its earlier resolutions.

It is evident that one dimension of the strife between Greeks and Turks in Cyprus is rooted in psychological factors—questions of identity and loyalty. In turn, the psychological distance between Greek and Turk is reflected in and reinforced by the prevailing institutional and social segregation of the past 15 years. This contemporary reality, however, is in part a surface reality and in part the culmination of developments extending over a period of nearly 100 years. Political integration theorists would not look beyond this apparent contemporary reality in Cyprus. They would ignore the fact that there was no preordained necessity or inevitability leading to the existence of two nationalities on Cyprus. To understand in meaningful and analytic terms the historical developments that brought division, one must view them as the historian Frederich Teggart would, in terms of the processes of change—"how things have come to be as they are."[5] In so doing, the discussion of historical social change in Cyprus starts with a consideration of the social and political system that prevailed in the centuries when Cyprus was part of the Ottoman empire from 1571 to 1878.

THE CYPRIOTS OF THE OTTOMAN EMPIRE

Throughout its history, the population of Cyprus has been an admixture of ethnic, tribal, and religious groups, but until the twentieth century whatever division and conflict existed was along lines other than nationality. During the Ottoman era the primary reference group for the mass of the population was the village and the attendant kinship system. Extending beyond the village, relatedness and identity reflected religion. There is evidence in fact that the Orthodox Christian population of the island welcomed the coming of the Ottomans, who overthrew the repressive Catholic rulers who had attempted to convert the population to Catholicism.[6]

In accord with the Islamic conception of the Ottoman empire, Christians (and Jews) were dhimis, a category above that of pagans and polytheists but below that of Muslims. As such, Christians and Jews were to be protected, although they were not to enjoy the privileges accorded the true believers. As a consequence religious freedom was permitted and the Eastern Orthodox Church and its clerical hierarchy was restored to the preeminence and power it had exercised in earlier centuries. The Ottomans organized their subjects into separate religious communities ruled in both civil and religious matters by their own clerics, called millets. By contrast to the modern nation-state, the proper function of the polity in the prenationalist Ottoman era did not include the welfare of its people; the

state was not of and for the people. Hence the religious underpinnings of the Ottoman empire did not imply, either for the
rulers or the ruled, any notion of participation in the decision-
making processes of the empire. Particularly after the demise,
during the sixteenth century, of the policy of recruiting Christian
children for palace service or for service in the Janissary Corps,
the obligations of the Christians to the sultan were limited largely
to the payment of various forms of taxes. The prevailing social
order, structured along religious lines, was perceived as legitimate by all concerned. The economic exploitation and the corruption of the Ottoman administrative taxation system, which in
the empire's later years accounted for many of the difficulties
encountered by the sultans, affected Christians, Jews, and Muslims
alike.

      The composition of the Cypriot population at the time of the
Ottoman conquest in 1571 is uncertain. Many Catholics fled or hid
their identity. Initially the Ottomans granted fiefs of Cypriot
land to officers in payment for military service rendered to the
empire. Soon thereafter, given the depleted population of the
island,[7] people from other parts of the empire—destitute peasants
from Anatolia, brigands and nomads, and even some skilled miners—
were transferred to Cyprus.[8] The influx of Muslims, only some of
whom were from Turkish tribes and some of whom may have been
Christian, nevertheless added to an already existing Arab Muslim
population. No accurate data on the religious composition of the
Cypriot population in the seventeenth or eighteenth centuries exists,
but most estimates indicate that in the eighteenth century there was
a preponderance of Muslims over Christians.[9] In fact there is
considerable evidence that up to the nineteenth century conversions
to Islam were common.[10] By the end of the nineteenth century,
however, this had been reversed and Christians predominated.[11]

      The intergroup conflicts that existed during the Ottoman era
clearly were not drawn along nationalist lines. The concept of
nationality was meaningless to the Cypriots during the period of
Ottoman rule. Individual Cypriots who had fought in or defended the
Greek War of Independence in 1821 were few and seemed to be
"mercenaries" rather than nationalists. Even in the twentieth
century when the Eastern Orthodox Christians increasingly began to
view themselves as Greeks, the Muslims continued to view themselves
as a religious, not a nationalist, group. In Turkey itself it was not
until the 1920s with Kemal Ataturk's revolution that the religious
premises of the Ottoman empire were abandoned and efforts were made
to establish Turkey as a secularized nation-state. The incipient
prenationalist trends of the pre-Ataturk era in the Ottoman empire
had left the Cypriot Muslims untouched, as did Ataturk's revolution
itself.

Conflicts during the Ottoman period in Cyprus did exist but seem to have been along class lines. As in many nonnationalist societies, there was little relatedness to or sense of identification between rulers and ruled. The way of life of the elite—their culture, values, beliefs, and behavior—were markedly at variance with that of the peasantry. The social structure in Cyprus was such that all classes were composed of both Muslims and Christians. The distinctions and behavioral consequences of religious differences were minimal by comparison to those of class. The influx into Cyprus of a Muslim population that settled as peasants on the land and conversions insured a peasant population composed of both Muslims and Christians. The Muslim peasantry was dispersed throughout the island; villages by and large were mixed Muslim and Christian and there were apparently numerous joint village ventures. This peasantry, Muslim and Christian, had little in common with and did not relate to or identify with the ruling oligarchy of Ottoman adminis - trators, Muslim and Christian landowners, and the Orthodox Church hierarchy. A third stratum, between the rulers and the peasantry, the tax farmers and tax collectors, again both Muslim and Christian, was dependent upon the rulers.

As the efficiency of the Ottoman empire declined, due to spreading corruption, the increasing exploitation of the peasantry— primarily through ruinous taxation imposed by Ottoman administrators, Orthodox bishops and local tax gatherers—peasant discontent, both Muslim and Christian, mounted. This discontent periodically erupted in peasant revolts. As a historian of Cyprus has stated, "small revolts in which Turks as well as Greeks were concerned, seem to have been continuously breaking out."[12] A peasant revolt of both Muslims and Christians was recorded as early as 1578. A major uprising in which the new Ottoman governor, Chil Osman, was killed took place in 1765 when the governor announced a decision to double the tax.[13] In the nineteenth century peasant revolts seemed to increase in frequency—1804, 1830, and a massive one in 1833. These rebellions in Cyprus stemmed from an exploitation that forced the peasants into a poverty more severe than they judged their due. The religion of the oppressors seemed of little importance to the oppressed, who were both Christian and Muslim.

Identification in terms of class interest was reinforced by other cultural commonalities. No European traveler or observer of Cyprus over a period of several centuries, and as late as the nineteenth century, comments on cultural distinctions or differences in "national character" between Muslim and Christian, although they comment on differences between the Cypriots and the Greeks of main- land Greece.[14] Intermingling of Christians and Muslims was frequent, as was conversion. Despite Islamic and Orthodox laws to the contrary, intermarriage was prevalent,[15] as was the interchangeable use by

Muslims and Christians of their respective places of worship. In addition, despite the millet system, in villages where municipal councils were elected this was done jointly by Muslims and Christians.[16] No separate municipalities for Muslims and Christians existed.

In view of the above discussion, a significant theoretical question poses itself. How did a society whose people for centuries, albeit perceiving differences along religious lines, nevertheless shared a common culture and related along class lines, evolve into two distinct nationalities? How did separate formal and informal insitutions, accompanied by increasing economic segregation, evolve for governing the two communities? How did two groups come to contend for the same territory?

Logically it would seem that a Cypriot nationalism should easily have emerged. If it is to be argued that existent religious differences were transposed into nationality differences, the problem remains as to why religion came to be viewed as psychologically significant whereas class identity was dismissed as irrelevant. It is hardly possible to claim as a generalization that religion is the foundation of national identity given the number of instances in which religious identity did not evolve into a single nationality and the number of instances in which different religions are part of the same nationality. An argument in terms of the revival of a latent national consciousness that had lain dormant for centuries is reminiscent of the views of the German romantic, a view hardly related to empirical realities and refutable by Cyprus's independent history and the admixture of many peoples on the island. During the Ottoman era in-groups and out-groups were defined in terms of religious and class lines, with class frequently cutting across religious barriers, while political authority was "legitimately" in the hands of the sultan and his representatives. The process of transformation of Cypriot society began with the imposition of British colonial rule.

THE NATIONALIZATION OF CYPRIOTS

British colonial rule (1878-1960) in Cyprus was rooted in the general conceptual framework that governed British rule of all colonies. The British contended that, although the indigenous population could be trained in certain skills, it differed innately from the British and consequently could not be assimilated. From this underlying precept, and as a matter of efficient administrative procedure for minimizing colonial costs, the British evolved the policy of indirect rule—a policy whereby British governance was exercised through existing institutions. Theoretically, the indigenous culture was therefore to remain formally intact. Such was the polity in Cyprus despite the changes from time to time in the colony's legal status.[17]

The imposition on any society of a new alien ruling elite and the adoption of policies designed to further the interests of the colonial power inevitably has an impact on the existing social system, no matter how indirect the form of rule. Among the more observable changes brought about by the British in Cyprus were the training of an indigenous civil service, the introduction of a new legal system, and the enactment of a literacy program. A new, modernized, largely British-trained Cypriot elite, both "Greek" and "Turkish," developed.* Not to be minimized was the impact of the establishment of British military bases on the island on Cypriot culture and on the economy.

More far-reaching than the above as a determinant of the future course of nationalist development and intergroup conflict between the Greek and Turkish communities was the manner of implementation of indirect rule. Such a policy presumes an understanding of social realities in the colony. However, this understanding was in terms of the Englishman's frame of reference. Granting a divide-and-rule policy, the British did not exploit existing psychologically relevant differences but redefined those differences within a British conceptual framework. Thus the meaning of religious differences and the millet system in Cyprus was comprehended by the British in nationalist terms.[18] Hence, the British took apolitical religious differences in Cyprus between Muslims and Eastern Orthodox and through indirect rule politicized them and transformed them into nationality groups. The generally shared culture and values were ignored, as were the common bonds among members of the same socioeconomic strata, irrespective of religion. By adopting a particula: set of educational and political policies, differences were exacerbated and redefined while commonalities were relegated to insignficance. As a consequence, the prospects for the development of a Cypriot nationality were nearly precluded.

Traditionally in Cyprus the primary structures for socialization were the kinship system and the church or mosque, the latter disseminating religious precepts. There were practically no formal schools.[19] It was the British in their campaign against illiteracy who established a formal educational system. By 1918 there were 729 elementary schools and several secondary ones.[20] But this

---

* As in many British colonies, the British trained a competent administrative elite, which resulted in a Cypriot bureaucracy that was more modernized and conformed to Weber's legal-rational model.

Interestingly, the leaders of the two ethnic communities in Cyprus today—Glafkos Clerides and Rauf Dentash—are British trained and former classmates.

new structure, rather than being unified, was divided. Two
boards of education were created, one Greek, the other Ottoman.
Control over these two educational systems was vested in Athens
and Constantinople, respectively. School teachers were imported
from Greece and from the Ottoman empire, curricula and texts
for use in the classroom were subject to approval by the respective
boards of education. [21]

   The establishment of a dual secular school system insured
the development of two political cultures; the Muslims and Orthodox
learned different languages, different histories, and different
ideologies. [22] The indigenous "Greek" and "Turkish" Cypriot
languages are variants of Greek and Turkish; so much so that they
are largely incomprehensible on the mainlands. A new generation was
reared in the rhetoric of their respective nationalisms. For the
Eastern Orthodox the transposition from an apolitical religious
reference group to a politicized nationally reference group was
relatively easy given the centrality of religion in the concept of
Greek nationality. In Greece proper the nineteenth century was the
era of the Megali idea, an irredentist nationalism that included Cyprus.
These nationalist goals were transmitted through the Greek Cypriot
educational system. As for the Muslims, the transformation to Turks
was a more difficult psychological process and a later historical
development. The absence of a Turkish nationalism in the nineteenth
or early twentieth century meant that religion rather than nationality
persisted as the operative distinction in the "Turkish" schools in
Cyprus. Even with the advent of Kemal Ataturk in the mid 1920s, his
secular nationalism was not a concept to which the Muslim Cypriots
easily related. It was not until the middle 1950s with the rise of a
Greek Cypriot nationalist movement advocating enosis (union)
with Greece, and with British insistence that Turkey be a participant
in negotiations regarding independence for Cyprus, that Turkish
nationalism found some roots in Cyprus.

   The educational policies pursued by the Bitish, by providing
for separate socializing structures, contributed significantly to
forestalling the development of an indigenous Cypriot nationalist
movement. The segregation of the two communities was further
reinforced by the political institutions that the British established in
Cyprus. In line with their notions of indirect rule and preservation
of existing culture, they created segregated institutional structures
by which the millet system was transformed and politicized. On
these separate religious communities with subordinate civil functions
stemming from religious precepts (the millets), the British superimposed a set of political institutions with political functions alien
to the millet system. Consequently, the religious underpinnings
of the existing communal system were abandoned, to be replaced

by secularism and ethnicity. The addition of political functions to the province of the millets further divided the two communities and fomented the development of two parallel social systems. Integrated formal and informal institutions that had existed traditionally were gradually dissolved as Cypriots were forced to live the totality of their lives within communal groups.

At the national level British colonial policy provided for the creation of a legislative council with advisory functions to the high commissioner and later to the British governor. The British contended that this legislative council, like those in many colonies, provided for representation of the indigenous people. Since in Cyprus the British perceived two ethnic groups, the legislative council initially consisted of twelve elected members, distributed more or less proportional to population (nine Greek and three Turkish) and six appointed British members.[23] However, no policies or programs were instituted that geared toward developing an identity or loyalty broader than that of Greek and Turk. The legislative councils themselves were secularized institutions that inevitably eroded religious authority. Concurrently, the representatives of the two communal "ethnic" groups in the legislative council began dealing with political and economic matters that had not been their concern within the framework of the millet system. Thus, administratively and politically dual, secularized institutions were established, with their authority stemming from the British.

The institutional separation between the two communities imposed at the national level was paralleled, albeit with less success, at the village level. One of the earliest acts of the British upon assuming power was the Municipal Councils Act, which provided for the election, separately, of Muslim and Orthodox members of the municipal councils; the total of members from each group was to be proportional to the numbers in the village.[24] Efforts to implement this and subsequent acts for the establishment of separate electoral rolls and for separate municipal councils did not meet with great success. As late as 1958, while negotiations were in progress for the granting of independence to Cyprus, the British were still making efforts to extend municipal segregation. One decree, in addition to ordering separate electoral rolls at the municipal level for the Greeks and Turks in mixed villages, ordered the establishment, if at all possible, of separate municipal councils.[25] The difficulty the British encountered in implementing segregation at the local level is reflective of how contrary these policies were to traditional village cultural and economic patterns, which were strong even this late in the twentieth century. Many of the problems with which municipal councils had traditionally concerned themselves—the digging of village wells; the sale, transportation, and distribution of farm produce—had been handled jointly by Muslims and Christians, and the British faced nearly insurmountable obstacles in changing these patterns.

Thus British colonial policy, while working within the traditionally existing framework, sharpened the divisions between the Muslim and Orthodox communities, extended the control and regulation of both over their members, redefined the communities in terms of nationalities, and located them within a modern political context. British policies, multileveled and multidimensional, affected all aspects of traditional Cypriot society. The British-created educational system disseminated notions of ethnicity while the administrative and political institutions further differentiated and polarized the two communities. In time the Cypriots came to view themselves just as the British did: separate antagonistic nationalities, Greek and Turk, fighting for political power and for control over the same territory.

The divisive policies of British colonial rule culminated in the institutional and legal structures set forth in the constitution of 1960, the year of Cypriot independence. It was this constitution that the British hailed as a model for peaceful coexistence of ethnic, racial, and all other groups. [26] The provisions of the constitution—ranging from mandatory individual membership in one of the two communities to two separate communal chambers governing the Greeks and Turks, to the divisiveness built into the ostensibly national institutions—further militated against national integration at any level. Constitutionally, it was as if two autonomous political systems were established, tenuously bound together in a shaky alliance within the organizational structure at the "national" level.

Since the constitution of 1960 was operative for less than three years and is now of only passing historical interest, mention will be made only of its most salient features. [27] It provided for separate representation of Turks and Greeks in the "national" institutions, legislative and executive, and granted veto power to each community within these structures. Thus, any effective decision making was impossible. An act passed by the majority in the legislature could be and often was vetoed by the Turkish minority in the national legislature. Even more important, however, Turks and Greeks were to be governed by their own parallel communal chambers, which in effect constituted the legitimate political authorities on the island. These communal chambers were provided with extensive taxing powers and could legislate on matters relating to personal status as well as on educational, cultural, and economic affairs. Reinforcing these powers of the communal chambers was the creation of two judicial systems within each community to interpret and enforce their respective laws.

That the central government was not supreme is evident. To the extent that national-level institutional structures, particularly governmental, may be an essential framework within which national integration can evolve, the Cypriot constitutional order was clearly one that militated against integration.

NATIONALIST MOVEMENTS

Although the constitution of 1960 was the culmination of British colonial policies and, as such, set the stage for intergroup conflict between Greek and Turk, a militant Greek nationalist movement had emerged in the island in the 1950s. Once the British through their policies had restructured Cypriot realities and had created the requisites for the development of dual nationalisms, Cypriots gradually became fertile ground for Greek and Turkish nationalist propaganda.

The first nationalism to take root was the Greek. In Greece itself the dominant foreign policy goal, at least until the 1920s, was territorial aggrandizement justified in terms of nationality. The massive defeat of the Greek army on the plains of Anatolia in 1922 at the hands of Kemal Ataturk's revolutionary forces signaled the collapse of the Megali idea (great idea) to reconstruct the Byzantine empire, and hence of many irredentist goals in Asia Minor. Cyprus, however, continued to be claimed by Greek leaders as territory that properly belonged to Greece.

Despite Greek irredentist claims, there was no Greek nationalist movement on Cyprus during the nineteenth century. During the Greek War of Independence in Greece in the 1820s there were instances of Orthodox Cypriots who joined the revolution.[28] Their motives undoubtedly were varied: profit, adventure, glory, and perhaps occasionally commitment to Greek nationalism. The violence on Cyprus in 1821 was mostly the result of the landing of Egyptian troops who plundered and killed Orthodox Christians and European merchants and traders, most of them Catholics.[29] This was traditional behavior on the part of rapacious army chieftains fighting for personal power, albeit at times within the framework of religious "wars." The Orthodox archbishop of the island, Kyprianou, admonished his flock to restore order and avoid violence.[30] In fact, despite agitation on the part of Greece, it was not until 1897, some 25 years after the beginning of British rule, that Greece succeeded in obtaining some volunteers from Cyprus for its short disastrous war against Turkey. Although by the latter part of the nineteenth century a segment of the Cypriot Orthodox leadership was petitioning Great Britain for union with Greece, these nationalist proclamations found

little support among the populace. As one student of the Greek
Cypriot nationalist movement, enosis (union with Greece), has
argued, it is significant that the nationalist movement was essentially
an effort by traditional elites, primarily the Church, threatened by
secular British colonial rule, to retain their traditional legitimate
authority.[31]

     A significant change in Cypriot social structure took place
during British rule. The Catholic merchant class had been decimated
by the Ottoman conquest in the late sixteenth century. During the
centuries of Ottoman rule the Cypriot economy regressed and even
agricultural production declined. Economic revival began during
the nineteenth century as Cyprus found outside markets for some
crops. The new indigenous merchant class was almost exclusively
Christian.[32] The traditional Islamic disdain for such economic
activities, in Cyprus as in the Ottoman empire as a whole, created
a merchant and trading class of non-Muslims.[33] Particularly
under secularized British rule, conversions back to Christianity
toward the latter part of the nineteenth century were thus in part a
consequence of the sanctions that Christianity provided for such
economic activity. By the twentieth century the social structure of
Cyprus was altering from that during Ottoman rule; an additional
class had emerged, the merchants, who by contrast to the other
classes in Cyprus were almost exclusively Orthodox Christians.
Thus, while under Ottoman rule the class structure cut across
religious divisions, by the time of Cypriot independence in 1960 an
affluent bourgeoisie was emerging that was almost exclusively
Christian.

     By the time the Greek Cypriot nationalist movement of
enosis reached the militant guerrilla phase in 1955 it was evident
that the class conflict that had existed during the Ottoman empire
and been manifest as late as 1931 was dormant and had been replaced
by nationalism. As is characteristic of nationalistic movements, the
specific grievances among different sectors of the population varied
but they were all subsumed under the banner of enosis with Greece.
The burgeoning middle class of merchants and traders, which had
replaced the Europeans and was far more modernized, hesitant at
first, eventually demanded freedom from colonial restrictions; the
Church hierarchy felt dispossessed by the secular authority that the
colonial power had legitimated, while many intellectuals and school
teachers were activated by the rhetoric of their "Greekness."

     Initially the Greek Cypriot movement had little impact on
the "Turkish" Cypriot community. Some Muslim leaders opposed the
movement in its nationalist form, concerned as much as the Greek
Orthodox religious hierarchy with retaining religious prerogatives.
There is little evidence that the movement as such antagonized the

"Turkish" Cypriots. In the early twentieth century, given the absence
of their own national identity, it appeared that the Muslims might
have been absorbed into the "Greek" Cypriot nationalist movement.
But in 1955 the rise of EOKA (National Organization of Cypriot Fighters)
a terrorist organization that attacked the British and British installation
for the purpose of achieving union with Greece, a hardening of attitudes
and a further polarization between Greek and Turk occurred. The
systematic British policies engendering divisiveness in Cypriot
society were reinforced by the British reaction to the EOKA movement.
The British began to employ Turkish Cypriots exclusively in the
police force to forestall attacks on the Greek Cypriot policemen, thus
making the Turkish the target of terrorist activities and dependent on
the British for protection. [34]

It was during this period that the newly emergent secular
leadership of the "Turkish" community acquired a Turkish identity;
an identity further reinforced once Turkey was brought into the
negotiations for independence in 1955 as an interested party by
Great Britain. [35] Henceforth the Turkish Cypriot community, as
will be discussed in the next section, became totally dependent on
Turkey. By 1956 an underground organization, Volkan, was formed
to combat the EOKA bands and a "Cyprus Is Turkish" party was
created. [36] The first interethnic conflict between Greeks and Turks
did not take place until 1957, when Volkan was organized by Turkey
and directed to combat the EOKA enosis movement. [37]

Most nationalist movements are viewed as progressive, and in
the post-World War II era the demand for nationalist independence
has been accompanied by a drive for economic development. Such
was not the case with EOKA. Although many sectors with differing
goals were involved in EOKA and even more so in the broader enosis
movement, EOKA—whose only articulated goal was enosis with
Greece—was a retrogressive guerrilla movement harking back to
an era when legitimacy was determined in terms of religion. [38]
The main thrust of opposition to British colonial rule was a response
to its secularization of Cypriot society. The Orthodox religious
hierarchy strongly supported EOKA and viewed enosis with Greece
as a means to reassert its traditional preeminence. [39] EOKA's reac-
tionary political coloration was symbolized by its leader, Colonel
George Grivas, a fanatic anticommunist who toward the end of the
Nazi occupation of Greece during World War II was leader of X (Chi),
a security patrol operating in the Athens area and dedicated to the
elimination of suspected communists. [40] In Cyprus itself EOKA's
targets were not only the British and British agents, but also
Greek Cypriots suspected of leftist sympathies. [41]

Although prior to independence in 1960 EOKA did attain mass
support and did incorporate diverse economic and social groups, its

neofascist ideology was repudiated after independence and EOKA's support for a continued struggle for enosis dissipated. Several factors contributed to this change. Basically, the Cypriot social structure had gradually undergone significant change. For the new political elite leadership of a sovereign state was more appealing than being a province of Greece. For the Greek Cypriot bourgeoisie the advantages of independence over enosis in the form of greater opportunities and a far higher standard of living than that prevailing in Greece were quickly apparent. For the labor unions, predominantly under the aegis of AKEL (the Cypriot Communist Party), an independent Cyprus meant higher wages for the workers and freedom from the repression of rightwing Greek governments. [42]

Underlying all this was a growing sense that the mainland Greeks viewed the Cypriots as inferior, a perception that was reinforced with the Greek dictator Papadopoulos' efforts to force President Makarios of Cyprus to submit to his demands while proclaiming that Greece was the center of "Greece of Christian Greeks." The seven-year Greek dictatorship (1967-74) in fact further alientated the Greek Cypriots and contributed to an increasing differentiation between themselves and the mainland Greeks. Never in support of the Grivas-led EOKA movement, AKEL, the Greek Cypriot Communist Party, was not about to accede to a situation in which its leaders and members were subject to arrest, imprisonment, and torture by the Greek military junta, nor were the liberal politicians such as Makarios's followers and members of EDEK (the Socialist Party), willing to subject themselves to rule by a military dictatorship with its attendant repression. Only the revived terrorist EOKA B proclaimed Greek patriotism and advocated enosis. All in all the psychological force of Greek nationalism abated, and within a dozen years after independence Greek Cypriots increasingly came to refer to themselves as Cypriots rather than Greeks. [43] Significantly, EOKA B's efforts in the 1970s to revive the enosis movement made little headway, failing to gain popular support.

The legacy of British colonial rule was embodied in the defunct consitution of 1960—two nations within the confines of a single state. Buttressing the constitutional and legal provisions imposing separateness were a set of attitudes and beliefs that pro-vided psychological legitimacy for two nationalities. Until 1974 in only two spheres was there any degree of integration; geopraphic (except for a few areas such as the capital Nicosia where a Turkish enclave extending toward Kyrenia had existed ever since the inter-communal strife in December 1963) and economic, whereby Turkish Cypriots worked in the Greek sector in Nicosia and in villages where there were joint Greek and Turkish cooperatives for farm produce.

Nevertheless, despite institutional and social segregation, attitudinal changes were taking place in the early 1970s among the Greek Cypriots, changes in the direction of reintegration in the name of Cyprus. It would be theoretically significant to investigate more thoroughly, given the process of increased segregation extending over a period of nearly 100 years, what factors precipitated the shifting attitudes of the 1970s. Particularly in light of the institutional framework that hampered rather than facilitated integration, it is of considerable import that in the past few years efforts were begun on the part of both Greek and Turkish Cypriots to demolish the barriers between the two communities. Joint professional meetings began to take place. Most significant, Greeks and Turks began to meet informally outside existing institutional channels to discuss strategy for reintegration and for preserving the independence of Cyprus. In 1974 a Cypriot organization composed of Greeks, Turks, Armenians, and Maronites, the New Cyprus Association, was formed with the avowed purpose of expressing loyalty to Cyprus. *

THE FOREIGN FACTOR IN NATIONAL INTEGRATION

The preceding analysis should make it evident that the division of Cyprus into two national entities was neither a historical given nor a preordained inevitability. British colonial policies were a major contributing factor to the divisiveness of Cypriot society—a divisiveness subsequently exploited by the Greek Cypriot nationalist movement. But developments in Cyprus during the last 15 years, including intercommunal strife, cannot be understood without scrutinizing the role of at least three other foreign powers: Greece, Turkey, and the United States. The policies and actions of these three, each motivated by its own national interests, it will be argued, thwarted

---

*In 1972 the writer met several Turkish Cypriots who were attempting to organize the Turkish community in opposition to the Turkish Cypriot leadership and working with Greek Cypriots for the preservation of Cyprus. In 1975 during the author's trip to Cyprus it became evident that the number of Turkish Cypriot dissidents had increased but that they operated clandestinely, as in any police state. Recently there have been reports of clashes between Turkish Cypriots and mainland Turks. For a discussion of the tensions within the Turkish Cypriot community, see Adamantia Pollis, "A Wedge Driven into Cyprus," The Nation 6 (December 1975): 586-89.

whatever potential existed for the unification of the two communities; hence they share responsibility for the crisis in Cyprus in 1974-75.

The legal foundations for foreign power intervention in Cypriot affairs was set forth in the maze of London and Zurich agreements and treaties of 1959 that provided for Cypriot independence. Consistent with the underlying constitutional premise that Cyprus consisted of two nations necessitating institutional structures to protect one against the other, Great Britain, Greece, and Turkey were given treaty rights on Cyprus. The Treaty of Alliance provided for the stationing of troops; Turkey was authorized to station 650 troops on the island, Greece 950. In turn, the Treaty of Guarantee gave Greece, Turkey, and Great Britain the right of intervention under certain conditions. Thus, "in so far as common or concerted action may not prove possible, each of the three guaranteeing Powers reserves the right to take action with the sole aim of reestablishing the state of affairs created by the present Treaty."[44] This complex of treaties was incorporated in the constitution of Cyprus. In addition, of course, Britain retained two military bases, one in Akrotiri and one in Dhekelia. Cypriot independence, it seems clear, was circumscribed; sovereignty was severely curtailed by the constitutional and treaty rights given to three foreign countries; the constituent power of its people was prescribed constitutionally and by international treaty while its legislative power was severely restricted.

The intercommunal violence that erupted between the Greek and Turkish communities in December 1963 was, in an immediate sense, a consequence of internal tensions with little if any direct outside instigation.* Analytically, however, foreign actions had created the conditions for violence. The constitutional framework itself precluded integration.[45] As discussed earlier, there were no national-level formal or informal institutional structures. It was the constitutional responsibility of each community to use governmental structures as devices for protecting its own interests; the two communities, by constitutional edict, were considered irreconcilable

---

*The leadership of the Turkish Cypriot community charged that the Greek Cypriots had a plan called Akritas (Grivas's pseudonym as leader of EOKA when it was fighting the British) drawn up by Greek army officers and the Greek Cypriot leadership in 1963 for the union of Cyprus with Greece. See Rauf R. Denktash, A Short Discourse on Cyprus (Nicosia, Cyprus, no date), pp. 29-36; the Greek Cypriots had planned the insurrection of December 1963 in order to provoke a Turkish invasion and partition. See Robert Stephens, Cyprus: A Place of Arms (London: Pall Mall Press, 1966), p. 181.

enemies. Also, exacerbating internal strife was the support and training both Greece and Turkey were giving to rightwing "extremist" irregular forces—the Nationalist Organization of Cypriot Fighters (EOKA) and the Turkish Defense Organization (TMT).

Inevitably, during the nearly four years of operation under the constitution, the Cypriot government failed to enact national legislation central to the concerns of any sovereign state. The national government had no legitimate authority and little power. Failure to enact tax legislation left the national government with no budget, while failure to enact legislation creating an army left Cyprus without a defense establishment.[46] Meanwhile, each community had its own taxing powers and each formed an army directed and controlled by Greece and Turkey respectively. Even the integrated Turkish-Greek police force began to divide along ethnic lines, with the Turkish police searching for arms being smuggled in from Turkey.[47] In order to resolve an obvious constitutional impasse, President Makarios in November 1963 proposed 13 amendments to the constitution, amendments geared toward forming a more unitary state by strengthening the powers of a majority national government.[48] The proposals were rejected by the Turkish Cypriot leadership. In December, as intergroup tensions kept mounting, a minor incident in Nicosia accelerated into a major conflagration between the two communities. These events brought the United Nations Peace Keeping Force (UNFICYP) into Cyprus, a force that in diminished numbers has been there ever since.[49] Clearly, the 1959 agreements were inadequate to the task of nation building in Cyprus.

Particularly as of 1964, a nonsignatory to these agreements, the United States, rapidly emerged as the most significant actor regarding Cyprus. The crumbling of Britain's empire and its demise as a world power left the United States in the role of "protector" of the free world, the inheritor of the British mantle. Thus, the task of defending Western strategic and military interests in the eastern Mediterranean, which in earlier decades would have been played by Great Britain, was now played by the United States. The United States, within the context of the cold war and later détente policies, became the major determinant of developments in Cyprus.

Between 1964 and 1974 events in Cyprus revolved around efforts by the United States, operating either directly on the Cypriot leadership, or more usually through Greece and Turkey, to bring about a Cyprus solution consonant with American security interests. The U.S. goal was and has remained the elimination of the threat that an independent, nonaligned Cyprus would pose to American security, by bringing Cyprus within the fold of the Atlantic Alliance. Its policies were nessarily flexible, given the need to accommodate, one way or another, its two NATO allies, Greece and Turkey. The

preponderance of power that the United States has employed, both
directly (through control and manipulation of groups within Cyprus)
and indirectly (through its two client states, Greece and Turkey)
has overshadowed and overpowered any potential within Cyprus itself
for the creation of a viable, independent Cyprus. Given the Middle
East setting and the leverage at the disposal of Greece, Turkey, and
the United States, Cyprus's ability to deal effectively with internal
strife was severely constrained and subordinated to great power
interests. Even further constrained were the prospects for the
attitudinal changes discussed earlier, whereby particularly the
Greek Cypriots began to identify and relate as Cypriots rather than
Greeks, to express themselves in behavior and institutional changes.

The linkages between international and domestic politics
becomes clear in analyzing the interrelationships among the two
Cypriot ethnic communities and Greece, Turkey, and the United
States. By the 1960s the leadership of the Turkish Cypriot community
was clearly a second-level leadership subordinated to Turkish
policy makers and serving essentially in an executive capacity for
decisions made in Ankara. Turkish government control over the
Turkish Cypriot community was achieved through several means,
including penetration of some Turkish Cypriot institutions,
economic dependence of the community on Turkey, exploitation of a
refugee problem and the populace's genuine feelings of fear, the
presence of a Turkish military force, and the formation of irregular
Turkish military bands.

The Turkish troops on the island far exceeded the number
provided for in the London and Zurich agreements.[50] In turn,
Turkish officers trained all Turkish Cypriot young men in the art
of war and in Turkish patriotism. The Turkish Defense Organization,
TMT, a group of terrorist irregular bands dedicated to "Cyprus Is
Turkish" or to taksim (partition) was supported by Turkey and led
by a Turkish officer from the mainland.[51] After the creation of
Turkish enclaves, particularly in parts of Nicosia and in an area
extending toward Kyrenia, the Turkish government annually subsidized
the Turkish Cypiot community.[52] These enclaves had little in the
way of productive economic activity that could provide employment
opportunities other than some village agriculture. By subsidizing the
Turkish Cypriots, some of whom were refugees from the December
1963 events, the Turkish government provided an income for individuals,
hence reducing economic pressure for leaving the Turkish enclave and
working in the Greek sector.

The Turkish Cypriot community has been no more monolithic
than the Greek Cypriot one. But gradually the Turkish government
operating through the Turkish Cypriot leadership, and the terrorist
organization TMT, has repressed opposition to Turkish policies;
dissidence in large measure has gone underground. Thus, whereas

the divisions and conflicts among EOKA B, the Greek Cypriot leadership, and the Greek government, given the relatively open society of the Greek Cypriot community, have been evident, the repressive mechanism of a police state in the Turkish Cypriot community has publicly created the false image of unity and consensus.

"Legal" opposition to the official Turkish Cypriot leadership, currently Rauf Denktash, has encountered increasing difficulties ever since independence in 1960. The three Turkish Cypriot political parties extant prior to independence were eradicated just prior to the first elections. Fazil Kutchuk of the United Front Party (or National Front) was elected vice president in 1960, only to be ousted a few years later by Denktash. Ever since the Turkish invasion and occupation of 40 percent of the island in 1974 a more vociferous opposition has been attempting to operate within the confines possible under the operative repressive conditions. In February 1975 Turkish Cypriot trade unions and the opposition press voiced strong protests against the proclamation of a Turkish Federated State of Cyprus and against what they claimed were Denktash's dictatorial actions in setting up a constituent assembly for the Turkish community.[53] Inevitably, however, under the guns of 30,000 Turkish troops, 99.4 percent of the Turkish Cypriots approved the constitution on June 8. By August 1975 a new opposition political party, the Populist Party, had been formed; its leadership includes Alper Orhon, an ousted minister of the Turkish Federated State of Cyprus, and Fazil Kutchuk, ousted former leader of the Turkish Cypriot community. The party defines itself as center-left and is strongly opposed to Denktash and his policies. Reflective of opposition views, cautiously presented, is the one Turkish Cypriot opposition newspaper, Halkin Sesi, owned by Fazil Kutchuk, which accuses the Denktash regime of suppressing the rights of the people and urges the Turkish Cypriots in the Greek area not to move to the Turkish-occupied areas because conditions there are deplorable.

However, the ability of the opposition to speak freely, to organize and propagate its views, is severely restricted. The most effective repressive structure was and remains the terrorist organization, the Turkish Defense Organization—TMT. As with EOKA, the activities of the TMT are not directed against Greek Cypriots but against their conationals. Terrorist bombings and assasinations committed by TMT members have been reported from 1962 to date. In 1962 two opponents of Kutchuk and the United Front Party, Ahmet Gurhan, editor of Combrist, and Ayhan Hikmet, a lawyer, both friendly to the Greek Cypriots, were found murdered,[54] while in 1965 a Turkish Cypriot trade union leader, Kavazoglu, was murdered along with a Greek Cypriot trade official. In the summer of 1975 TMT agents terrorized the Turkish Cypriot population and in the Greek area they threatened the Turkish Cypriots with reprisals if they associated with Greek Cypriots or failed to move to the Turkish occupied area.

By the fall of 1975, of the 8,000 to 9,000 Turkish Cypriots in the Greek area approximately 200 to 250 remained. In July 1975 it was reported that 8 to 10 Turkish Cypriots were executed because of their ties to Greek Cypriots. Financed and supported by Turkey, TMT has been one of the organs used by Turkey to impose an authoritarian regime on the Turkish Cypriot populace, subservient to Turkish interests.

TMT and EOKA B have served the same function within their respective communities. TMT's goal of takism ("partition") has complemented EOKA B's goal of enosis; a fulfillment of both goals would divide Cyprus with the largest area going to Greece. While TMT has served the interests of Turkey and EOKA B the interests of Greece, both in turn have served the interests of the United States.

However, the relationship between TMT and the Turkish Cypriot leadership has differed from that between EOKA B and the Greek Cypriot leadership. TMT, in cooperation with the Turkish government, succeeded in subverting the autonomy of the Turkish Cypriot leadership. By contrast, the Greek Cypriot leadership remained relatively independent both of EOKA B and of the Greek government. Turkey has not hesitated to publicly demonstrate domination of Turkish Cypriot policy. In November 1963 when Kutchuk received Makarios's proposals for constitutional amendment, he expressed a willingness to consider them but Turkey immediately repudiated them.[55] In 1967 when Kutchuk was under attack by Turkish patriots advocating taksim he defended himself and his policies in a newspaper he owned. The Turkish government ordered him to stop defending himself and to stop opposing the Turkish nationalists.[56] Inevitably, although under very unclear circumstances, Kutchuk was ousted in 1971,[57] to be replaced by Rauf Denktash, considered a reliable spokesman for Ankara's foreign policy and a reliable ally of the West. Even in January 1975 when Denktash accepted the Greek Cypriot proposal for the reopening of the Nicosia airport under United Nations auspices, the Turkish government effectively overruled him.[58] The announcement of the formation of the Turkish Federated State of Cyprus in February 1975, the administrative incorporation of this area into the Turkish province of Mersin, the expulsion of Greek Cypriots from Turkish-occupied areas, and the continued rule of this territory by the Turkish army are clear indications of the lack of autonomy of the Turkish Cypriot community and its leadership. The current Turkish Cypriot reality can hardly be interpreted as necessarily indicative of the attitudes, beliefs, or goals of the Turkish Cypriots. An authoritarian Turkish Cypriot political system, directed and dominated by a foreign power, precludes any accurate evaluation of the views of the Turkish Cypriot population.

Any actions or statements in the Turkish Cypriot community supportive of Cypriot independence would run contrary to Turkish foreign policy and in turn to United States policy and therefore have warranted suppression. In part Turkish support of taksim has been argued in terms of Turkish security interests that are threatened by a Greek-dominated or an independent Cyprus. That Turkish policy in turn has reflected American goals is perhaps illustrated best in an article by Ismet Giritli in 1967. He stated, while discussing Cyprus:

> Turkish foreign policy continues to be determined
> by the basic facts of Turkey's international position
> rather than by changing moods of internal politics.
> The basic fact is awareness based on experience of
> old and familiar Russian expansionism and therefore
> a desire to seek or accept Western-American support. [59]

Within this context, no Turkish Cypriot leadership desirous of maintaining an independent, nonaligned Cyprus would be acceptable to Turkey or to the United States (see below for a discussion of the U. S. position).

Similar efforts to control the leadership of the Greek Cypriots, to quash dissent, and to bring Greek Cypriot policy into line with Greek or American foreign policy also were made by Greece. However, Greece failed in its efforts to dominate Greek Cypriot politics and to make its leadership the spokesman for Greek policies. The political leadership of the Greek Cypriot community resisted such control and in the process of resistance became increasingly committed to the maintenance of an independent, nonaligned Cyprus. Makarios pursued a policy often contrary to the objectives of Greek and U. S. foreign policy.

Makarios alternated between resistance to and compromise with the pressures exerted on him by the various Greek governments. [60] That he was able to maintain a high degree of autonomy for the Greek Cypriot political system is attributable in large measure to the overwhelming popular support among the Greek Cypriots. Two political parties—the Communist Party, AKEL, and the Socialist Party, EDEK—both in opposition to Makarios on many domestic issues nevertheless supported him in his efforts to maintain Cypriot independence. [61] In turn, a popular mandate facilitated Makarios's ability to gain support from the nonaligned countries, particularly the Arab countries, and from the Soviet Union. Time and again, faced with intercommunal conflict he thwarted Greek, Turkish, and U.S. plans for NATO consideration of the issues and appealed to the United Nations, where he could be assured of at least a measure of third world and Eastern bloc support.

During the dictatorship of George Papadopoulos in Greece (1967-74) Makarios alternated between compromise and resistance in his dealings with the Greek military junta's efforts to impose a totalitarian regime on the Greek Cypriot community. The Greek dictator engaged in a variety of political strategems; announcing that Athens was the center of Hellenism and demanding obedience from Makarios; demanding that Makarios replace his cabinet officers with those acceptable to Papadopoulos; setting up the Cypriot bishops to demand Makarios's resignation as president, claiming that he had violated canon law and threatening him with excommunication. Makarios went through the motions of compromise but made few concessions; he replaced two cabinet members, ignored the bishops' threats—in fact had them defrocked[62]—and finally publicly attacked Ioannides and his dictatorial regime.* On the other hand, his power base remained weak since he had balked at ousting the junta officers of the Cypriot National Guard, which in July 1974 executed a coup against him and made an abortive assassination attempt.

Makarios's ability to partially fend off Greek pressure solidified his popular support; a support due in part to marked changes in the social structure of Cyprus, particularly within the Greek Cypriot community after 1960. It was not only the leadership as represented by Makarios that became committed to an independent Cyprus but the Greek Cypriot populace as well. Enosis as a goal of the Greek Cypriots lost support, while the Greek Cypriots began to identify themselves as Cypriots rather than Greeks, symbolized by the increased use of the Cypriot rather than the Greek flag.[63] The middle class in particular grew and prospered and enjoyed a standard of living higher than in Greece—$840 per capita income for Greece and $970 for Cyprus, inclusive of the Turkish Cypriots, in 1960.[64] In addition, the trade unions, dominated by a communist leadership, did not relish union with Greece, which had consistently been repressive of leftwing movements even before the Papadopoulos dictatorship.

---

*One such letter, considered the precipitating factor for the Cyprus coup of July 15, 1974, was sent by Makarios to the Greek dictatorship days before the coup against his regime. He specifically accused the Ioannides regime of planning his assassination and he demanded the withdrawal of the Greek officers from the National Guard—a demand he had refused to make for the previous six years. See The Observer, July 7, 1964, and Steven V. Roberts, in the New York Times, July 16, 1974.

The Papadopoulos dictatorship in Greece had a marked psychological impact on the Greek Cypriots. Its anachronistic, traditionalist values ran contrary to the secularization and modernizing developments in both the economic and political spheres in Cyprus, further intensifying the differentiation of the Greek Cypriots from the Greeks on the mainland. Although supporting Archbishop Makarios as their president, the modernized sector repudiated the dominance of the Greek Orthodox Church, its Hellenism, and its appeal to traditionalism. One political consequence of these attitudinal changes was the formation in 1971 of the Socialist Party of Cyprus (EDEK) led by Vassos Lysarrides, which began to organize on a mass base. Its membership includes Turkish Cypriots and it argues for reconciliation with them and reintegration of the island. Significantly EDEK, although socialist in ideology, has the support of much of the indigenous middle class, largely because of its stance on independence, its opposition to foreign powers, its antiimperialist position.

The failure of political pressure on Cyprus led the Greek regime to rely increasingly on the threat and use of force as a means of attaining domination over the Greek Cypriots. As a consequence, during the past few years Cyprus had been perennially on the verge of civil war—a civil war not between the Greeks and Turkish Cypriots but within the Greek Cypriot community. As discussed earlier, there was no Cypriot army; the military force for the Greek community was the National Guard, which was officered exclusively by officers from mainland Greece. Particularly during the Papadopoulos reign these officers were selected for their loyalty to Papadopoulos, their fascist ideology, and their opposition to Makarios. The Greek troops, in excess of those permitted by the treaty of London and Zurich, which Makarios had demanded to be withdrawn by Greece in 1969, were gradually infiltrated back.

Reflective of the significance of force and violence as a determinant of historical developments, regardless of the attitudes, beliefs, and loyalties of a given population, were the activities of the EOKA terrorist bands in Cyprus. Under directions from mainland Greece, these bands were reorganized in 1971 as EOKA B and, like their Turkish Cypriot counterpart, directed their activities against their fellow nationals while receiving external support from Greece and from the United States.[65] Grivas, the guerrilla leader of EOKA in the 1950s when it operated as a nationalist, anticolonial movement, who had returned to Greece after independence, returned to Cyprus in 1964 after apparently accepting the Acheson plan for partition of Cyprus, was expelled by Makarios, and returned once again— clandestinely with the approval of Papadopoulos—in 1971.[66] EOKA B then mounted a propaganda campaign for enosis, assassinated supporters of Makarios, and plotted and planned assassinations and coups to oust Makarios with the assistance of the officers of the Cypriot National Guard. Grivas's banner of enosis, his attacks against Makarios, and his terrorist activities—assassinations and kidnapings—found few supporters or followers among the population.

Clearly, Makarios had a broad political base and he possessed legitimate political authority. Nevertheless, he had little in the way of force to protect his position against the onslaught of Greece and Turkey. The Palace Guard he had organized and a police force loyal to him had few arms and supplies that could countervail the power of the well-supplied and financed EOKA B and the Greek-officered Cypriot National Guard. Greece used EOKA B and the National Guard as its instruments of force to attain its objectives in Cyprus. The Papadopoulos regime had set as one of its goals the solution of the Cyprus crisis, a solution satisfactory to both Greek and American security interests; Cyprus was to be destroyed as a nonaligned country with a strong internal communist force (AKEL) since this posed a potential threat to Western security interests in the eastern Mediterranean. Abortive coups and failed assassination attempts against Makarios became commonplace.[67] Eventually, however, the force of arms won out and shortly after Grivas died in January 1974 a successful coup was executed against Makarios in July 1974 under the direction of Greece, toppling Makarios's government, although bungling the assassination attempt against him.*

Just as the Turkish invasion and control over 40 percent of the island and the actions of Turkey and the Turkish Cypriot leadership, in particular Denktash, have been reacted to negatively by the Turkish Cypriots and have aroused a consciousness of being Cypriot, so the Greek Cypriots, conscious of themselves as Cypriots, are increasingly critical of their own leadership. Widespread opposition has developed against Glafkos Clerides, the chief negotiator for the Greek Cypriots and acting President for several months before

---

*The new short-lived leader of Cyprus after the coup was Nicos Sampson, head of an EOKA assassination squad in the 1950s and known as a professional killer. Makarios's escape, the widespread repudiation of Sampson, except by the United States, and the collapse of the military dictatorship in Greece led to Sampson's replacement by Glafkos Clerides; Makarios returned to Cyprus on December 8, 1974. The New York Times in an editorial on July 16, 1974, called Sampson "a confessed murderer, professional bully boy," while a bibliographical sketch stated that his reputation in Cyprus "was about like that of Al Capone in Chicago." New York Times, July 16, 1975.

Makarios' return to Cyprus after the coup in July 1974. Stemming from his probable role in the coup against Makarios, his "realistic" stance regarding a bizonal federation, his pro-United States position, his acceptability to Turkey and his well-known rightist views, he is considered a spokesman for Greek and American interests. Makarios, in turn, is beginning to be perceived as losing his effectiveness as a leader in defending the interests of the Cypriot nation as evidenced by his retention of Clerides.

An analysis limited to the relationships of Greece and Turkey to their respective Cypriot communities would appear to indicate that two foreign powers, with traditionally conflicting national interests, attempted to extend their hegemony over their communities in Cyprus. However, although at times Greek and Turkish national interests have been and are in conflict, most sharply of late on the question of oil rights in the Aegean, and although their respective nationalist rhetoric places constraints on actions, both are members of NATO, both have been committed to the cold war, and both have been client states of the United States. The foreign policy objectives of both Greece and Turkey have been to strengthen their own security, in light of the threat posed by a nonaligned Cyprus with a strong communist party, by incorporating Cyprus within the Western military alliance. Time after time Greece and Turkey have agreed on a solution to the Cyprus "conflict," only to find its implementation Thwarted by Makarios. Thus, Greece and Turkey agreed on the constitution of 1960 and on the Acheson plan in 1964, and Greece and Turkey insisted in 1971 on a Greek and Turkish governmental representative to participate in the intermittent intercommunal talks between the two Cypriot communities, ostensibly as constitutional experts. And it was in June 1971 that Greece and Turkey apparently made a "secret" agreement at a NATO meeting to end the independence of Cyprus and partition the island.[68]

The status of Greece and Turkey as client states of the United States sets the context within which their policy vis-a-vis Cyprus was formulated. Inevitably, the United States, most often but not always acting through its clients, was a major determinant of developments within Cyprus. Shortly after the December 1963 intercommunal violence on the island, the United States attempted direct negotiations with the Cypriots and proposed the Acheson-Ball plan as a solution. This plan, a form of double enosis, would have united a large part of the island with Greece, while the northeast section would become predominantly a Turkish base under Turkish sovereignty. This porposal, accepted by Greece and Turkey, was categorically rejected by Makarios. Thereupon the premier of Greece, George Papandreou, reversed his position by declaring his support of Makarios and rejected the Acheson-Ball plan.[69]

The consequent U.S. intervention in Greek governmental affairs and the determining U.S. role in the selection of the Greek political leadership is perhaps nowhere more evident than in the immediate withdrawal of support from Papandreou and the instigation of the series of events by organs of the U.S. government, such as the CIA, segments of the Greek political oligarchy, and Greek military officers, that led to the military coup of 1967.[70] An understood condition for the new Papadopoulos regime's survival was its success in solving the Cyprus crisis and in ousting Makarios.[71] As discussed earlier, Papadopoulos was thwarted time and again by Makarios, and hence lost credibility with the United States. Even the support by the United States, through the CIA, of Grivas and his EOKA bands, did not lead to success. Papadopoulos's overthrow by Brigadier General Dimitri Ioannides, a less cautious and more ideologically committed man, opened the way for the coup in Cyprus in July 1974, a coup whose success was assumed, particularly in view of the already existing agreement with Turkey.

Whatever the specific international situation, the United States has been consistent in its goal of incorporating Cyprus into the eastern Mediterranean defense system and in viewing Makarios as a formidable perennial obstacle. While the United States has used the British bases on the island—consistently for U-2 flights[72] and for "spy" flights during and after the recent Middle East crisis[73]— Cyprus has nevertheless been viewed as a potential threat to American interests, especially in light of fears that the British may withdraw from their bases. In fact, the urgency of incorporating Cyprus within the NATO framework became more immediate after the Arab-Israeli war of June 1967 and the continuing Middle East crisis. The Middle East conflict, in conjunction with the previous loss of American bases in Libya and the increased presence of the Soviet fleet in the Mediterranean, intensified American concern for securing a safe, reliable ally in Cyprus, as a bulwark for the defense of Israel. Under Makarios's leadership, the United States viewed Cyprus as a potential "Cuba" in the Mediterranean.[74] Undoubtedly it was this sense of urgency that prompted the United States to support the Cypriot coup of July 1974 and to tacitly approve the Turkish invasion. *

---

*The former U.S. ambassador to Greece, Henry Tasca, has testified before the House Select Committee that the CIA was the U.S. representative in Greece during the Ioannides dictatorship, while Ioannides through his lawyer has contended that the United States assured him that, if he executed a coup against Makarios, Turkey would not invade Cyprus. Talory B. Belcher, former U.S. ambassador to Cyprus, testified that senior Cypriot officials knew

The United States, in working through Greece and Turkey during the past decade as the vehicles for implementing its objectives, has further strengthened the political reality of the identity of Greek with Greek Cypriot interests and of Turkish with Turkish Cypriot interests, although on a psychological level this identity is being reversed. Thus Secretary of State Henry Kissinger and more recently the European Economic Community have been negotiating for an agreement regarding Cyprus with Greece and Turkey, assuming that any such agreement would be tantamount to one with the Greek and Turkish Cypriots. The major obstacles to such an agreement have been the Greek Cypriot leadership in the form of Makarios,* the Socialist Party, and the Cypriots themselves.

Nevertheless, the United States may be witnessing a loss of power, with regard to both Greece and Turkey. Gradually, a shift of decision making may be taking place in these countries that could lead to an erosion of the United States's eastern Mediterranean defense system. Although the evidence indicates that the current Karamanlis government in Greece, which followed the collapse of the military junta resulting from the Cyprus coup, is agreeable to an "American" solution to the Cyprus crisis, the Greek government must face increasingly anti-American public opinion. Particularly with the recent revelations regarding American support of the Greek dictatorship, former Greek dictator Ioannides's statements implicating the United States in the Cyprus coup,[75] the survival of the Karamanlis government may well be contingent on increasing independence from American domination.

By contrast to Greek-United States relations, those of the United States with Turkey have been strained for over a decade, as

---

that the CIA was paying Ioannides to subsidize EOKA B. Summaries of the testimony transcripts were provided upon request from the House Select Committee on Intelligence, October 1, 1975.

*It is significant that Turkish political leaders view Glafkos Clerides, the chief negotiator, with favor. See, for example, Haluk Ulman, "Geneva Conferences," Foreign Policy (Ankara, Turkey) 4, nos. 2-3 (1974):48. Ulman, a deputy of the Republican People's Party of Turkey, attended the Geneva conferences in 1974 to discuss a solution to the Cyprus crisis after the Turkish invasion. He stated," I believe that the most realistic man on the other side of the conference was Mr. Clerides." Makarios and his supporters, the Socialist and Communist parties, are arguing for an independent, nonaligned, integrated Cyprus.

Turkey embarked on a policy of increasing independence from the
United States. Gradually, unrestricted, unilateral use by the
United State of its military bases in Turkey has been restricted.[76,]
Anti-Americanism in Turkey predated its emergence in Greece by
approximately a decade. And very recently Turkey has been attempting
to cement its relations with the Arab world.

     Specifically on Cyprus, there is for the moment a confluence of
Turkish and U.S. interests, but American leverage over Turkey has
significantly diminished. It is more than doubtful whether a repetition
of the Johnson letter[77] of 1964 or a comparable U.S. action—
threatening Turkey not to invade Cyprus—would be effective today.
Turkey has been sending immigrants into the Turkish-occupied area
of Cyprus, estimated at 12,000 to 20,000 as of the fall of 1975, thus
gradually changing the demography of the island. All in all, America's
apparent success in partitioning Cyprus and thus incorporating it into
NATO may come at the very time when NATO allies in the eastern
Mediterranean have become disaffected with NATO. However,
it should be stated that the conservatism of Turkish Premier Demirel,
his general pro-Western stance, as much as Premier Karamanlis's
conservatism, pro-Western stance, and dependence on the United
States, may be a temporary brake on the consequences of widespread
anti-Americanism in both countries.* However, Turkey in its
renegotiations of the agreement with the United States for the reopening
of the U.S. bases, closed during the congressionally imposed embargo
on U.S. military aid to Turkey, is further restricting U.S. prerogatives
and demanding higher payment. With regard to Cyprus, evidence is
mounting that intensified militant nationalism in Turkey may be leading
to a long-run policy of annexation of Cyprus, with or without U.S.
approval.

------

    *Greece's alienation from NATO may be accelerated by the
replacement of the United States by France as the chief arms supplier
to Greece (Le Monde, April 5, 1973). France, as early as January
1972, recommended some form of defense cooperation between France
and Greece to offset the Soviet fleet's presence in the Mediterranean.
On August 25, 1974, Le Monde reported that the French were favorable to
sending technicians to Greece and aiding the Greeks in developing an
arms industry. Karmanlis, it was stated, is receptive to this French
concept of an alternative Mediterranean counterforce. As of this
writing, negotiations between the United States and Greece are in
progress regarding the status of U.S. bases in Greece. It seems
clear that whatever the outcome, U.S. "rights" will be curtailed.

Significant developments within Cyprus itself make a "peaceful" solution of the Cyprus crisis along the lines of American strategic concerns increasingly difficult. As a result of the Turkish invasion there are approximately 200,000 Greek Cypriot displaced persons. Contrary to logical expectations, the recent events in Cyprus, rather than polarizing the population even further, have created a greater sense of Cypriot identity. Awareness of the disastrous consequences of Greek and U.S. involvement in Cypriot affairs, including the destruction of the economy and with it the ruination of the middle class, has engendered among the Greek Cypriots an awareness of shared commonalities with the Turkish Cypriots. Pervasive among the Greek Cypriots is a reexamination and a critique of their past actions, including their neglect of the Turkish Cypriots. The Turkish Cypriots, mostly peasants, are resentful in turn of being uprooted from their land where they had lived in peace with their Greek Cypriot neighbors, to be resettled in other areas—in former Greek homes stripped bare by the Turkish troops—with Turkish neighbors from the mainland to whom they do not relate and with whom clashes have already taken place.

Several groups currently operative in Cyprus include Greek and Turkish Cypriots in their membership. Of the political parties, both EDEK, the Socialist Party, and AKEL, the Communist Party, have close liaison with Turkish Cypriots—their members at the moment are undisclosed for fear of reprisals by TMT. Representative of the attitudinal changes in Cyprus is the formation at the beginning of 1975 of the New Cyprus Association, which includes members from all ethnic groups whose stated goal is to work for the creation of conditions leading to "feelings of love and loyalty for Cyprus, our Country."[78] Not a political party per se, it specifically calls for the reintegration of the Cypriot communities and has been working toward this end among both Greek and Turkish Cypriots. And on the horizon lurk two prospects: (1) the emergence of a guerrilla movement intent on maintaining an independent, sovereign, nonaligned Cyprus[79] and (2) after further demographic changes, the incorporation of the whole island by Turkey.

CONCLUSIONS

It is beyond the scope of this essay to deal with Greece, Turkey, and the United States at the level of international politics. Discussion of these countries has been undertaken only to the extent that it has provided additional insights into the question of political integration in Cyprus and the processes leading toward partition.

The above scrutiny of the Cypriot experience indicates that over the decades the two communities, Greek and Turkish, became increasingly segregated. The process of division began with British colonial policies, augmented by the direct controls exercised by Greece and Turkey and the indirect control of the United States, and fomented by nationalist movements. By the 1970s the island's population was segregated along psychological, social, economic, and political lines, and after 1974, territorially.

In turn, the institutional framework imposed structural barriers to the evolution of commonalities and a shared perception of the legitimacy of the political regime. The prospects are that Cyprus will be partitioned, probably under the temporary rubric of "bizonal" federation, rationalized as an inevitable and just consequence of the existence of two conflicting ethnic groups.

What internal developments in Cyprus would have taken place without British colonial policies, without subsequent Greek and Turkish governmental actions that further polarized the two communities, and without the U.S. efforts to divide the island is difficult to ascertain. Compounding the difficulties of integration stemming from international factors was the imposition of parallel governmental, economic, and social institutions, which in themselves militated against integration. It can be argued that without the systemic factors internal developments might well have been markedly different since the salient determinants would no longer have been foreign powers and the structuring of the Cypriot reality would not have been contingent on Great Britain, Greece, Turkey, and the United States.

Theoretically, the above analysis of the processes whereby divisiveness came to characterize Cypriot politics and society points to the inadequacy of prevailing models in accounting for political integration or disintegration. Political integration for nation-states is contingent upon a given set of attitudinal, behavioral, and institutional factors. A reconceptualization of the very approach to issues of integration seems in order. The pervasive assumption that there is congruence between the legal existence of an independent state and the analytically valid unit for investigative purposes must be abandoned. In other words, the processes of integration and its determinants may be found outside rather than inside the boundaries of the political unit, namely, the state being investigated. Thus, as with Cyprus, it may be that in some cases international factors are the crucial variables accounting for internal developments.

The case of Cyprus indicates not only that the use of external force has been a crucial factor of political disintegration but that internal realities themselves—such as institutional structures, the rise of nationalities, attitudinal and behavioral variables—were in large measure the consequence of systemic (international) factors.

Additional case studies of political integration using this approach
would provide evidence either confirming or negating the generalizations
that can be drawn from the case of Cyprus.

The case of Cyprus raises a related theoretical question.
If external factors largely accounted for the increasing divisiveness
and segregation of the communities in Cyprus, and their identity
with two separate sovereign states, what accounts for the recent
attitudinal changes of increased differentiation among the populace—
both Greek and Turkish—from Greece and Turkey? What accounts
for the apparent emergence of the notion of a multiethnic Cypriot
nation to which loyalty is owed, even in the face of force and
violence? The perception of reality seems to be altering, and
with it the operative cognitive structure. Can such attitudinal
changes—changes in attitudes, beliefs, and loyalties—affect
political realities given the absence of an appropriate institutional
framework and the determining role of external factors? Again,
case studies of other countries may yield greater insights into
the process of integration and disintegration.

NOTES

1. See Makarios's Thirteen Points in Greek Communal
Chamber, Cyprus Today (Nicosia, Cyprus), November–December
1963, p. 1.

2. Ministry of Finance, Cyprus, Statistical Abstract of 1964.
In 1960, of a total population of 577,000 some 80 percent were
"Greek," 18 percent "Turkish," and the remainder other minorities
such as Maronites and Armenians. There has been no overall population
census since 1960. More recent estimates place the total population
at 632,000. See Economic Consequences of Turkish Invasion (Nicosia,
Cyprus: Public Information Office, October 1974), p. 1.

3. Interview, Nicosia, Cyprus, 1972.

4. Rauf R. Denktash, A Short Discourse on Cyprus (Nicosia,
Cyprus, no date), p. 26.

5. Frederich J. Teggart, The Theory and Processes of History
(Berkeley: University of California Press, 1960), p. 116.

6. See almost any history of Cyprus, such as Doros Alastos,
Cyprus in History (London: Zeno, 1955), p. 182.

7. George Hill, A History of Cyprus 1511-1948, vol. 4
(Cambridge: Cambridge University Press, 1952), pp. 18-20.

8. Ibid.

9. Theodore Papadopoulos, Social and Historical Data on
Population 1570-1881 (Nicosia: Cyprus Research Center, 1965).
This is the most comprehensive compilation of data on the Cypriot

population, based on several population censuses undertaken by the Orthodox Church and the Ottomans for tax purposes during Ottoman rule and by the British in 1881. Nevertheless, there are several questions regarding the original data and there are significant omissions, particularly in the author's analysis and interpretation. For example, he ignores an Arab-speaking population and makes no distinctions among the various Christian categories.

10. Ibid., pp. 32-35.

11. Ibid. See also J. Hackett, A History of the Orthodox Church in Cyprus (London: Methuen, 1901), pp. 527-28.

12. Most histories of Cyprus attest to these revolts. See, for example, Alastos, Cyprus in History, pp. 275-76. H. D. Purcell, Cyprus (New York: Praeger Publishers, 1969): pp. 189-92, cites evidence of extensive uprisings by the Turkish Cypriots against the Ottoman rulers.

13. See Alastos, Cyprus in History, and Purcell, Cyprus.

14. See, for example, Sir Samuel White Baker, Cyprus as I Saw It in 1879 (London: Macmillan, 1879).

15. Archilles C. Aimiliandides, "The Evolution of the Law Concerning Mixed Marriages in Cyprus," Cypriote Studies II (Leukosia, Cyprus) 1938, p. 209 (in Greek).

16. See Sir Stanley Fisher, Municipal Council Law, 1882, in The Statute Law of Cyprus 1878-1923 (London, 1923), for a discussion in terms of the efforts made to establish separate municipal councils.

17. See Adamantia Pollis, "Intergroup Conflict and British Colonial Policy: The Case of Cyprus," Comparative Politics 5, no. 4 (July 1973): 575-79, for a more detailed analysis of British colonial rule in Cyprus.

18. See Stewart E. Easton, The Rise and Fall of Western Colonialism (New York: Frederick A. Praeger, 1964); S. N. Eisenstadt, The Political Systems of Empires (New York: The Free Press, 1963), for an overall discussion of the consistency of British colonial policy and how it differed from that of other colonial powers.

19. William W. Weir, Education in Cyprus (Larnaca, Cyprus, 1952), pp. 54-56.

20. Ibid., pp. 113-16.

21. Ibid.

22. See Paulos Ksioutas, "Foreign Words in Our Language," Cypriote Studies I, 1937, pp. 133-74 (in Greek), for efforts to preserve the "Cypriot" language.

23. See C. W. J. Orr, Cyprus under British Rule (London: R. Scott, 1918), pp. 97-99.

24. Fisher, The Statute Law, Municipal Council Act, 1882.

25. Cited in Parliamentary Debates, vol. 594, pp. 767-68.

26. See Sir Anthony Eden's comments in Parliamentary Debates, Commons, vol. 595, pp. 563-64.

27. Stanley Kyriakides, Cyprus: Constitutionalism and Crisis in Government (Philadelphia: University of Pennsylvania Press, 1968) for a detailed analysis of the Cypriot constitution.

28. John T. A. Koumoulides, Cyprus and the War of Greek Independence 1821-1829 (Athens: National Centre of Social Research, 1971), pp. 106ff. Although the author attempts to argue that the Cypriots in the early nineteenth century were Greek nationalists, his own data indicate that the few individuals who became involved in the Greek War of Independence did so for a variety of motives.

29. See ibid., pp. 100-04, where it is evident that the Egyptian troops mostly plundered the European merchants who were the wealthiest sector of the population.

30. See ibid., p. 37, for Archbishop Kyfrianou's pronouncement to his flock.

31. Kyriacos C. Markidis, "Social Change and the Rise and Decline of Social Movement: The Case of Cyprus," American Ethnologist 1, no. 2 (May 1974).

32. M. Attalides, "Forms of Peasant Incorporation in Cyprus During the Last Century," paper presented at the New York Academy of Sciences Conference on Regional Variations in Modern Greece, February 1975 (mimeographed), for a discussion of the Greek merchant class in Cyprus in one district.

33. A. Suat Bilge, Le Conflict de Chypre et les Cypriotes Turcs (Ankara: Faculté des Sciences Politiques de l'Université d' Ankara, 1961), pp. 13-14. The author discusses the preference of Turkish Cypriots for administrative and military positions.

34. See Markidis, "Social Change," pp. 319-20.

35. Cited by James Callaghan (M.P., Cardiff, South East) in debate on second reading of Cyprus bill, July 14, 1960, in Parliamentary Debates, Commons, vol. 626, p. 1634.

36. Robert Stephens, Cyprus: A Place of Arms (London: Pall Mall Press, 1966), p. 147.

37. See Charles Foley and W. I. Scobie, The Struggle for Cyprus (Stanford, Calif.: Stanford University Press, 1975), p. 115.

38. Markidis, "Social Change."

39. Foley and Scobie, The Struggle for Cyprus. A theme running through this journalistic account is the support given by the Church and Archbishop Makarios to EOKA—a support, however, marked by tension and conflict. A break between Makarios and EOKA came prior to the London and Zurich agreements.

40. See George Grivas, The Memoirs of General Grivas, trans. (New York: Frederick A. Praeger, 1966), in which he personally concedes that anticommunism was one of his main objectives.

41. Sp. Linardatou, "Cyprus till Independence," in A. G. Xydis, Sp. Linardatou, and K. Hatziargiri, Makarios and his Allies, 3rd ed. (Athens: Gutenberg Press, 1974) (in Greek), p. 318. He quotes Grivas as stating in 1958: "With regard to the threats of the communists I decided to confront it in the same manner, in which I confronted the threats from any other traitor. . . . This problem of course was not simple because every execution of a communist traitor. . . ." (author's translation). See also Stephen G. Xydis, Conflict and Conciliation, 1954-58 (Columbus: Ohio State University, 1967), p. 71, which cites a document whereby the communists are denied membership in EOKA.

42. T. W. Adams, AKEL: The Communist Party in Cyprus (Stanford, Calif.: Stanford University Press, 1971), is the only history of the Cypriot Communist Party, unfortunately filled with errors and misinterpretations.

43. See A. G. Xydis, "The Psychological Complex" (in Greek), in Xydis, Linardatou and Hatziagiri, Makarios, pp. 31-32. The author, a Greek diplomat, attests to this shift in attitudes.

44. Provisions of the Tready of Guarantee by Cyprus, Greece, and Turkey and the United Kingdom; Great Britain, Cyprus (London: Her Majesty's Stationery Office, 1960), pp. 86-87.

45. See Xydis, "The Psychological Complex," p. 28; Kyriakides, Cyprus, p. 51, for Makarios's objections to the constitution and the pressures for acceptance.

46. See Kyriakides, Cyprus, pp. 77-103, for a detailed discussion of the legislative stalemate in Cyprus in 1960-63.

47. Stephens, Cyprus: A Place of Arms, p. 182; the author argues that the split in the Cypriot police force predates the December 1963 crisis.

48. See Cyprus: The Problem in Perspective (Republic of Cyprus, May 1971), Appendix 1, pp. 14-20.

49. See James Stegenga, United Nations Force in Cyprus (Columbus: Ohio State University Press, 1968), for a discussion of the United Nations Peace Keeping Force in Cyprus in 1964-67.

50. Stephens, Cyprus: A Place of Arms, p. 200, estimates that in 1965 Turkey had about 1,000 men in Cyprus and the Turkish Cypriots some 12,000 men under arms. There is no reason to assume that the number was reduced in later years; other estimates place the number of Greeks at closer to 10,000. See Thomas Ehrlich, Cyprus: 1958-1967 (New York: Oxford University Press, 1974), p. 99.

51. James Hughes, "The Cypriot Labyrinth," New Left Review, June 1966, pp. 49-50.

52. Denktash, A Short Discourse, p. 25. In 1972 Rauf Denktash was claiming that for eight years, "Turkey has been paying the salaries of every single Turk in the Turkish administration; refugees have lived on Turkey's aid and live in houses built by Turkey," as a result of the fact that the Makarios government refused to recognize the Turkish Cypriots' legitimate rights.

53. See Paul Martin, "Turkish Cypriot State Takes Shape as Constituent Assembly Is Set Up in Nicosia," Times (London), February 25, 1975.

54. Hughes, "The Cypriot Labyrinth," pp. 49-50; See also, AKEL, Victims of Facist Terrorism (Nicosia, Cyprus: AKEL, no date), pp. 10-15.

55. Stephens, Cyprus: A Place of Arms, p. 180.

56. Purcell, Cyprus, p. 378.

57. Ibid. Purcell reports a series of bomb explosions in May 1967 outside the homes of leaders loyal to Vice President Kutchuk.

58. See Steven V. Roberts in the New York Times, January 24, 1975, p. 3.

59. Ismet Giritli, "Turkey Since the 1965 Elections," Middle East Journal, Spring 1967, p. 361.

60. See Xydis, "The Psychological Complex," p. 28, for discussion of the secret meetings between the premiers and foreign ministers of Greece and Turkey on February 10 and 11, 1959, for accepting the constitution and treaties binding on the forthcoming independent state of Cyprus. This article is probably the best analysis of the continuing tension and conflict between the Cypriot leadership of Makarios and the Greek governments.

61. See E. Papaioannu, "For the Independence and Progress of Cyprus," World Marxist Review 9, no. 12 (December 1966), for AKEL's decision to support Makarios.

62. New York Times, July 15, 1973. The three bishops were defrocked by the Middle East Orthodox Synod on July 14, 1973.

63. The writer was able to ascertain this shift in self-identification in the course of three field trips to Cyprus in 1970, 1972, and 1975, including interviews with many Greek Cypriot elites and nonelites.

64. World Bank Atlas, 1969 (Washington, D.C.: World Bank, 1970).

65. J. Bowyer Bell, "Violence at a Distance: Greece and the Cyprus Crisis," Orbis 18, no. 3 (Fall 1974): 796, discusses the fact that EOKA was trained and financed by KYP, the Greek CIA. On CIA involvement, see Laurence Stern "Bitter Lesson: How We Failed in Cyprus," Foreign Policy 19 (Summer 1975): 43, 52. The author strongly implies that the CIA may have transmitted funds through Greece to EOKA B using Andreas Potamianos, a wealthy playboy, as the intermediary.

66. See Van Coufoudakis, "United States Foreign Policy and the Cyprus Question: A Case Study in Cold War Diplomacy," in Theodore A. Coulombis and Salle M. Hicks, eds., U.S. Foreign Policy Toward Greece and Cyprus (conference proceedings) (Washington, D.C.: 1975), pp. 123-24. See also "Archbishop Makarios Strikes Back," Financial Times, July 10, 1974.

67. See Guardian (London), October 8, 1973, on planned coups against Makarios which became common. A major coup attempt in February 1972 was followed by another attempt in 1973.

68. Coufoudakis, "United States Foreign Policy," pp. 123-24.

69. See Xydis, "Thy Psychological Complex," pp. 35-38.

70. See John A. Katris, Eyewitness in Greece (St. Louis: New Critics Press, 1971), pp. 44-45; Elizabeth B. Drew, "Democracy on Ice: A Study of American Foreign Policy Towards Dictatorship in Greece," Atlantic Monthly, July 1968; and Stanley Karnow, The Atlantic Monthly, February 1975, for detailed discussions of the role of various U.S. agencies (including the CIA) in the 1963-67 period and the U.S. role in the April 1967 coup.

71. See Xydis, "The Psychological Complex," p. 38.

72. Benjamin Welles, in the New York Times, December 2, 1970, p. 5, cites the admission by the State Department that the British base at Akrotiri had been used for American reconnaissance air flights. On U.S. aerial reconnaissance, see Stern, "Bitter Lesson," p. 58.

73. Daily Telegraph (London), March 1, 1975, p. 5.

74. See David Fairhall, "Bitter Lemons," Guardian (London), May 29, 1974, for a discussion of the strategic value of the British bases in Cyprus to NATO. See also Stephens, Cyprus: A Place of Arms, pp. 200-01.

75. Interview given by Mr. Alfantakis, Ioannides's lawyer, to Curtis Ingham, Ms. Magazine, May 1975.

76. See Adamantia Pollis, "United States Foreign Policy Towards Authoritatian Regimes in the Mediterranean," Millennium: Journal of International Studies 4, no. 1 (Spring 1975): 42-43, for a discussion of cooling U.S.-Turkish relations and U.S.-Greek relations.

77. Coufoudakis, "United States Foreign Policy," pp. 114-16, for discussion of the Johnson ultimatum.

78. New Cyprus Association (pamphlet) (Nicosia, Cyprus, 1975).

79. News release, Office of Public Information, Republic of Cyprus, Nicosia, Cyprus, June 23, 1975, announcing that on June 23, 1975, Yasir Arafat, leader of the Palestine Liberation Organization, after a meeting with President Makarios of Cyprus, promised him unqualified support for an independent demilitarized Cyprus.

CHAPTER

3

INTERNAL AND EXTERNAL FACTORS IN THE FAILURE OF NATIONAL INTEGRATION IN PAKISTAN
Inayatullah

Recent critiques of the dominant theories of political development and national integration have exposed several implicit biases. First, these theories have generally assumed a universal trend toward homogenization of diverse cultures within a nation-state as well as in the global community, and a progressive enlargement of political units absorbing smaller territorial units. When this trend is obstructed, slowed down, or reversed, it is considered a breakdown in modernization—a political regression. All phenomena that spoil the symmetry of this trend are characterized as parochial, primordial, fissiparous, and disruptive. These theories are biased in favor of the national elite attempting to build a nation.* They fail to recognize the aspirations of the regional or ethnic counterelite to influence policies of the national elite and the direction of the process of national integration. [1]

---

*The term "national elite" is used in this study for the study of the political elite that sees the whole nation as its political constituency and makes and implements national integration policies. The term "regional counterelite" is used for the elite that perceives a given region within a nation as its political constituency and struggles to protect the interests of this region by demanding changes in the policies of the national elite. These two concepts have their logical counterparts, the national counterelite and the allied regional elite, but these concepts have not been used in this study because the struggle over issues of Pakistani integration occurred primarily between the national elite and the regional counterelite.

Second, these theories attach disproportionate significance to internal variables in a society in which national integration is taking place, ignoring the role of the international environment in determining and limiting the policy options of the elite.[2] These theories generally assume that the internal power structure and the technical assistance programs of Western countries are positive factors for integration. Therefore, whenever national integration fails to take place it is primarily due to negative internal conditions. This bias could be the result of the influence of older theories of social evolution of the nineteenth century.[3] It could also be the result of a gap between the theories of international politics and those of development and modernization.

For an adequate analysis of national integration, the process through which a people living in a given territory or terrorities come to develop a level of solidarity adequate to sustain a common political organization and authority structure, one needs to take into account three sets of variables and their interaction:

1. Initial primary conditions such as a society's geophysical characteristics, degree of unity and diversity of culture, patterns of social structure integration, and composition and character of power structure.
2. The dynamics of demand and policy interactions between the national elite and the regional counterelite within the local and international setting, and the consequences for national integration.
3. The structure of international power and the society's place in this structure.

It can be assumed that geographical compactness; relatively even distribution of natural resources and wealth between different regions; homogeneity of culture and a commonly accepted national language; an egalitarian, flexible, and open class structure; and a broad-based, progressive power structure would be conducive for national integration. Absence of these conditions or presence of contrary conditions would favor a low level of integration, malintegration, or disintegration.

Within the context of primary societal conditions, a national elite attempts to absorb and contain the aspirations of the regional counterelite through various policies that rely either on an ideological appeal or a sharing of political power, or a distribution of economic and utilitarian rewards, or on coercion, or a combination of all or some of these. The effect of these policies varies with the quality of the internal conditions and external setting, the sequence in which the policies are pursued, and the demands of the regional counterelite. These conditions can generate an "integrative circle" or a "disintegrative circle." Favorable primary conditions and internation environment plus an adequate, timely, and accommodative response by the national elite at an early stage in the articulation of regional demands could start an integrative circle. Unfavorable internal and external conditions plus a repressive response to the manifestation of regionalism could generate a disintegrative circle, which may be difficult to reverse if the accommodative response comes from the national elite at too late a stage.

The flows from the international setting as mediated by the structure of international power may affect the process of national integration in several ways. First, the national elite and the regional counterelite are influenced by the structure of international power. When this structure is extremely polarized and expansionist, the dominant powers attempt to penetrate the whole international political arena and expand their zones of influence at each other's cost. This may require creating satellite allied nations, bringing into power subordinate and subservient elites in those nations, and helping them remain in power by providing necessary assistance if they are threatened. This could dispose the national elite to pursue one set of integrative policies in preference to another. Generally, the national elite is less disposed to accommodate regional demands when it is assured of external support.

To subvert the alliance between a dominant power and a national elite the opposing dominant power may offer greater rewards to the elite or penalize it by assisting the regional counterelite to press for more radical regional demands, such as carving out a separate country. Perceived or actual assistance to a counterelite from an antagonistic power may dispose the national elite to adopt a repressive policy toward regionalist demands in the belief they emerge not from genuine grievances but from instigation by an outside power. Furthermore, the polarization between internationally dominant powers may sharpen the antagonism between their satellites, disposing them to subvert each other's national integration.

The flow of resources, ideology, and technology from the international environment can affect the national integration process indirectly. It can increase the national elite's capacity to buy off regional disaffection; or, if these resources are used to favor some regions, it can accentuate disaffection. The latter instance can result in the exploitation of one ethnic group or region by another. The flow of technical assistance may bring with it a preference for certain strategies of development which may be insensitive to national integration problems. When development is orientated only to economic growth and skewed against regional or ethnic distributive justice, it may incite regional disaffection.* Seizing upon this disaffection or independently, an antagonistic dominant power may export a counterideology supportive of regional demands, as well as provide support to the regional counterelite, thus compounding the difficulty of national integration.

The present study of failure of national integration in Pakistan, as reflected in the separation of East Pakistan and the emergence of Bangladesh, is undertaken to suggest the analytical utility of studying problems of national integration in the framework described above.

PRIMARY CONDITIONS RELATED TO NATIONAL INTEGRATION OF PAKISTAN

Pakistan emerged in 1947 with a mixture of primary conditions both favorable and unfavorable to the development of national integration. First, the country lacked physical contiguity, its two wings were separated by 1,200 miles of Indian territory, and the east wing was almost totally surrounded by Indian territory. This factor decisively contributed to the separation of the east wing by making its military defense difficult, as became apparent in the 1965 war and especially the 1971 war. Physical discontinuity limited the flow of labor and manpower from one wing to the other, making it impossible to develop a single integrated economy. The multiplier effects of greater investment in west wing could not spread to the east wing. Consequently, all public investment decisions became either/or decisions, the gain of one wing came to be seen as the loss of the other, giving rise to a demand to create two self-sufficient economies. Finally, by limiting physical contacts, the separation favored the growth of two separate and divergent cultures in the two wings and made the evolution of a common national language difficult.

A second primary condition, to a great extent unfavorable to national integration, was the distribution of population, land, and natural resources between the two wings. East Pakistan had 56

---

*For instance, the growth-oriented policies of many developing countries, developed with Western technical expert advice, have been skewed in favor of more prosperous regions and more entrepreneurial ethnic groups, promoting, to a degree, regional and ethnic disparities and consequent regional disaffection.

percent of the population but only one-sixth of the total area; it had
one of the highest population densities in the world and was subject
to highly unfavorable environmental conditions such as frequent
cyclones and floods. Except for the production of jute, it did not
have abundant natural resources. It did not inherit much industry:
at the time of partition, jute mills were left in Calcutta, India.

In contrast, although West Pakistan was also poor, it had
certain advantages. It had a relatively favorable land ratio. It
inherited an excellent network of irrigation systems. It was better
endowed with mineral resources. It inherited some industry.
The refugee population migrating to the west wing brought with it
greater professional and entrepreneurial skills. This imbalance
in wealth and numerical strength created several complex problems
in national integration.

First, under the Western type of parliamentary democracy,
which Pakistan initially tried unsuccessfully, the east wing's numerical
majority should have given it considerable political power over, if not
necessarily domination of, central institutions. But this could not
happen as the numerically smaller west wing possessed the effective
bases of political power—wealth and bureaucratic organizations.
This imbalance brought Pakistan to several constitutional impasses
and political crises. Second, this imbalance helped transform the
relations between the two wings into those between a metropolitan
power and a colony. The east wing became the market for protected
industries located in the west wing. It earned foreign exchange
through jute, which supported the further expansion of industry and
wealth in the west wing as well as the import of foreign consumer
goods. This relationship was a major issue in Pakistani politics,
giving rise to East Pakistan's demand for greater autonomy and
economic self-sufficiency.

A third primary condition unfavorable to national integration
was the lack of a common language. Urdu, which was intitially
declared the national language, was spoken only by a small minority
in urban areas of West Pakistan and a still smaller number in East
Pakistan. Bengali, the language of the majority of East Pakistan,
was virtually unknown in West Pakistan. The effective language of
communication between the secular elite of the two wings, therefore,
remained English, the official language of the central government until
the last days of the united Pakistan. Furthermore, attitudes toward
the place of language in local culture differed. The Bengalis showed
great attachment to their language and pride in their literature and
literary accomplishments.[4] The urban-educated Punjabis, on the
other hand, preferred Urdu over Punjabi, the language of the majority
of refugees from India, and considered the lingua franca of India's
Muslim community.

These linguistic complexities created severe problems in national integration, including a demand for equal status of Bengali with Urdu and a demand by Sindhi, Pakhtun, and Baluchi regionist elites for the preservation of their linguistic heritage in the face of the expanding influence of Urdu and English.* Furthermore, absence of a common national language restricted direct communication between the national elite and the masses, thus limiting the elite's capacity to create direct political support for integrative policies in both regions. The issue of national language also was related to the availability of jobs, at least in the central government. If Urdu became the only national language, this would have put the Urdu-speaking refugees and Urdu-preferring Punjabis at an advantage vis-a-vis Bengalis in competion for jobs. Hence their concern to have Bengali recognized as one of two national languages.

The negative effects on national integration of physical discontinuity, imbalance in numerical strength and distribution of wealth and resources, and linguistic diversity were reinforced by the regional cultural diversity and weak common cultural bonds.

The common bond of Islam and a consciousness of common Muslim history provided a basis for national solidarity. Regional and ethnocultural diversity lay dormant under these sentiments, but gradually came to the surface and gained ascendancy over the sense of national cohesion under appropriate internal and external stimuli.[5] The development of Muslim national identity preceded the emergence of the state of Pakistan and was an important factor in sustaining it for two decades, but it was neither widely diffused in all classes of Muslims nor sufficiently intense in all regional Muslim communities in India as to submerge local and regional loyalties. The following brief analysis of the emergence of Pakistan supports these points.

Islam spread into India gradually over a dozen centuries under the umbrella of Muslim political power, although not necessarily due to it. In spite of Mughal Emperor Akbar's efforts to create an eclectic national political religion embodying elements from Islam, Hinduism, and other religions that could strengthen Mughal rule in a united India, the Muslim urban and rural aristocracy as well as the

---

*Until 1955, Pakistan was divided into five provinces called East Bengal, Punjab, Sind, North West Frontier province (NWFP), and Baluchistan, and several princely states with a certain degree of autonomy. These five provinces corresponded roughly to five linguistic and cultural regions. In 1955 the four provinces in the west and some princely states were merged into one province, named West Pakistan, under a formula known as "One Unit." East Bengal was then renamed East Pakistan.

urban commercial classes maintained their Muslim political identity and refused to be submerged in the engulfing Hindu culture. [6] By contrast, the Muslim masses in the village, some of them converts from lower Hindu castes but almost all aware of their religious and ritual separateness from Hindus, did not possess a clear Muslim political identity; their sense of separateness was localized, usually apolitical and unrelated to the concept of a Muslim political community or state.

With the loss of Mughal political power to the British, the Muslim aristocracy and the urban classes felt insecure about their future status in the heterogeneous Indian society. This insecurity was compounded by radical changes in politics, economics, and social organization during British rule. Under the British not only the size of the Indian urban classes grew but also the level of interaction among them. With the expansion of the scope of polity, greater physical mobility, the spread of education and means of communication, the Indian urban classes—which previously were ensconced in their communal and ethnic social structures and interacted only peripherally—found themselves in competition over distribution of new opportunities.

In this competition, the Muslim urban classes found themselves seriously disadvantaged against the more Westernized and skillful Hindus, as they were slow in acquiring the new values, attitudes, and skills that the Hindu urban upper classes were relatively quick to adopt. This heightened awareness of disadvantage in an unequal competition reinforced the preexisting separate identity focused on Islamic and Muslim cultural symbols. [7] The sense of identity was further strengthened by anxieties and insecurities created by the Hindu revivalist movements aimed at the reconversion of Muslims and the elimination of Muslim cultural influence from India. [8]

The emergence of the so-called representative and democratic central and provincial institutions under the British, who assigned political power to number, further heightened the sense of separateness of the numerically smaller Muslims.

These disabilities and uncertainties generated three responses among the Muslim upper and middle classes. First, there was a new and vigorous intellectual fermentation focused on the superiority of Islamic cultural tradition as reflected in the writings, in particular, of Shibli, Hali, and Iqbal. Second, there developed a greater sense of identity with the Muslim world outside India, as demonstrated by the Khilafat movement in the early 1920s. Finally came the demand for a separate state or states for the Muslims of India.

The consciousness of a single separate Muslim community in India in search of a state was not initially pervasive among all urban Muslims of India. First, there was uncertainty as to whether it was one Muslim community or several that sought transformation into a political community. The poet-philosopher Iqbal, considered the founder of the concept of Pakistan, only suggested a Muslim state in northwest India, without specifying the political status of Muslims in Bengal. The Lahore Resolution, the most important formal stipulation about the creation of the new state, provided for "sovereign states." The resolution was indeed amended in 1946 to make room for one Pakistan, and the Muslim League always maintained that it wanted a single Pakistan in its struggle for the achievement of a new country. But the fact that the resolution originally did not aim at the creation of a single state was an implicit recognition of at least two separate Muslim communities that, as part of larger Muslim nation, should struggle together to create independent Muslim states.[9]

Second, not all Muslims believed that the preservation of their community and culture required the protection of a Muslim state. A small number of Muslims, including some distinguished scholars of Islam organized into Jamait-Ul-Ulema-i-Hind, did not believe their Islamic/Muslim identity constrained them to demand a separate Muslim state. The number of such politically articulate Muslims in one province, the Northwest Frontier Province, allied to the Indian Congress favoring a united India, was significant enough to make it necessary for the British to test whether the province should join Pakistan or India. Finally, when confronted with the possible partitioning of Bengal into two parts, with West Bengal remaining in India and East Bengal becoming part of Pakistan, there was a lingering ambivalence among some Muslim leaders in Bengal, who wondered aloud in 1946 whether the cost of partitioning a culturally homogeneous, united Bengal was worth the benefit of a new Muslim state.

At the time of its creation Pakistan was a country bound by the vague sense of Muslim identity among upper and middle urban classes and by the feeling of security that the refugees fleeing from India found in their new environment. But under this Muslim identity lay hidden explosive regional, linguistic, and parochial identities that limited or subverted the broader consciousness. Within the Muslims of Pakistan there existed at least five distinct subcultures: Bengali, Punjabi, Sindhi, Pathan, and Baluchi. Yet another layer of culture was brought to Pakistan by mostly Urdu-speaking refugees. The partition of the subcontinent still left the country religiously heterogeneous, in spite of large-scale migration of Hindus from Pakistan (especially the western part) and emigration of Muslims from India to both wings; about 22 percent of the population of East Bengal was Hindu and a small number in Sind (1.5 percent of the total population of Pakistan) decided to stay in that province, making Hindus about 13 percent of the total population of Pakistan, according to the 1961 Pakistan census.

After the establishment of Pakistan, Islam, the unifying ideological force and rallying point of Indian Muslims in their struggle for Pakistan, turned out to be a divisive force as well. The problem of definition of an Islamic state, for example, tended to divide the Ulema and the Western-educated elite, which considerably exacerbated constitutional controversies in the early 1950s. As the issue of the Islamic state became dominant in politics, and as being a Muslim was conceived to confer special status and obligations on citizens, there developed a demand for declaring Ahmadis a minority community in 1953.* The anti-Ahmadiya movement assumed such intensity and magnitude in West Punjab that the army had to be called in to restore law and order.[10] Attempts to affirm the Islamic character of the state also revived the old controversy about joint and separate electorates. This divided the West Pakistani politicians, who supported a separate electorate, from East Pakistani secular regionalist politicians, who supported a joint electorate, expecting it would ensure an overall Bengali majority in Pakistani politics by including the Hindus of East Pakistan in the common electorates with Bengali Muslims.[11]

East Pakistani society became, immediately after the partition, a relatively egalitarian and homogeneous population with a large class of peasants forming the base of a pyramid. This homogeneity increase as the rapidly multiplying population and slow economic development created a large rural proletariat. At the top of the pyramid was a newly emergent relatively secular professional urban class of lawyers, teachers, and so on, who were highly politically oriented. The absente landlord class created by the British either vanished with the departure of high-caste Hindus or was liquidated through legislation.

West Pakistani society, on the other hand, remained highly stratified and feudalistic despite some timid attempts to change its structure. The hold of the big landlords on the rural power structure, and indirectly on national politics, was considerable.[12] Also, the pattern of migration and government economic development policies brought into existence a new class of rich industrialists and traders in West Pakistan who not only amassed a large amount of newly created wealth but also indirectly exercised great influence over

---

* Ahmadis are a religious group that believes in the claim of Mirza Ghulam Ahmad of Qadian (India) to prophethood, which other Muslims regard as repudiation of the doctrine of finality of the Prophet Muhammad (a doctrine considered essential to Muslim belief). This group was declared a religious minority in Pakistan in 1974.

national politics.[13] As a consequence no horizontal social
integration could develop between different classes in each wing.[14]
Interwing marriages were rare even among urban Pakistanis. The
rural Pakistanis were tied up in their limited local kinship socal
organization.

The presence of two different types of social structure existing
in physical isolation from each other created incompatible political
interests and made it difficult to develop a stong national structure.
Integration between the two wings occured only through regionally
bifurcated and weak political structures and West Pakistan dominated
the strong administrative institutions. The regional orientation of the
political and administrative institutions and the power imbalance between
East and West Pakistan were not conducive to the national integration
of Pakistan, as later analysis would show.

In the absence of strong and cohesive patterns of cultural and
social structural integration, Pakistan was bound by three seemingly
integrative institutions: the Muslim League, the British-trained and
predominantly West Pakistani military and civil bureaucracy, and a
federal structure.

The Muslim League in a short time gained widespread support
among the Muslim elite as well as the masses in various provinces
for the creation of Pakistan under the leadership of Muhammad Ali
Jinnah. However, to win support from different Muslim classes and
ideologically divergent groups, the league remained unspecific on
major socioeconomic issues. This was later to confront Pakistan
with immense divisions.[15] Further, the structure of the Muslim League
was so highly centralized and authoritarian that regional Muslim
leaders who challenged the judgment of the supreme leader could
find no place within it.[16] Among those who disagreed with Jinnah
and left the league were two Bengali stalwarts, Hussain Shahid
Suhrawardy and A. K. Fazulul Huq, who in the first decade of
Palistani politics successfully challenged the dominance of the
league and sealed its fate in East Bengal.

The high extent to which Jinnah's charismatic personality
became the driving force behind the Pakistan movement and the
pivot of the Muslim League was a rough measure of the fragility of
this organization. Finally, the Muslim League and the movement
it led did not have to wage a long struggle that could weld the divergent
groups, classes, and regional cultures into a single Pakistani national
entity. Within seven years of its demand, Pakistan was created.
Besides, the struggle for the country under the Muslim League was
more tumultuous than disciplined. Its elite and constitutional
character were transformed by a mass and heroic struggle only a
short time before creation of the country. After achieving its
objective, the creation of Pakistan, and after the death of Jinnah, the

Muslim League soon disintegrated due to the increasing
struggle for political power and spoils among its leaders and the
shifting of power from political to bureaucratic institutions.

The second integrative institution that Pakistan inherited
was the civil and military bureaucracy. In its initial stages,
indeed, the British-trained civil and military bureaucracy played
a crucial role in sustaining the country, creating civil order,
accommodating and rehabilitating a multitude of refugees, building
an infrastructure for economic development, and in the case of the
military, preserving the integrity of the country. But soon the
disintegrative potential of this institution became dominant as it
became more and more involved in national politics. Both civil
and military bureaucracies were predominantly West Pakistani;
of course this was partly due to the fact that the share of Bengali
Muslims in the Indian Central Service was rather small. [17] The
civil bureaucracy's regional character was to an extent rectified, but
the military bureaucracy retained its regional character even up to
the separation of East Pakistan. This affected the process of
national integration in several ways.

First, the regional imbalance in the composition of the
bureaucracy and the pace of rectification became a significant
political issue, dividing the national elite and the Bengali counterelite. The Bengali counterelite also alleged, with some justification,
that Bengalis were assigned less important posts in less important
ministries. [18] Secondly, initially the paternal and occasionally
arrogant attitude of West Pakistani civil servants working in senior
positions in East Pakistan toward Bengalis invested them with the
image of colonial rulers from West Pakistan in the minds of the
Bengali intelligentsia. Third, as the bureaucracy became more
powerful in national affairs, and its role expanded with greater
government intervention in the economy and society, the predominantly
West Pakistani bureaucracy working in a national capital far from the
east wing was considered insensitive to Bengali development needs
and unamenable to Bengali political control. Finally, due to their
regional character, the armed forces could not earn the status of
a national institution, especially as they became more and more
involved in partisan national politics. This fostered divisions in
the armed forces, culminating in the rebellion of Bengali soldiers
and officers in March 1971. To some extent the ferocity with which
the Pakistani armed forces attempted to suppress the Bengali
rebellion was due to its regional and partisan character.

The federal government structure was a third integrative
institution inherited by Pakistan and considered an effective device
for maintaining diversity of regional culture within a common political
structure. The Lahore Resolution in fact recommended such a struc—

ture for the two envisaged states. After the creation of Pakistan, the federal features of the 1935 act were incorporated in the Indian Independence Act, which remained the constitutional framework until the 1956 constitution was introduced. Consequently, constitutionally and formally the provinces of Pakistan enjoyed considerable autonomy. But in practice the imperatives of maintaining a certain degree of cohesion and coordination in the weak newly created state, lack of experienced Bengali administrators to run the administration, the centralized organization of the Pakistan Muslim League, the combination of political and constitutional functions in the trusted leader of the new nation, emasculated the federal character of the new state.[19] This process continued even when a certain degree of stability and order had come to the country, culminating in the abolition of a federal structure in favor of a unitary form of government under Ayub. Thus, Pakistan was deprived of a possible political device for remaining a united country with autonomous constituent units, a device that the Bengali counterelite demanded should be effectively instituted.

This review of the impact of primary conditions on national integration indicates that Pakistan lacked most of the conditions that could foster and sustain adequate national integration. Compensatory mechanisms in the form of adequate and flexible policies toward national integration probably could have sustained the country for a longer period. But as subsequent sections of this essay suggest, such policies were not adopted and probably were not feasible in view of the constraints imposed by the perception of the ruling elite about the nature of national integration, as well as the dynamics of internal and international power.

NATIONAL INTEGRATION THROUGH
IDEOLOGICAL APPEALS, 1947-54

Aware of predominantly unfavorable conditions for national integration, disposed to overemphasize the Islamic bond between Muslims of various regions in its struggle to create Pakistan against the vehement opposition of the All India Congress, facing overwhelming problems in creating an economic and political infrastructure, the ruling Muslim League elite was conditioned to view the problem of national integration from a specific perspective. The basic premises of this perspective were:

1. The Pakistani Muslims should develop a common culture bearing imprints of Islam and the regional and ethnic identities should be dissolved into the larger Pakistan/Muslim identity. To

facilitate the emergence of this culture, Urdu must be given the status
of a national language.

2. That in order to maintain Pakistan as a cohesive entity
and save it from disintegrative regional forces, Pakistan must evolve
a strong unitary political structure, allowing the provinces only
limited political autonomy.

3. That the Muslim League, which fought for the creation of
Pakistan, should be the sole party trusted to preserve Pakistan and
foster national integration. Emergence of opposition parties was
viewed as a threat to Pakistan's integrity and national solidarity.[20]

From these premises emerged integrative policies during
the early years of Pakistan that were essentially unsympathetic and
hostile to any manifestation of regional cultural diversity, especially
when it also undergirded a demand for greater political autonomy
from the national elite and challenged the monopoly of the Muslim
League to rule Pakistan. They placed a narrow limit on the assertion
of regional, cultural, and political identity, which was to be suppressed.
The challenge to the Muslim League's concept of national integration
and policies came from East Pakistan in three forms. (For the purpose
of present analysis, mainly concerned with the separation of East
Pakistan, challenge to the league's integrative policies from political
groups in West Pakistan is ignored.)

First, when Jinnah and the Bengali Muslim League leadership
in 1948 declared that Urdu would be the sole national language of
Pakistan, the Bengali intelligentsia refused to accept it. Later
reiteration of this position by the Basic Principle Committee set
up to formulate basic principles for constitution making, and the
Bengali prime minister's declaration in Dacca on this subject,
prompted a strong movement for getting Bengali recognized as one
of the two national languages. This led to a confrontation between
police and student and the deaths of four students on February 21, 1952.
Nascent Bengali regionalism in Pakistan had its first martyrs.
Later, when the regionalists came to power at the provincial level,
a Shahid Minar (martyrs' tower) was erected to symbolize this
sacrifice and February 21 was celebrated as an official holiday in
East Pakistan. Now Bengali regionalism had its martyrs as well
as a physical symbol.

The second challenge to the Muslim League's unitary,
assimilative policy came in the form of a demand for greater
autonomy and a greater share in national political power for East
Pakistan. Initially, to an extent, stirred by language movements
and other factors, the fight for autonomy occurred within the
committees formulating constitutional proposals, led by the Muslim
League faction from East Pakistan. But when the Bengali counterelite

found that the Muslim League leaders in the central government could not realize this demand, they preempted it and made it a major demand of the opposition parties in the 1954 election.

A third challenge to the league's concept of national integration came from Bengali leader Hussain Shahid Suhrawardy, who set about organizing a nationwide opposition party. He had only limited success in West Pakistan but found politically stirred East Pakistan much more responsive to his appeal; there his party, the Awami League, gathered a considerable following among the urban classes and intelligentsia. This party, united with several other opposition parties, successfully defeated the Muslim League in the 1954 elections for the legislature of East Bengal.

The Muslim League's conception of national integration and its response to the challenge of Bengali regionalism was shaped by its perception of the counterelite, by its historical experiences, and by the threatening external environments.

The Bengali counterelite that challenged the Muslim League's political hegemony and policies was composed of two elements: (1) the communist leaders (predominantly Hindus), who in the face of the ban on the Communist Party in Pakistan had gone underground and were working in other opposition political parties, [21] and Hindu Congress which was not considered loyal to Pakistan (despite its protestation to the contrary[22]) and (2) the old Muslim Leaguers like Bhashani, Huq, Suharwardy, who had defected from the league on various grounds and whose loyalty to Pakistan was considered by Muslim Leaguers to be no more than their loyalty to the league.

In its struggle for a separate country and a separate cultural base, the Muslim League had overemphasized the community of outlook, sentiment, and interest among Indian Muslims and deemphasized the diversity, and when the league was confronted with the reality of this diversity after Pakistan was created, it found abandoning its old perception difficult.

This perception was in fact reinforced by the threatening external environment. The league was possessed by the fear that Pakistan's right of separate existence was not recognized by its neighbor, India, which it thought was bent upon Pakistan's destruction and reabsorption. Several events apparently lent support to these fears. First, the Indian government agreed to transfer to Pakistan its share of assets only after Gandhi brought political pressure on the cabinet through his standard political methods. Second, India's readiness to manipulate the overthrow of the Muslim ruler of the princely State of Junagarh, which had acceded to Pakistan, and the use of force to annex Hyderabad State, which had been ruled by a Muslim ruler, further added to Pakistan's sense of insecurity. Third, war between India and Pakistan erupted over Kashmir, a princely state adjacent to Pakistan with a high majority of Muslim

population and a Hindu ruler; to Pakistan this demonstrated the
continued refusal of India to accept and to apply to Kashmir the two-
nation theory on which the existence of Pakistan was based. Indian
control of Kashmir further added to Pakistan's fears of strangulation
by India, as several rivers flowing through Pakistan originated in
Kashmir. In 1950, after communal riots both in India and Pakistan,
responsible Indian leaders made threats of war against Pakistan; this
was averted by a 1950 pact between the prime ministers of the two
countries.[23] Later, developments in Kashmir brought the two
countries to the brink of war. The disagreement over the distribution
of water plus Pakistan's refusal to devalue its rupee following
devaluation of the Indian rupee, further strained relations.

Pakistan's neighbor to the nortwest, Afghanistan, also showed
hostility to the fledgling state by refusing to vote for its admission to
the United Nations and demanding that Pakhtuns in Pakistan, who had
joined the country after casting an overwhelming vote in favor of
Pakistan, should be given the option to establish an independent state.
These Afghan demands were not purely out of commitment to the right
of self-determination for ethnic minorities; they were seen as reflecting
an irredendist claim as well as an ambition for access to a seaport.[24]
After the creation of Pakistan, Afghanistan continued stirring up
trouble on Pakistan's northern borders with the hope that, if Pakistan
fell as some Indian leaders predicted, it could extend beyond the
international boundaries established by the British. The Pakistani
elite also perceived a certain degree of collaboration between India
and Afghanistan and suspected the Soviet Union of supporting
Afghanistan's efforts to create difficulties for Pakistan.

The relationship between India and Afghanistan not only
reinformed the Muslim League's conception of national integration
but also provided a policy weapon with which to fight those considered
internal enemies. A military threat from India to a small and
relatively weak country provided the Pakistani ruling elite with a
device for welding the heterogeneous nation into one entity.[25] It
could convincingly claim that cultural diversity and greater provincial
autonomy would expose the country to external dangers and internal
subversion through collaboration between the radical wing of the
regional counterelite and India.

But gradually the fear of the external enemy wore off as the
grievances of ethnic and regional groups became more acute and the
regional counterelite could argue that this fear was being used as
an excuse to ignore regional demands. Furthermore, use of this
fear to promote national integration proved counterproductive in
some ways. The 20 percent Hindus in East Pakistan could not
evolve a firm commitment to Pakistani identity in the face of a
continuously tense relationship between India and Pakistan, which

produced frequent communal riots and suspicion about their loyalty. Furthermore, emotionally and politically alienated from the ruling elite of the Islamic Republic of Pakistan, the Hindu leaders in East Pakistan sought greater solidarity with Bengali Muslims, supporting autonomist movements in East Pakistan with the hope of winning the trust of Bengali Muslims, security for themselves, and possible separation of East Pakistan from West Pakistan.

The hostile relations between India and Pakistan further generated disintegrative pressures indirectly. Apparently the east wing had to carry a greater share of the cost of these strained relations and less of the benefits. For instance, Pakistan's decision not to follow India in devaluing its currency with devaluation of sterling, to which both currencies were tied, led to an almost complete stoppage of trade between the two countries. This particularly affected the East Pakistani economy, which produced jute for jute mills in Calcutta. Also, the trade stoppage led to the substitution of Chinese coal for Indian coal. This set a trend toward reduction of trade between the two countries, which eventually proved more costly to East Pakistan than to West Pakistan. Similarly, Pakistan's confrontation with India on Kashmir could not bring any material rewards to East Pakistan except satisfaction of seeing Kashmir Muslims get the right of self-determination. But to West Pakistan it added a vital territory. Thus, the East Pakistani counterelite could consider a policy of confrontation with India more costly to East Pakistan and beneficial to West Pakistan, which dominated the policy-making structure, including foreign policy.[26]

Pan-Islamic ideology as well as a sense of insecurity in relation to India moved Pakistan to seek closer identification with Muslim causes and Muslim Middle Eastern countries.[27] While this possibly had some positive integration effects as the Muslims in both wings supported this policy, it also had internal costs. First, the Middle Eastern-orientated foreign policy did not receive as much support from the Bengali counterelite, which thought Pakistan should take as much interest in Muslim countries of Southeast Asia, which was much closer to East Pakistan.[28] Second, greater identification with Muslim countries, of course, further added to the alienation of the Hindu minority in East Pakistan. Both factors added to the strength of regional sentiments.

NATIONAL INTEGRATION THROUGH PARITY, 1955-58

During the phase of Muslim League domination, Pakistan was an embryonic administrative state with a political facade. The first governor general, Jinnah, laid considerable stress on stability, law and order, and the creation of administrative structure, and relied more on the bureaucratic machinery to achieve this purpose than on the quarreling and factious politicians.[29] This strengthened as well as increased the power of the bureaucracy in Pakistan from the beginning and laid the foundation of what has been called "imbalanced polity" or "overdeveloped bureaucratic superstructure."[30] With increasing fragmentation of the Muslim League in West Pakistan after the death of Jinnah and Liaqat Ali Khan, and its defeat in East Pakistan, constitutional impasses on various issues, anti-Ahmadya movements, hostile external environments, and availability of outside military and financial aid further strengthened this over-developed superstructure, which became more organized and skillful vis-a-vis the inexperienced politicians and unorganized apolitical masses. As the bureaucracy was West Pakistan-based and dominated the greater share of bureaucracy in the national elite meant greater power for West Pakistan in national decision making.

The victory of the counterelite in East Bengal (as it was then called) presented the civil servant-dominated national elite with a dilemma. It could either reject the results of the elections and engage in a confrontation with East Bengal or accept a certain degree of accommodation with the new forces until they could be overwhelmed through political manipulation. The elite adopted the second course. As a result, a new integrative formula was evolved to accommodate certain demands of the Bengali counterelite. The demand of Bengalis for equal status of Bengali with Urdu was conceded. East Bengal was assured greater provincial autonomy. A "parity formula" was evolved by which both east and west wings were assigned equal weight in allo-cation of seats in the central legislature. The Bengali demand that the principle of parity should be extended to recruitment to central civil services as well as allocation of development funds also was conceded. To avoid the possibility of an alliance between smaller provinces in the west wing and East Bengal, all West Pakistani provinces and a large number of princely states were merged into what was called "One-Unit."[31] The new integrative formula was enshrined in the constitution of 1956.

The new integrative consensus, however, proved short-lived. First, the One-Unit was not acceptable to the two provincial regional elites of NWFP (North West Frontier Province) and Sind, especially those who had a stake in the regional ethnic identity of their provinces and found their power reduced in the larger constituency of West Pakistan. Besides, with One-Unit political decision making became more centralized and they could not easily influence it. Consequently the West Pakistan provincial assembly passed a resolution to dissolve One-Unit. This position of the ethnic elite in the small provinces of

West Pakistan was supported by the radical wing of the East Pakistan counterelite, National Awami Party (as it was then renamed), led by Maulana Bhashani.

The promised provincial autonomy for East Pakistan did not materialize either, as the national elite frequently intervened in the provincial politics of East Pakistan, taking advantage of the schism that developed there. This elite frequently dismissed ministries and imposed central rule. Of course, this intervention was occasionally prompted by pressures from rival political parties in East Pakistan and by a concern that the Hindu minority in the provincial assembly was using its power between the two competing parties, the Awami League and the Krishak Sramik Party, to nullify certain extraordinary measures aimed at control of smuggling from Pakistan to India to protect the Pakistani economy.[32] Furthermore, the pressure from the powerful organized industrial and commercial interest groups from West Pakistan, and the lack of availability of coalition partners in the central government to the representatives of East Pakistani regional elite made it impossible for them to hold power in the center for long.

Attempts to redress the imbalance in the allocation of resources initiated during the government of Suhrawardy ended when President Mirza's Republican party withdrew from the coalition with the Awami League. The end of Suhrawardy's coalition government also ended any realistic chances that the integrative formula would be implemented in spirit and letter. The radical counterelite in East Pakistan, estranged from the Awami League and Suhrawardy, became dissatisfied with the level of autonomy granted to East Pakistan and pressed for greater autonomy leaving only defense, foreign affairs, and currency with the central government.[33]

Increasing apprehension that the fragile integrative formula would collapse, plus the fear that greater politicization of national life through the approaching 1958 elections could bring into power more and more of the radical counterelite and threaten the domination of the central institutions by civil and military bureaucracy led to the 1958 military coup.* This was a coercive device to reduce the power of the regional counterelite by curtailing political participation and to end the integrative policy oriented to sharing of power between the

---

*The explanation of the military takeover differs with different political groups. The regionalist counterelite stresses fears by the military that regions would acquire greater autonomy after elections. The center-oriented politicians considered fear of loss of political power by Mirza the crucial factor. It appears that all these factors were involved to a varying degree.

two wings.[34] All central and provincial legislatures were dissolved. Political parties were banned. A number of radical regionalists in both wings were detained.

The emergence of civil and military bureaucracy as a dominant political force also was helped by external factors. In the early 1950s the cold war between the Western bloc under U.S. leadership and the Soviet Union and its satellites extended itself to the subcontinent, to an extent, prompted by the fall of mainland China to the Communists, the Korean war, and the defeat of French colonial power in Indochina. The Americans sought political allies in the East to build a defense perimeter around the Soviet Union and China, for which they needed military bases. Beset with internal economic and political problems and entertaining fears of two of its big neighbors, the Soviet Union and India, Pakistan sought a military alliance with the United States and readily joined the cold war on the side of the West, entering first into a mutual defense treaty with the United States and then into two military pacts, the Baghdad Pact (later CENTO) and SEATO.[35] This had the crucial consequence of upsetting the internal-external balance of power in Pakistan and thus hastening its eventual disintegration. First, this alliance earned Pakistan the hostility of the Soviet Union, which abandoned its neutrality on two major issues confronting Pakistan: the dispute with India on Kashmir and the dispute with Afghanistan on the so-called "Pakhtunistan" question. The USSR provided military assistance as well as trade facilities to Afghanistan, thus encouraging it to pursue an actively hostile policy toward Pakistan and to instigate rebellion among tribes on Pakistan's northern border. Second, Pakistan's alliance with the West further froze its relationship with India, which considered that Pakistan had brought the cold war to the subcontinent in an effort to get the military wherewithal to wrest away Kashmir. Third, joining the Western pacts initiated a sort of alliance between Pakistan's two hostile neighbors, which finally culminated in a friendship treaty (August 1971) between the Soviet Union and India that provided India with both military assistance and diplomatic support to dismember Pakistan.

Alliance with the West also upset the internal balance of power in Pakistan by bringing in military assistance, financial and technical aid, as well as a preference for capitalist policies and strategies of economic development and by closely tying Pakistan to the international capitalistic economies.[36] These factors compounded the integrative problems of Pakistan in several ways. First, military assistance and economic support helped to enlarge the size of the civil and military bureaucracy as well as to modernize it, and thus increased the bureaucracy's hold on politics, and eventually gave it a political monopoly after a 1958 military coup.[37] Second, it enabled

the Pakistani central elite to expand the military apparatus in West
Pakistan; the ratio between forces deployed in the west and the east
ranged up to seven to one. This had multiplier effects on the economy
by generating greater employment opportunities in West Pakistan and
contributing to the widening of regional disparities.

Third, the Western economic assistance was unevenly distributed. West Pakistani industry and agriculture, especially irrigation
projects, received a much greater share.[38] Of course, it could be
argued that the availability of aid itself did not lead to the discriminatory policies against East Pakistan. But the issue should be seen
in the larger setting of the aid. The Western aid not only was provided within the framework of a predominantly free enterprise economy
but was intended to strengthen that framework. Within this framework
the aid was more utilized in the regions with greater absorptive capacity and more favorable basic conditions for further growth, which led
to uneven development.

Thus, alliance with the West indirectly strengthened both the
capitalist free enterprise system and the government's capacity to
massively intervene to stimulate the private sector, which favored
the more developed provinces.[39] The regional disparities, in turn,
further stimulated and strengthened the feelings of relative deprivation and the demands for greater political and cultural autonomy.
The East Pakistan counterelite, especially its radical wing, generally
demanded a neutralist foreign policy and withdrawal from the Western
pacts, partly moved by their antiimperialism stand and partly realizing the negative effect on regional disparities of alliance of the
bureaucratic-military regime with the West.

NATIONAL INTEGRATION THROUGH POLITICAL CONTROL AND
ECONOMIC DEVELOPMENT IN THE AYUB ERA, 1958-68

Imposition of martial law in 1958 was the end of the new shaky
balance of power between the East Pakistani counterelite and the civil
servant-dominated national elite. The new regime came out with a
new diagnosis of the problems of national integration and with a few
new strategies for achieving it. Unlike the Muslim League, which
claimed that it brought Pakistan into existence and therefore had the
exclusive right to control its politics, the new regime regarded
politics and political process itself as a major evil from which most
of the problems of national integration sprang.[40] The domination of
this process by the urban professional politicians and landed aristocracy was believed to have increased the malintegrative potential
of politics. Consequently, the first strategy of the new regime was

to restrict the arena of politics as far as major national issues were
concerned and to enlarge it for the discussion of local issues.[41] As
a result, the regime abolished national and provincial legislatures,
banned political parties, controlled mass media, and disqualified
from politics for a period the established politicians who could challenge the regime. It introduced the Basic Democracies system, a
four-tiered system of local government that served as an electoral
college for election of the provincial national assemblies and president.
This brought into the local political process a rural upper-middle
class and undercut the traditionally powerful landed aristocracy and
urban middle and upper classes, which were the base of power of the
politicians. The system enabled the regime, on the one hand, to
penetrate deeper and control more effectively a large sphere of society
that had remained mostly outside government control and to divert the
attention of the new recruits away from troublesome national integration problems to local problems.

Considering that demand for greater provincial autonomy would
dry up if the administrative inconveniences that the urban classes
encountered in a centralized polity were removed, the new regime
introduced several measures for decentralizing administrative power
from the central capital to the provincial capitals. Several public
corporations were bifurcated. To develop greater responsiveness to
provincial needs, the old practice of an official belonging to central
services but working in the provinces was abolished and only officials
belonging to the province were posted there.[42]

The new regime also recognized that relative economic deprivation and regional disparity were significant sources of national integration problems and needed to be removed.[43] It believed economic
reward could prove an effective substitute for the clamor for political
participation and would erode the power of the politicians. Consequently, to remove regional disparity East Pakistan's share of public
investment was increased to surpass that of West Pakistan. A pledge
of parity in foreign aid allocations was given.[44] These efforts brought
considerable stimulation of the East Pakistani economy; its rate of
growth for the first time surpassed that of West Pakistan.[45]

The regime also departed from the Muslim League's traditional
strategy of seeking national unity through invocation of external threat
and Islamic ideology. Instead, it sought to deemphasize the links of
Islam to national unity. The name, Islamic Republic of Pakistan, was
dropped. An Islamic research institute was established to develop
and project an image of Islam that facilitated rather than impeded
modernization. An effort was made to ease tension with India to the
extent of offering a joint defense of the subcontinent if India would
agree to peacefully resolve all outstanding issues.

The new regime also sought to calm regionalism by forbidding the reopening of what it considered settled regional issues, such as the status of national language, One-Unit, and parity. It also diluted the Muslim League's policy of creating a unitary culture by assimilating regional cultures, instead encouraging the preservation and development of regional cultures. Through the Bureau of National Reconstruction, the Bengali Academy of Dacca received considerable financial support for development and promotion of Bengali literature. The bureau also produced and distributed literature aimed at creating a common consciousness of the struggle for independence, the interdependent interests of the two regions, and so on.

These "pragmatic" policies of nation building by Ayub to an extent failed to produce the expected results and in some respects proved counterproductive, due partly to the internal dynamics of Pakistan's development and partly to external changes and foreign policies.

The administrative state that Ayub Khan built restored the balance of power in favor of West Pakistan, which prevailed in the early 1950s. The national elite came to be essentially dominated by the military and civil bureaucracy, with a collaborative relationship with a new industrial and commercial class and gradually with the landed gentry in West Pakistan. As East Pakistan's participation in the bureaucratic elite was limited, [46] it was virtually excluded from the national elite. Under the restrictive political framework this elite structure could not be effectively challenged by East Pakistani counterelite whose members either were disqualified from politics under the Elective Bodies Disqualification Order (EBDO) or were behind bars. The limited participation allowed under Basic Democracies was focused on local issues; as the system owed its existence to the regime and was thoroughly supervised by the bureaucracy, it could not become a challenge to its exclusive and authoritarian structure.

It soon became evident that the new system could not contain the opposition groups, especially the highly politically mobilized intelligentsia and students of East Pakistan, so a facade of participant structure was added under a new constitution; this was expected to pacify these groups without undermining the national elite's power. The 1962 constitution stipulated a presidential system and a central legislature, both indirectly elected by an electoral college of Basic Democrats, and revival of political parties. But the addition of a political facade to the administrative state did not reflect any significant change in the power base of the ruling elite, which remained the civil and military bureaucracy. It only symbolized Ayub's reluctant acceptance of the impossibility of building a partyless apolitical administrative state in Pakistan of the 1960s.

The expectation that the enlarged role of Bengalis in the central bureaucratic apparatus would provide an avenue for participation by the East Pakistani intelligentsia was not fully realized. First, East Pakistanis were not satisfied with the pace of growth in their share of the bureaucracy. Besides, the Bengali civil servants generally were in junior positions and therefore could not exercise much influence in favor of their province. Even a few who rose to higher positions were generally assigned posts in less important ministries. The military elite remained dominated by West Pakistan.[47] According to the calculation of Sayeed, "in 1965, out of the seventeen highest officers in the Pakistan army—one general, two lieutenant generals and fourteen major generals, only one East Pakistani held the rank of Major General. Indeed, according to Government figures, East Pakistanis constitute no more than 5 percent of the officers in the Pakistan army."

Initially, the Bengali civil servant at the center was in general a pliant tool for administering central policies. But gradually, in the absence of effective political articulation by the regional counterelite, they took a stand on regionalist issues in internal debates. Thus, fissures began developing within the administrative state.

The regional counterelite's resentment against its exclusion from effective participation in the power structure increased, especially after promulgation of the new constitution. The Ayub regime's response was generally repressive. The intensity in repression increased with the enunciation of the "Six Point" formula by the Awami League. Members of the regionalist counterelite were frequently arrested, their meetings banned, and the press news about antigovernment demonstrations censored. Ayub Khan also threatened to use weapons if the regionalists did not temper their demands. This policy of repression culminated in the arrest of a number of Bengali civil and military officers and some politicians, including Mujib. These repressive measures proved counterproductive, gaining greater popularity for the radical counterelite and their demands.[48]

The regime's strategy for winning the political loyalty of East Pakistan through greater economic development of the province also failed to produce the desired results. Indeed, the allocation of public funds for development of East Pakistan increased, as did the rate of economic growth of East Pakistan compared to earlier periods. But this did not satisfy the East Pakistani urban classes and intelligentsia, for within a mixed economy with free enterprise dominant, the weak private sector in East Pakistan could not develop as fast as the more developed private sector in West Pakistan; thus, East Pakistan as a whole remained far behind in economic development.[49]

Furthermore, within the framework of free enterprise, which the Ayub regime had strengthened in Pakistan, the newly emerging Bengali commercial and industrial classes (which to an extent the

policies of the Ayub regime have created), suffered disabilities in
relation to their West Pakistani counterparts, just as the Muslim
urban industrial and commercial classes had in relation to economically advantaged Hindu classes in united India. Consequently, they
gravitated more and more toward the creation of a separate and protected economic market in East Pakistan.[50] They supported the
radical regional counterelite in its two economies demand, just as
the urban Muslim classes in India had earlier supported the demand
for Pakistan. The sociological processes that brought Pakistan into
existence were now operating to bring about its disintegration. Besides, East Pakistan's hard currency earnings, with an export surplus
in the world market but a deficit of trade with West Pakistan, gave rise
to charges of colonialism and exploitation. In the politically charged
climate of the mid-1960s these charges evoked greater support for
radical regional demand, and they could not be countered with the data
showing the greater pace of development in East Pakistan during the
1960s compared to the 1950s.

The regime's cultural policy of supporting the development of
Bengali language and literature also ran into difficulty. Obviously the
regime wanted to encourage the development of a Bengali language
with a dominant imprint of Muslim literary tradition and to rid it of
the influence of the Sanskritized Bengali of Indian Bengal. Ayub
occasionally expressed the need for evolving a common language and
once proposed that the Sanskrit script in which Bengali was written
be replaced by the Quranic script. The Bengali governor of East
Pakistan, Monem Khan, took an open stand for eliminating Hindu
influence on Bengali and banned the import of literature from West
Bengal. The regime also discouraged the use of Tagore's song,
generally popular in East Pakistan. The Bengali intelligentsia saw
this policy as an attempt to distort the original character of their
language, leading to a "resurgence of linguistic nationalism" in the
late 1960s that manifested itself in celebration of Tagore's birthday,
use of Bengali for writing signboards and car plates, and pressure
for introducing Begali as medium of instruction in schools, colleges,
and universities.[51]

The East Pakistani counterelite's response to Ayub's authoritarian regime and its integration policies came in the form of the
"Six Points" formula, which was aimed at creating two separate
economies and currencies; a federal structure with a weak center
and only two powers, defense and foreign affairs; and a parliamentary
form of government with a unicameral legislature elected on the basis
of adult franchise. It also suggested the creation of a separate militia
or a paramilitary force for East Pakistan.

In the context of the administrative state that Ayub had built
and the exclusive power structure on which it rested, the Six Points

were indeed a prescription for dismantling this state. The demands
reflected the realization by the East Pakistan counterelite that the
country could not evolve a strong, common, central framework that
would allow equal participation for the two wings. Therefore, the
only solution to East Pakistani problems, they thought, was to seek
a high level of self-sufficiency and low dependence on the center.

Reaction to the Six Points in West Pakistan was strongly
unfavorable. Various political parties in West Pakistan and some in
East Pakistan considered it a plan for secession and division of the
country. The national elite viewed it similarly and rejected it out-
right. Ayub refused to accept the formula in the round table conference of political leaders in his last days. The formula evoked similar
reactions from the Yahya Khan regime and from Pakistan People's
Party leader Bhutto in the first quarter of 1971, although both had
remained reticent earlier on this subject.[52]

Dissatisfaction with restricted political expression among the
enlarged and modernized urban middle classes, pessimism after the
1964 elections concerning the prospects that the Ayub regime could
be changed through electoral methods, rising economic inequalities
between classes and regions, and greater assertion of radical autonomist movements in East Pakistan and in small provinces in West
Pakistan, and the corruption of the regime itself unleashed a powerful
movement against the Ayub regime. Basically, the attack came from
politically deprived urban classes, students, professional groups,
and laborers under the banner of greater democracy, greater economic equity, and greater regional, political, and cultural autonomy,
although the mixture of these three elements differed in different
parts of the country. The regionalist Bengalis, Pakhtuns, Sindhis,
and Baluchis sought change in the regime to secure their regional
demands. The urban classes in the big cities of Punjab and Karachi
demanded the overthrow of the regime for greater political freedom
and greater economic equity, without necessarily seeking the reversal
of the integrative policies and structures. This overwhelming tide of
opposition of urban classes brought down the Ayub regime and martial
law was imposed by a new military regime headed by Yahya Khan,
the commander-in-chief of the armed forces.

Meanwhile, by the beginning of the 1960s significant changes
had occurred in the external environment of Pakistan, which considerably changed the foreign policy context of Pakistan, creating some
immediate integrative problems as well as unleashing forces toward
eventual disintegration. With the cooling down of the cold war in the
1960s and the development of new military technology, the military
bases built by the United States in countries on the periphery of the
communist world became less important. Consequently, the political
and military value of former American allies including Pakistan

somewhat declined. There developed a schism between the two communist giants as well as antagonism between China and India, precipitating the 1962 border war. As a consequence of both these developments, India moved closer to the Soviet Union. After its "China war," India received considerable military assistance from Pakistan's Western allies; Pakistan resented this on the ground that its security was endangered by further tilting the military balance in favor of India, making it impossible for India to arrive at a settlement of the Kashmir dispute. The Pakistani national elite demanded that its Western allies extract from India an acceptable solution of Kashmir as a price for military assistance, something the Western powers, in their zeal to save Indian democracy and to contain a supposedly expansionist Communist China, refused to do.

The decision of the Western powers to provide military aid to India, despite the protests by Pakistan, was a major setback for Pakistan's foreign policy; Pakistan viewed itself as abandoned in what it perceived as a hostile environment. Pakistan did not have a realistic option of seeking support from the Soviet Union, with which it had a long history of hostility or at least cool relations. In any case, the Soviet Union would not have let itself be placed in a situation where it had to antagonize its old friend India for a new, and presumably dubious, ally. Within this context, the Sino-Indian conflict and the military superiority that China demonstrated in that conflict tempted the Pakistani elite to solicit the friendship of the only major power available for this purpose—China. The Chinese, themselves isolated from their former ideological and military ally and confronted with India supported by the West and the Soviet Union, warmly reciprocated Pakistan's friendly gestures. Soon an informal alliance developed.

This led to a further cooling of relations between Pakistan and the United States. Pakistan became less enthusiastic about its participation in Western military pacts, particularly SEATO, a natural corollary of its new alliance with China. The development of a close relation between Pakistan and China was interpreted by the Indian leadership as a collusion to encircle India to disturb its borders.[53] This further deepened the mutual hostility between the two countries, culminating in the September 1965 war.

These shifts in international power relations and alliances involving India and Pakistan were to prove a decisive factor in Pakistan's later disintegration. Their impact was accentuated by the second Kashmir war between India and Pakistan in September 1965. The war considerably strengthened the new regional alliances. Sino-Pakistani relations were further consolidated as the Chinese provided badly needed military, economic, and diplomatic support to Pakistan. To create military pressure on India, the Chinese served an ultimatum on India. U.S.-Pakistani relations took a further dip as the United States suspended military supplies to Pakistan. Sino-Indian hostility was further aggravated. The Soviet Union took an apparently neutral posture in this conflict, in order to further wean Pakistan away from the West and to keep it from becoming too closely allied to China—now the Soviet Union's major political and ideological rival in Asia.[54]

The impact of the 1965 war on national integration proved largely negative. Initially, sentiment for solidarity with the war efforts and with the nation heightened. The reports of bravery by Bengali soldiers and pilots on the western front gave East Pakistanis confidence in their military skills and capability. But overall, the impact of war on national integration was negative. First, East Pakistan's military vulnerability became apparent to the East Pakistani intelligentsia. Foreign Minister Bhutto's statement that East Pakistan was not attacked by India because of fear of Chinese intervention further added to East Pakistan's sense of insecurity, as it was virtually an acknowledgment that the West Pakistan-based army could not defend East Pakistan, a repudiation of the established military strategy. Feeling also grew in East Pakistan that the national elite considered solution of the Kashmir problem more important than the security and safety of East Pakistan, as it had risked a war over Kashmir that could have endangered East Pakistan.[55] Consequently, the East Pakistan regional counterelite added renewed stress on self-sufficiency ciency in defense of East Pakistan to demands for political autonomy and two economies. Finally, the September war also tended to slow Pakistan's economic development as more resources had to be diverted to military expenditure, especially with the drying up of the flow of U.S. military assistance to Pakistan. This meant a further slowing down not only in East Pakistan's economic growth but also in progress toward regional parity, the cherished hope of East Pakistanis. In 1966 Sheikh Mujibur-Rehman presented his Six Points formula, which stimulated and strengthened regional sentiments. Finally, the war increased discontent with the authoritarian regime of Ayub and led to its rapid decline by generating internal dissension in the national elite, by accelerating inflation, and by creating a belief among the West Pakistani intelligentsia that Ayub Khan had bartered away on the negotiating table in Tashkent what was supposedly won in the military field. The end of this regime marked the failure of the policy of promoting national integration through accelerated economic development and restriction of political activity. Another national integration strategy had failed.

The new configuration of regional policies and international alliances also had implications for the relationship between the central ruling elite and the regional counterelite. The Awami League, the core organization of the counterelite, increasingly demanded a friendly relationship with India and other neighbors and opposed the hostile foreign policy toward India as a device for scaring Pakistanis into artificial unity and thereby forgetting their regional grievances and demands.* The Awami League also found support for its stand for greater economic development of East Pakistan from the United States, which was now estranged from the national elite because of its friendship with China.[56] The National Awami Party broke into two sections—the pro-Peking and pro-Moscow groups.[57] The pro-China National Awami Party (Bhashani group) found the foreign policy of the ruling elite acceptable, although it continued to press for socialism and withdrawal from Western pacts. As a result of external changes, in the East Pakistani counterelite the internal schism between the rightist Awami League and the leftist National Awami Party (NAP) widened.

THE "POLITICAL" SOLUTION OF INTEGRATIVE PROBLEMS: THE YAHYA REGIME, 1969-71

The end of the Ayub regime was the end of the administrative and economic strategy for achieving national integration. It also exhausted the three main possible options in this field:

1. The Muslim League's policy of maintaining unitary culture and a strong center through religious ideological appeals and invocation of the fear of India.
2. The sharing of power with the East Pakistani regional counterelite on the basis of a parity formula.
3. Enlargement of the East Pakistani share in economic development and the bureaucracy within the framework of a West Pakistani-dominated administrative state.

To be acceptable and effective, the new regime of Yahya Khan had to try a new solution to the old problem. None of the old solutions

---

*In a speech broadcast from Radio Pakistan on the occasion of general elections for the national assembly in 1970, Mujib-ur-Rehman, the president of the Awami League, said, "We believe in peaceful coexistence with all states and in particular our neighbors. We believe that normalization of our relations with our neighbors would be to the best advantage of our people." The implications of this statement in relation to India were obvious to West Pakistanis.

was acceptable to the now much more powerful East Pakistani counterelite. Even the power-sharing solution under a parity formula, once
acceptable to this elite, was rejected as the Six Points formula of
Awami League was aimed at the dilution of central power and not at
obtaining a greater share of it.

As part of a new strategy of national integration, the Yahya
regime accepted the major demands of the regional counterelite of
both east and west wings as well as those of national opposition parties.
The One-Unit was dissolved. The parity formula was abandoned in
favor of creating a unicameral national assembly elected on the basis
of adult franchise in which the number of seats for each province would
be in proportion to population, to frame the future constitution of the
country. A Legal Framework Order was issued defining the basic
principles to guide constitution making. It provided for a federal
structure in which provinces were to be given maximum autonomy
consistent with a strong center capable of discharging "its responsibilities in relation to external affairs and to preserve the independence
and territorial integrity of the country." The new constitution was to
be framed within 120 days of the meeting of the first session of the
assembly and had to be approved by the president to become operative.[58]

The political response to the new strategy of national integration
from the regional counterelites in both wings was positive. Their two
basic demands of ending One-Unit and scrapping the parity formula
were accepted. The East Pakistan counterelite could hope that after
the election the Legal Framework Order would not be interpreted in
such a way as to negate their Six Point formula of maximum autonomy.
In any case, the new order provided them with an opportunity to
dominate the national assembly and to frame a constitution of their
choice. The Yahya regime, on the other hand, had hoped that the
election would not necessarily give total control of the national
assembly to the East Pakistan counterelite, and that the counterelite
therefore would be forced to bargain with other centrist parties and
to dilute their demand for maximum provincial autonomy, which
could weaken the center and threaten the traditional power structure.
The regime did not expect that it was unleashing forces that would
undermine the power structure and drive it to rescue itself by
repressive measures.

The expectations of both parties were not fully realized. The
Awami League swept the polls in East Pakistan. In West Pakistan
the center-oriented Pakistan People's Party under the leadership of
Z. A. Bhutto emerged victorious in Punjab and Sind.[59] Each party
failed to elect a single member in the other wing. A serious political
bifurcation so far unknown in Pakistan had occurred, setting the stage
for the disintegration of the country. Mujib, who considered his

electoral victory due to the popularity of his Six Point formula,
secured from the newly elected members of his party to national and
provincial assemblies an oath of allegiance to frame Pakistan's future
constitution on the basis of this formula and declared that there would
be no compromise on the Six Points. Yahya Khan, after meeting with
Mujib, got the impression that the Six Points were negotiable. Bhutto,
in a latter meeting with Mujib, did not get a similar impression; he
then worked to mobilize public opinion in West Pakistan to force Mujib
to compromise on the Six Points and to share power with him. Mujib
refused to share power with Bhutto, as he could frame the new constitution with the help of the regional autonomists from the west wing.
Subjected to these cross-pressures, Yahya Khan first called the
National Assembly and then, under pressure from Bhutto, postponed
it. This led to the Bengali civil disobedience movement and the final
round of negotiation in the third week of March 1971.[60]

The failure of these negotiations by Yahya, Mujib, and Bhutto
to arrive at a settlement acceptable to all, pressure from the military
hawks who saw in a constitution framed on the basis of the Six Points
the destruction of the preeminent role of the armed forces in Pakistani
politics, suspicion that Mujib was set on the path of secession, and
the threat to the safety of Urdu-speaking Biharis and other West Pakistanis in East Pakistan led to military action against the Awami
League, which started a civil war in Pakistan.

Some external factors also were at work in the defeat of the
Pakistani armed forces and the disintegration of Pakistan at the end
of 1971. First, Indo-Pakistani relations, which since the inception
of Pakistan had remained tense, could not be improved with the
Tashkent agreement under the auspices of the Soviet Union. These relations worsened after Pakistan's success in barring India from the
Conference of Heads of Muslim States held in Rabat, Morocco, in
1970 and communal riots in Gujrat, India, the same year. The two
major issues that were the perennial source of strain between India
and Pakistan—Kashmir and the diversion of water from the Ganges
River by India by building the Rarakha barrage—remained unresolved.
Furthermore, Indian fears of Sino-Pakistani collaboration were
intensified as the old silk route between Pakistan and China was
opened in 1969. Pakistan's role in facilitating détente between China
and the United States added to India's fear of isolation as well as its
hostility toward Pakistan.

Within this context, when the Awami League won an overwhelming electoral victory, India could see the possibility of a new pro-India
regime emerging in Pakistan, as the Awami League had scarcely
concealed its leaning toward the big neighbor. Consequently, India
attempted to strengthen the Awami League when it launched a civil
disobedience movement by forbidding the flight of Pakistani planes

over Indian territory, thus severing a vital link between the two wings of Pakistan. If this move had any effect on acceptance of the Awami League's demands, it probably was negative as the military elite, suspecting collusion between Mujib and India, was less willing to entrust him with the country's destiny.

Meanwhile, the strained relations between the Soviet Union and Pakistan, which had improved since the mid-1960s, again started deteriorating as Pakistan refused to be drawn into the Russian-proposed regional economic cooperation and planned Asian security system, which Pakistan thought were both directed against its friend China. The Pakistani role in arranging Sino-American secret contacts (Henry Kissinger flew to Peking secretly in 1971 from Pakistan) did not endear Pakistan to the Russians. Consequently, when the Pakistan military initiated action against the Awami League, President Podgorny sent a letter to Yahya Khan warning him of the grave consequences of continuing such action. And when India, expecting to go to war against Pakistan in support of the rebels in East Pakistan, sought assurance of Soviet assistance to neutralize Chinese support to Pakistan, the Soviet Union obliged India by signing a Treaty of Peace, Friendship, and Cooperation that implied total Soviet commitment and support for Indian intervention in East Pakistan.

While a coalition was developing between the East Pakistani secessionists, India, and the Soviet Union, Yahya's regime—primarily due to its rash and ruthless action against the Awami League—found no assurance from China that it would intervene militarily on its behalf if it were attacked by India.[61] Pakistan's old ally, the United States, which had suspended military and economic assistance during the 1965 war and urged Yahya Khan to seek a political solution, could not offer Pakistan more than qualified diplomatic support. Consequently, the balance of political, diplomatic, and military power had seriously turned against Pakistan. India, assured of the support of the Soviet Union and encouraged by the isolation of Pakistan due to the international moral outrage sparked by its military action against the rebels, and in addition burdened by the economic weight of several million refugees, intervened militarily in East Pakistan in support of the rebels and took advantage of what an Indian scholar called a "chance of the century" to dismember Pakistan. The intervention ended only when Pakistan's military surrendered in mid-December 1971 and the new state of Bangladesh had been born.

CONCLUSIONS

This essay has analyzed the conditions that resulted in the separation of East Pakistan from Pakistan. The analysis was made within a conceptual framework taking into account not only the effect of internal primary societal conditions and the policies of the national elites and the demands of the regional counterelite, but also the effects of the international environment. The analysis has been guided by a conscious effort to be neutral with respect to the conflicting claims of legitimacy of the concept and policies of the national elite and those of the regional counterelite of national integration.

This analysis has attempted to demonstrate that primary societal conditions, the interaction between the regional counterelite's demands and the national elite's policy response, and the international environment are three crucial variables that determine the success or failure of national integration. Each variable interacting with the other two makes a critical contribution.

Had Pakistan possessed the favorable primary conditions for national integration such as geographical contiguity, a relative balance in resources, wealth, and organizational skill between the two discontiguous wings of the country, a common language, and an adequate level of structural and cultural integration, the demands of the counterelite from the east wing would not have confronted the national elite with such difficult integrative problems. Nor would the national elite have responded to these demands as it did. The regional elite's demands for recognition of Bengali as one of the two national languages, for greater provincial autonomy, for a joint electorate, for separate economics, and for a certain degree of self-sufficiency in defense, emerged from the facts of geographical discontiguity, cultural diversity, relative economic underdevelopment, and lack of effective political participation in the national power structure, which was monopolized by the West Pakistan-dominated civil and military bureaucracy.

The national elite's responses to these demands were usually inadequate, evasive, substitutive, or coercive. When some demands were accommodated, this was done reluctantly and grudgingly, which did not initiate what we earlier termed an integrative circle. If the national elite had instead fully appreciated the constraints of the primary conditions and responded to the regional demands adequately and realistically, an integrative circle could have been initiated. If, for instance, East Pakistan had been permitted to translate its numerical majority into effective political power in the early 1950s, something the Yahya regime attempted half-heartedly and ineffectively in 1970, and if Bengali had been accorded similar status to Urdu without intense political agitation and some bloodshed, an integrative circle might have been initiated. Similarly, if East Pakistan's right to develop at a pace comparable to West Pakistan had been effectively conceded in the 1950s, something the Ayub regime did grudgingly in the early 1960s, and if "robber barons" in West Pakistan had been restrained through effective economic policies from exploiting the

poor in general and East Pakistan in particular in the name of economic growth, the disintegrative cycle need not have moved as rapidly
as it did.

The inadequate policy responses of the national elite were themselves influenced, although not necessarily determined, for the most
part, by the primary conditions. Geographical discontiguity and the
absence of a common language restricted the national elite's ability
to develop a nationwide structure of political mobilization and articulation and thus know and anticipate the intensity of feelings behind
regional demands. Furthermore, differences in social structure and
political culture between the two wings had erected communication
barriers between the national elite and the regional counterelite.
Moreover, the increasing dominance of the national power structure
by the overdeveloped superstructure of the West Pakistani bureaucracy
hampered the development of political channels for communication of
regional demands as well as the political solution of such demands.

The international environment impeded Pakistan's national
integration in several ways. First, the sense of insecurity in the
national elite of the fledgling state, which was in fair measure the
consequence of militant actions by Pakistan's big neighbor, India,
was not conducive for developing accommodative and flexible policies
toward the regional demands of East Pakistan. Perceiving that some
elements in the East Pakistan counterelite were in collusion with India
to subvert it internally, and that demands for equal status of Bengali
as well as greater autonomy for East Pakistan were attempts to weaken
Pakistan's unity, the national elite initially reacted to these demands
negatively.

It is possible that, if Pakistan had come into existence in more
peaceful circumstances, and if tension between India and Pakistan
on communal riots and the Kashmir problem had not been as acute, if
the Kashmir wars had not erupted, and if the presence of a sizable
Hindu minority in East Pakistan had not added to the anxieties of the
national elite, its response to regional demands in the early 1950s
might have been different and possibly more accommodative. Pakistan's strained relations with India were exacerbated by lack of
resolution on Kashmir and the Farakha barrage problems, the eruption
of a second Kashmir war, border conflict between China and India,
and the development of an informal alliance between Pakistan and
China that India interpreted as a collusion against it. Under these
circumstances India developed a vested interest in forming a pro-
India state on its eastern border. The electoral victories of the
Awami League in 1970 and the failure of negotiation between Pakistani
leaders provided India with an opportunity to establish such a state.

The extension of the cold war between the two superpowers to
the subcontinent in the mid-1950s further weakened Pakistan's capacity

to tackle its integrative problems effectively. To overcome its sense
of insecurity and tempted by offers of military and financial aid, Pakistan joined the cold war on the side of the West. This brought military
and economic assistance, which assuaged Pakistan's sense of insecurity but also strengthened the power of the civil and military bureaucracy to control the internal political process and to impose bureaucratic and restrictive solutions to its integrative problems. To
penalize Pakistan for siding with the West and later with China, as
well as for its refusal to be drawn into an Asian security system and
regional economic cooperation, the rival superpower, the Soviet
Union, threw its military and diplomatic weight behind India. This
enabled India not only to successfully intervene militarily in support
of the rebels in East Pakistan, but also to dismember Pakistan.

The provision of aid also tied Pakistan to capitalist international
economies and reinforced its preference for growth-oriented free
enterprise policies of economic development. This accentuated the
regional disparities between the two wings of the country and further
strengthened forces of separatism.

NOTES

1. Walker Connor, "Nation Building or Nation Destroying?"
World Politics 24 (April 1972): 319-55; M. Kesselman, "Order or
Movement? The Literature of Political Development as Ideology,"
World Politics 21 (October 1973): 139-54.
2. Terrence K. Hopkins, "Third World Mobilization in Transitional Perspectives," The Annals (American Academy of Political and
Social Science) 386 (1969): 126-36; Egil Fossum, "Political Development and Strategies for Change, Journal of Peace Research 1 (1970):
21-22.
3. Inayatullah, Transfer of Western Development to Asia and
Its Impact (Kuala Lumpur: Asian Centre for Development Administration, Occasional Papers Series no. 1, 1975), pp. 13-14.
4. Rounaq Jahan, Pakistan: Failure in National Integration
(New York: Columbia University Press, 1972), p. 13.
5. T. N. Madan, "Two Faces of Bengali Ethnicity: Muslim
Bengali or Bengali Muslim," Developing Economies 10 (March 1972):
80-81.
6. I. H. Qureshi, "The Development of Pakistan," in Guy S.
Netraux and François Crouzet, eds., The New Asia (New York:
Mentor, 1965), pp. 232-36.
7. Hanna Papanek, "Pakistan's Big Businessmen: Muslim
Separatism, Entrepreneurship and Partial Modernisation," Economic
Development and Cultural Change 21 (October 1972): 2-4.

8. Khalid Bin Sayeed, Pakistan—The Formative Phase 1857-1948, 2nd ed. (London: Oxford University Press, 1968), pp. 21-24.

9. Ibid., pp. 113-17.

10. Leonard Binder, Religion and Politics in Pakistan (Berkeley and Los Angeles: University of California Press, 1961), chapter 9.

11. Khalid Bin Sayeed, The Political System of Pakistan (Boston: Houghton Mifflin, 1967), pp. 83-84, 171.

12. Talukder Maniruzzaman, "Group Interests in Pakistan Politics, 1947-1958," Pacific Affairs 37 (1966): 84.

13. Ibid., pp. 89-91; Papanek, "Pakistan's Big Businessmen," pp. 28-29.

14. Wayne Wilcox, "Problems and Processes of National Integration in Pakistan," in Anwar S. Dil, ed., Toward Developing Pakistan (Abbotabad, Pakistan: Book Service, 1970), pp. 117-24.

15. Khalid bin Sayeed, Pakistan, p. 181.

16. Ibid., pp. 182-93.

17. Ralph Braibanti, "Public Bureaucracy and Judiciary in Pakistan," in Joseph La Palombara, ed., Bureaucracy and Political Development (Princeton, N.J.: Princeton University Press, 1963), pp. 363-67.

18. Jahan, Pakistan, pp. 98-100.

19. Keith Callard, Pakistan, A Political Study (London: Allen and Unwin, 1957), pp. 155-63; Sayeed, Pakistan, chapter 9.

20. Callard, Pakistan, pp. 37-38.

21. Marcus F. Franda, "Communism and Regional Politics in East Pakistan," Asian Survey 10 (1970): 591; Jahan, Pakistan, pp. 40-41.

22. Muhammed Kamlin, "Domestic Instability as a Factor in Pakistan's Foreign Policy, 1952-58," unpublished Ph.D. thesis, University of London, October 1968, pp. 194-98.

23. S. M. Burke, Pakistan's Foreign Policy: An Historical Analysis (London: Oxford University Press, 1973), p. 57; G. W. Choudhury, Pakistan's Relations with India, 1947-1966 (London: Pall Mall Press, 1968), pp. 187-208.

24. Burke, Pakistan's Foreign Policy, pp. 73-74.

25. Karl von Vorys, Political Development in Pakistan (Princeton, N.J.: Princeton University Press, 1965), p. 151.

26. Khalid Bin Sayeed, "Southeast Asia in Pakistan's Foreign Policy," Pacific Affairs 41 (Summer 1968): 231.

27. Burke, Pakistan's Foreign Policy, pp. 66-67.

28. Stanley Maron, "The Problems of East Pakistan," Pacific Affairs 28 (1955): 143; Sayeed, Pakistan, pp. 230-44.

29. Sayeed, Pakistan, pp. 299-300.

30. Fred W. Riggs, "Bureaucrats and Political Development: A Paradoxical View," in La Palombara, ed., Bureaucracy, pp. 123-36;

Hamza Alavi, "Bangladesh and the Crisis of Pakistan," Socialist Register, 1971, pp. 303-04.

31. Jahan, Pakistan, pp. 47-48; Talukdar Maniruzzaman, "National Integration and Political Development in Pakistan," Asian Survey 7 (1967): 878.

32. Talukdar Maniruzzaman, "Group Interests in Pakistan," pp. 95-96.

33. M. Rashiduzzaman, "The National Awami Party of Pakistan: Leftist Politics in Crisis," Pacific Affairs 43 (Fall 1970): 395.

34. Wayne Wilcox, "Political Change in Pakistan: Structures, Functions, Constraints and Goals," Pacific Affairs 41 (Fall 1968): 341-55.

35. Kamlin, "Domestic Instability."

36. Hamza Alavi and Amir Khusro, "Pakistan: The Burden of US AID," New University Thought, Fall 1962, pp. 14-48.

37. Robert La Porte, Jr., "Pakistan in 1971: The Disintegration of a Nation," Asian Survey 12 (February 1972): 98.

38. According to a calculation based on data published by the government of East Pakistan's Planning Department, in 1947-70, East Pakistan received 17 and 30 percent and West Pakistan 62 and 64 percent of foreign development aid and U.S. commodity aid, respectively. The remaining went to the central government. Jahan, Pakistan, pp. 34-35.

39. Sayeed, The Political System, p. 290.

40. Jahan, Pakistan, pp. 54-55; Talukdar Maniruzzaman, "'Crises in Political Development' and the Collapse of the Ayub Regime in Pakistan," Journal of Developing Areas 5 (January 1971): 224.

41. Shahid Javed Burki, "Group Politics in a Praetorian Society— A Case Study of Ayub's Pakistan," (Cambridge, Mass.: Harvard University, Center for International Affairs, 1970).

42. Vorys, Political Development, pp. 158-59.

43. Jahan, Pakistan, p. 65.

44. Ibid., pp. 68-75; Vorys, Political Development, p. 160.

45. Talukdar Maniruzzaman, "National Integration," p. 879.

46. Jahan, Pakistan; Braibanti, "Public Bureaucracy," p. 265.

47. Sayeed, The Political System, p. 195.

48. Ibid., pp. 210-11; Jahan, Pakistan, pp. 159-70.

49. Jahan, Pakistan, p. 74.

50. Maniruzzaman, "National Integration," p. 880; Alavi, "Bangladesh and the Crisis of Pakistan," p. 313; Papanek, "Pakistan's Big Businessmen," pp. 31-32.

51. Jahan, Pakistan, p. 163.

52. Zulfikar Ali Bhutto, The Great Tragedy (Karachi: Vision Publications, 1971), p. 27.

53. Choudhury, Pakistan's Relations with India, pp. 277-78.

54. Burke, Pakistan's Foreign Policy, pp. 349-52; G. W. Choudhury, "Pakistan and the Communist World," Pacific Community 6 (1975): 111-15.

55. Burke, Pakistan's Foreign Policy, pp. 337-38; Kamruddin Ahmad, A Social History of Bengal (Dacca: Progoti Publishers, 1967), pp. 171-72; Jahan, Pakistan, pp. 166-67.

56. Sayeed, The Political System, p. 291.

57. Rashiduzzaman, "The National Awami Party," pp. 398-99.

58. Jahan, Pakistan, pp. 187-88; La Porte, Jr., "Pakistan in 1971," pp. 98-100; Wilcox, "Problems and Processes," pp. 74-77.

59. Craig Baxter, "Pakistan Votes—1970," Asian Survey 11, no. 3 (March 1971): 210; Mustaq Ahmad, Politics Without Social Change (Karachi, 1971).

60. David Dunbar, "Pakistan: The Failure of Political Negotiations," Asian Survey 12 (May 1972): 447-53.

61. G. W. Choudhury, "The Last Days of United Pakistan: A Personal Account," International Affairs 49 (April 1973): 231-32.

4

CORPORATION THEORY AND POLITICAL CHANGE: THE CASE OF ZAIRE
Wyatt MacGaffey

The lack of a satisfactory definition of "integration" in political science, despite the amount of attention given to the subject, derives from the ambivalence of the concept itself, which refers both to effective administrative control of a given territory, usually a state or a major subdivision of a state, and to a consensus among the population regarding the legitimacy of that control, in opposition to the claims of potential or actual competitors, internal or external. Such consensus, made up of a more or less explicit ideology and of strong personal sentiments and motivations in individuals, is believed to grow so slowly as to be for the purposes of practical politics virtually an absolute and autonomous force, and therefore, with respect to current political realities, in large measure irrational. It is implicitly assumed, in intelligent commentary on international affairs, that in the normal and desirable state of affairs administrative boundaries and policies correspond to sentimental consensuses, which indeed generate and maintain them. A "nation," according to this point of view, is the political expression of "nationalism" in an appropriate population.

Since this ideal state of affairs can rarely be identified in the real world, supplementary assumptions are necessary. The imminent disintegration of a nation is attributed to the relative strength of particularistic loyalties known as "tribalism" if, from an American perspective, the populations involved speak exotic languages, and otherwise as "ethnic ties." Tribalism is the same kind of irrational phenomenon as nationalism but inferior to it, as representing a lower level of political maturity which, in the context of modern politics, is also anachronistic. Accordingly, the American public is asked by authoritative commentators to believe, and apparently does on the

121

whole believe, that political conflicts in Nigeria at the time of the
Biafran war, or in the Democratic Republic of Congo during 1960-65,
for example, are matters of age-old ("traditional") tribal animosities
that the national administration, prematurely instituted in advance of
the development of nationalist sentiments, is scarcely able to contain.

The tautological form of this nonexplanation (in which political
conflict alone reveals the strength of the "isms" that supposedly
account for it), and its inappropriateness as an account of real events
in Nigeria, Congo, and elsewhere, have been repeatedly pointed out,
yet the formula is still with us. Its persistence can be attributed to
its appeal as a statement of a political ideal, that of an ethnically
united community, to which we aspire and assume others should. This
ideal, supposedly necessary and universal, serves as a standard for
political judgments, congratulations, and expressions of disappoint-
ment.

Integration at any level implies discontinuity at the next higher
level, or the disintegration of a potentially more comprehensive unit.
One commentator's nationalism is another's tribalism, chauvinism,
imperialism, or revanchism; the labels have no empirically descriptive value. The strength and autonomy credited to irrational factors
allow us to overlook political and economic factors that are actually
present, but in their historical particularity are difficult to elicit or,
in some instances, embarrassing. Lastly, the cookie-cutter approach
emphasizing the internal structures of groups, distracts attention
from the role of external factors. Every group, whether or not it is
subordinate to another of higher order, belongs to a series of like
groups whose boundaries and their maintenance constitute a "system."
Every nation, for example, is such because its identity and boundaries
are recognized by other nations. Modification of the boundaries, or
of the conditions of boundary maintenance, directly affects the internal
organization of the groups: conversely, internal developments frequently carry across boundaries.

Adequate political analysis demands the use of a consistent and
realistic theoretical vocabulary, dependent on a set of interdependent
concepts and capable of direct application to empirical data. Since
national integrity and its maintenance marks off, at best, only a particular level of political activity, and not a special kind of politics,
the concepts and vocabulary used must apply to all kinds of polities
and their transformations. Such an analytical framework can be
found in the theory of corporations elaborated by M. G. Smith in his
collected essays in political theory, Corporations and Society, 1974.[1]
A summary of this point of view is followed in this essay by a brief
application of it to the history of Zaire, 1875-1975.

Government, according to Smith, is the regulation of public
affairs. Public affairs are the affairs of publics, and their regulation

consists of the continuous but analytically distinguishable processes
of making decisions (politics) and carrying them out (administration).
The public whose affairs are to be regulated is a corporation, defined
as a (1) presumptively perpetual (2) civil personality, with a (3) rule
segregating its membership from others, (4) some actual personnel
or members, (5) a distinct set of affairs that are their concern,
(6) autonomy to regulate the affairs, and (7) procedures and (8) organization for doing so. Subtypes of corporation exist when certain of
these eight closely related characteristics are absent.[2] Besides the
perfect corporation, the corporation aggregate or corporate group,
the most important subtypes include the corporation sole, or office,
which has a membership of one and therefore lacks internal organization; second, the corporate category, which lacks the capacity to
regulate its own affairs; and third, the commission, a type of office
to which recruitment is intermittent or contingent. Publics do not
include statistical cohorts, mobs, crowds, casual assemblies, or
mass communication audiences.

In the simplest possible polities, those of band-organized
hunters and gatherers, a single type of corporation aggregate, the
band, is the only internally autonomous corporate form. In more
complex polities we find corporations of several types, differing in
scope, that is, in the affairs attributed to them; in base, that is, in
the rule of recruitment; in their mode of articulation with other corporations, for example, parallel or hierarchical; and in their characteristic internal organization and procedures. The polity also may
include a variety of categories, commissions, and offices. The
United States, for example, includes corporations such as the state
of Pennsylvania, the American Political Science Association, General
Motors, and the Graduate Wives Club of the University of California
at Los Angeles. It also includes corporate categories such as blacks
and old-age pensioners, both of which lack the internal organization
necessary for continuous monitoring of their own affairs, although
both include local groups that have this capacity. It includes offices
such as the Presidency, and commissions such as that of special
prosecutor for Watergate affairs. The most complex as well as the
simplest societies can thus be contemplated within a single perspective; in each instance the primary data are provided by an inventory
of corporate forms and their contents.

The functions of a corporation, that is, the content of its affairs,
must be determined by inspection. Only one can be predicted and
that is government itself. The mere existence of a corporation en-
dows it with internal and external relations whose form and content
are maintained or changed by continuous political action. Although
the type of corporation that has no other raison d'être than itself may
be regarded as a limiting case, we are all familiar with examples

of this type, the law of whose operation is as famous as Parkinson's Law.[3]

Functions can be distinguished only analytically, since any action, and especially any complex action, will exhibit several functional dimensions simultaneously. As Smith says, government itself is an aspect of action, not a distinct type of action such as playing hockey. The inventory of activities, social groupings, norms, ideas, values and orientations, together with material resources necessary to carry out any function in a particular society, may be called an institution. An institution is a standardized way of getting something done. In practice, both for the analysis of any one society and for comparative purposes, anthropologists find it convenient to list religion, education, government, law, domesticity, and economy as the major institutions. The area, not necessarily continuous, within which a particular set of institutions is replicated demarcates a society. For Smith, a society may contain several autonomous polities of the same type, or on the other hand a single administrative structure may include several societies. The latter condition is that of pluralism, to which Smith has devoted several well-known and controversial essays.[4] As the aspect of action that is concerned with regulation, government has a special and in Smith's view paramount importance, comparable to that attributed to the economy by Marxists.[5]

Government is in the first place an administrative process in which rights and responsibilities legitimately allocated to groups and individuals are routinely exercised. Administration is authoritative, and characteristically hierarchical in form. Second, government consists in political activity intended to maintain or to change the existing distribution of rights and responsibilities. Here we must distinguish between changes anticipated by the existing administrative structure, as for example the election of a new President, and changes in the structure itself, for example, a coup d'état or the redefinition of the scope of the Presidency to include the authority to make war without reference to Congress. Political activity means the exercise of power, not authority, and is characteristically segmentary in form. "Segmentary" (or contrapuntal) is a term used in anthropology to describe the relationship of opposition between formally similar segments or divisions of a political community in competition with one another over some common issue. It is contrasted analytically with "hierarchy," implying authoritative subordination of one unit to another. The distinction between politics and administration, for example, was implicit in an argument before the Supreme Court in 1974, in which lawyers for the White House held that the special prosecutor, an appointee of the President, could not enter into adversary relations with him.

In simple societies corporations tend to be multifunctional and the structure of government undifferentiated. In principle, in a segmentary lineage system, the lineage consisting of the descendants of ancestor A, which as a lineage allocates to its member certain rights and duties, will divide in case of an internal dispute into two lesser lineages tracing their descent to A's children B and C, respectively. Lineages B and C, which for administrative purposes are constituents of A, become, for the duration of the dispute, political factions contraposed in dispute over the decision to be made. If the dispute, which may be about the compensation to be paid to a member of B for theft committed by a member of C, can be settled, no change occurs in the constitution of lineage A. Alternatively, failure to settle the dispute in a routine way may lead to the dissolution of A as a unit within which a normative distribution of rights is recognized, or to a change in its internal structure, that is, the boundaries and articulation of its constituent lineages. The genealogy that nominally explains the organization of the lineage will then be revised to describe the new state of affairs.

Much the same kind of relations, to which the same vocabulary is applicable, occurs in highly differentiated systems, although indigenous commitment to a particular normative order, and consequent concern with judgments of illegitimacy, may obscure the analysis. In differentiated systems, corporations are relatively specialized in their functional responsibilities, with organization, procedures, and rules of recruitment adapted accordingly. There have been many examples of governments in which only politically disqualified persons, such as slaves (the Ottoman empire) or women (the Fon kingdom of Dahomey) were eligible for administrative office, although in practice, as Americans know, the separation of functions, and therefore the structure of government, is never perfect and is always itself a focus of political activity. J. Edgar Hoover's FBI, although normatively subordinate to the Justice Department, could and did enter into coordinate political relations not only with the Justice Department itself but the White House and the Congress, on whose personnel Hoover reportedly kept politically useful files; this activity, as some complained at the time, tended to constitute the FBI as a fourth branch of government.

At any time, a given administrative structure allocates rights, including resources, which may in turn contribute to the political power of the holders and be used by them to change the structure of authority. Power, however, is wherever you find it; it does not follow from Smith's definitions that power can be generated only within a corporation, although careless readers have come to this conclusion.[6] Members of a lineage in dispute with another may call upon agemates, neighbors, affines, or clients to help them. Hoover would not have been as powerful without the support of people in Congress and elsewhere.

For the purposes of this essay, more or less expedient and temporary alliances of this sort, organized for political purposes, that is, to influence public decisions, will be called factions. A faction with long-term goals will need to develop its own administrative apparatus if it is to be effective; familiar examples include the communications or steering committee, the caucus, the lobby, and the political party. Any faction whose interests are regarded as transcending those of its individual leaders becomes a corporation, like the Democratic Party, if it does not already have a corporate framework, and if it is large enough it will develop its own internal politics, generating lower-order factions.[7]

Smith explicitly disclaims interest in causal relations. All that he holds is that changes of function, whether developed from within or imposed from without, will eventually be inscribed by political action on the forms and contents of corporations. In this connection the most important characteristics of corporations are their bases, that is, the rule of recruitment, and their scope, that is, the content of their affairs, these characteristics being critical for the articulation of any given corporation with others.

The theory permits orderly classification and comparison of political events, but it also has predictive value, in the following sense. Although he does not presume to say why or when change will occur, Smith argues in the provocative last chapter of Government in Zazzau, and in "A Structural Approach to the Study of Political Change," that change in a governmental structure can only occur in a particular sequence, which is the logical order of the articulation of its constituent units.[8] For example, it can be shown that political discrimination handicapping corporate categories in national politics are (in order of their discriminatory application) race, religion, and ethnicity. These are the principles, roughly speaking, to which the expression "WASP" refers. In practice, the system of discrimination means, for example, that a Protestant of English extraction has a better chance to be President than an Irish Catholic. With respect to change, it means that the discrimination against Catholics and Jews, and hence the revision of the jural identity of these categories in the political system, is likely to disappear earlier than discrimination against blacks, which involves a principle (race) more fundamental to the system as a whole.

In terms of corporation theory, as used here, the concept of "integration," as used in political science, would include "government," namely, the capacity to regulate the affairs of a given public. Such a public need not, however, be identified with a bounded

territory. The role of ideological and sentimental consensus, like
that of force or fraud, is given no privileged position in the theory but
is treated as a matter for empirical inquiry. Smith adds:

> It will be noticed that throughout this discussion there has
> been no need to assume that societies or their structures
> constitute systems, whether analytical or constructivist,
> natural, moral or symbolic, open or closed, homeostatic
> or other, nor to what degree or under what conditions.
> Such metaphysics are only essential in functionalist analy-
> ses of social situations and processes; but instead of
> furthering our understanding of concrete social phenom-
> ena, those conceptions merely obscure them.[9]

CORPORATIONS BASED ON DESCENT

The application of corporation theory may be illustrated by a
review of the history of what is now Zaire, formerly Belgian Congo,
and in the nineteenth century simply a large area in Central Africa
inhabited by many different peoples. The most westerly of these
peoples, the BaKongo, gave their name to the colony. The accompanying table lists the principal institutional features of the area
under successive regimes.[10]

An inventory of the corporate forms characteristic of Kongo
society in the mid-nineteenth century includes matrilineal descent
groups, offices associated with them, and the commissions of priest
and chief. BaKongo were differentially incorporated in their society
through their membership in unorganized nominal clans. The affairs
of these clans were trivial and since they lacked machinery of any
kind to regulate them they are called categories. The important governmental units were the local sections of such clans, distinguished
by their relationship to particular tracts of land as well as by a
matrilineal genealogy that described their internal organization.
Local clans were divided into houses and the houses into lineages,
but this was not a segmentary lineage system since the processes of
segmentary fission and fusion were not continuous. Segments at each
level were administratively specialized: clans were exogamous,
exchanging the domestic services of their members in marriage with
other clans; houses owned land and the persons of their members,
and engaged in transactions respecting these properties with houses
of other clans or of the same clan; lineages owned movable property
and were responsible for the debts of their members and the distribution of inheritances. Each of these groups, although not the

DEVELOPMENT OF PRINCIPAL INSTITUTIONAL FEATURES

	Public domain	Private domain
Kongo (until 1885)	Descent groups, slavery; chiefs, priests	Domesticity; magic and healing; subsistence
Belgian Congo (1885-1960)		
Bureaucratic (European)	Government; companies; international churches; statutory law	
Customary (African)	Descent groups; customary law	Domesticity; magic and healing; subsistence
Democratic Republic of Congo (1960-65)		
Bureaucratic	Government; companies; international churches; statutory law	
Customary	Descent groups; customary law; indig-enous churches	Domesticity; magic and healing; subsistence
Zaire (1966-)	Goverment; law; MPR	Domesticity; magic and healing; Christianity

categorical, had a representative headman. Besides these corpora-tions sole and aggregate, the inventory includes only two more types, the titles of priest and chief, both of which were commissions rather than offices because both were recruited, by initiation, only when local circumstances warranted, rather than automatically on the death of the previous incumbent. Only in some areas, where the functions they served were continuously in demand, did these com-missions become offices, but their authority was always precarious and each was recognized within a small area only.

Simple though it is, or perhaps because of its simplicity, this organization has been misconstrued by ethnographers in two respects.[11] First, it has been seen as a miniature nation-state, with the local clan as the population of a discrete territory and the clan head as its sovereign. Second, the importance of tradition and ascriptive status

has been exaggerated. Descent was not, in fact, a record of the
children born to a line of women; it was a legitimating inscription
upon the past of the outcome of current political processes that redefined the boundaries of groups. In such struggles the active political
units, or factions, were not the dispersed descent groups themselves
but local groups, which consisted typically of the coresident members
of a landowning house, plus their resident extralineal children and
grandchildren, who were members of other clans. Such a group was
pitted against other houses of the same clan and their respective
extralineal adherents. The structure of political factions, that is to
say, was based upon voluntary association and patrifiliation, not
matrilineal descent. The network of patrifiliation, which was also that
of marital alliance, stretched from local clan to local clan across the
countryside and had neither centers nor clear territorial boundaries.
The outcome of factional struggles was eventually recorded in matrilineal genealogies in such a way as to show, for example, that one
house was senior to another and entitled to provide the clan head; or
it might be recorded in the succession of a particular man to a charismatic title. Political failures became slaves, either because they
were actually sold to other houses or because their pedigrees were
rewritten to deny them birthright membership in the houses they
belonged to. The resources deployed in such struggles were derived
from the trade crossing Kongo territory from the interior to the coast.

The rise and fall of matrilineal houses, expressing the authoritative distribution and redistribution of rights with respect to individuals, produced no general change in governmental organization,
for which the list of corporate forms, their contents, and modes of
articulation remained the same. Radical change was effected from
without, following upon the imposition of colonial rule in 1885. At
the conference of Berlin in that year, the major European powers
divided the African continent among themselves and agreed that
Leopold II, king of the Belgians, could have the Congo basin, the
heart of Africa, as a personal dominion. The new state, conquered
for the king by a motley collection of European and African mercenaries, was taken over by Belgium as a colony in 1908 when Leopold
ran into political and economic difficulties. By forbidding what may
be called capital transfers, namely all transactions in which individuals were sold, executed, or transferred between descent groups, the
colonial government deprived those groups of much of their autonomy
and caused the swift disappearance of chiefs and priests. Subsequently,
the policy of indirect rule restored some measure of autonomy to
descent groups, permitting them once again to modify their own
boundaries and memberships, by instituting a complex system of
supposedly traditional litigation over land rights, under cover of
which certain aspects of slavery were revived. A new kind of chief,

also supposedly traditional but in fact essentially a low-level bureau-
crat, was invented to articulate the indigenous and colonial structures
of government.

BUREAUCRACY AND PLURALISM

At the beginning of the twentieth century Kongo society as a
whole was divided between three colonies, which were themselves
examples of a bureaucratic type of corporation carrying out military,
capitalist, and industrial functions new to that part of Africa. Within
Belgian Congo, Kongo was only one of many societies that together
made up the indigenous or African sector of a new, plural society
that included among its affairs the maintenance of its boundaries
against other states and, internally, the relations of its corporate
constituents.

As a primary constituent of the new state, the African sector
collectively fitted the definition of a corporate category, of which
Smith says that:

> Being . . . thus constitutionally incapable of undertaking
> routine actions to regulate any distinctive affairs, and
> whether or not subdivided into groups of variable scope
> and continuity, categories are either regulated by abstract
> rules which . . . impose disabilities on the members, or
> they are subject to positive regulation by other units. A
> corporate category whose members by virtue of their
> categorical status remain subject to regulation by others
> is differentially incorporated in the society in which
> those who regulate it are characteristically organized
> as a corporate group. [12]

The controlling corporate group in this instance, that of the
colonizers, also was culturally distinct in being European rather
than African. Among the affairs of the controlling group was the
maintenance of the fundamental cleavage between the two sectors of
the colony and the differentiating disabilities imposed upon the African
sector, the conquered population. Among the means used to this end
were to forbid Africans access to the factors of production, except
to the extent necessary for subsistence, to forbid the development of
the procedures and organization necessary to transform the subordinated category into a corporate group capable of challenging the
regime politically and effecting changes in its structure, and to restrict managerial roles in all institutions to Europeans.

From about 1900 to 1960 Congolese were subject to two different sets of institutional constraints within the colonial framework. As members of incorporated indigenous societies they were subject to so-called customary or traditional law, affecting primarily their domestic lives and the newly restricted functions of descent groups. In the public domain they belonged permanently or temporarily to bureaucratic corporations such as churches, schools, administrative districts, the army, and commercial and industrial companies. Often these creations of the colonial power deliberately took over functions previously carried out by indigenous organizations, which were thereby restricted in their scope or entirely abolished; public worship, education, and justice are good examples. [13]

With very little reference, then, to the internal political dynamics of the area, except as they were expressed in military opposition to conquest, the colonial enterprise combined into a new and much larger government a large number of polities, greatly differing among themselves. By force, persuasion, and often without intending to, the colonial regime transformed the internal structure of indigenous governments, to a far greater extent than the idea of indirect rule admitted, but it also created, in its own institutions, a new set of political goals to which Congolese could aspire, and new resources they might employ, including literacy, printing, bureaucratic methods and models, and the capacity to influence foreign audiences.

In the 1920s and 1930s Congolese attempted to form churches of their own. They held that religion was a private matter, but the authorities immediately saw these nascent organizations as a public threat and destroyed them. Responsible officers were specifically instructed to watch out for the development of hierarchical structures, that is, of administrative competence.

The essence of colonial policy, therefore, was to eliminate from the public domain all corporate groups controlled by Congolese except those (the descent groups) whose function was, under bureaucratic supervision, to regulate contracts in the private domain, that is, marriage, filiation of children, household subsistence, neighborliness, and the like. This political emasculation was justified in colonial policy literature as being a realistic response to the supposed absence of "modern" economic and political "isms" among the Congolese, in other words, to their "primitive mentality." When the existence of such "isms" could not be denied, they were characterized negatively. Protonationalistic political activity, for example, was routinely attributed by Belgian writers to "xenophobia."

INDEPENDENCE

In the 1950s, largely as a result of changing external conditions following World War II, Congolese were able to form two kinds of quasi-bureaucratic corporation, both at first allegedly private in their functions. The two kinds were cultural associations and, once again, churches. Together they rapidly became political factions exercising power in the public domain, directed toward revising the fundamental constitutive rule of the colony, the rule excluding Congolese from administrative and political office. The position taken by Kasavubu at the round table in Brussels is of great interest in this regard, he having seen as clearly as Nkrumah the primacy of the political kingdom.[14]

The disintegration of Belgian Congo, as described by Crawford Young, was hastened by the formation of new factions whose elements withdrew their support from the existing administrative structure. The Flemish and Walloon constituents of metropolitan Belgium allied themselves differentially with groups of Congolese, as did representatives of religious interests and the Belgian political parties. In Congo itself, "the colonial trinity" of church, state, and capital dissolved when the Catholic missions, and less explicitly the companies, decided that the nationalists were more promising allies for the long run. The missions in particular foresaw that it would be better for them, in a future independent Congo, to be remembered as the friends rather than the opponents of the independence movement. Thus the first explicit public demand for a new regime came to be issued by a group of educated men sponsored by the Scheut Fathers. The prospect of autonomy in the management of their own affairs divided the Congolese into coordinate groups, known as tribes to the foreign press, which often drew upon traditional bases but did not correspond in form or function to anything that had previously existed: Young speaks of "super-tribalism" and "artificial ethnicity."[15] Some of these new groups were specifically fostered, not to say invented, by foreign interests, and all the important ones were allied to foreign individuals or organizations.

Considering the speed of Kasavubu's victory and the fundamental character of the constitutional revision it entailed, what the world press chose to call the chaos of the Congo was in fact a remarkably orderly process. What has been going on since 1960 may be summarized as the following four empirically simultaneous and analytically interconnected processes: (1) the redefinition of all bureaucratic corporations on new bases; (2) the redistribution of political and administrative functions; (3) changes in the scope of the state; and (4) elimination of pluralism.

First, we consider the redefinition of corporations. Under colonial rule, all offices of any importance were filled by Europeans. Initially, the new rules of recruitment (1960) provided for a distinction between political offices, to be filled by nationals, and administrative and technical offices, to be filled by foreigners. Political offices were filled by a variety of means, overt and covert, including election, appointment, and force, and they multiplied in number, so that the resources of the public treasury were redistributed without regard to other functional efficiencies. On the other hand, politics and administration being distinguishable only analytically, the foreign advisers inevitably retained a considerable political importance. They were gradually replaced by technically qualified Zaireans, until under Mobutu, starting in 1965, all offices in the government proper, including those that once carried policy responsibilities, were at least nominally filled by technocrats charged with carrying out the policies of Mobutuism. Simultaneously, a separate political hierarchy was created and staffed by a combination of election and appointment. The core of this new hierarchy was the Popular Revolutionary Movement (MPR).[16]

This revision in the bases of offices began in government but was extended somewhat later to both the churches and the commercial and industrial companies. Foreigners have been restricted increasingly to technical roles filled by temporary appointment, but independently the government has sought to incorporate the political aspects of all major organizations into the MPR, which has units at all levels in factories, schools, and localities. Most firms have been wholly or partly nationalized, to reduce their autonomy.

In terms of redistribution of function, under colonial rule the primary political opposition obtained between the colonizers and the colonized. The colonizers monopolized authority and used the administrative apparatus of the state as a political instrument. After independence, the primary focus of political activity was control of the government itself, which rapidly took on a segmentary form; that is, it tended to dissolve into a system of competing groups. The boundaries of administrative units at all levels remained virtually unchanged, but their hierarchical relations were frequently altered. Provinces and lesser regions became the cores of political factions, and their administrative functions were made secondary to political functions. Majority parties sought maximal autonomy for the units they controlled, whereas minority parties formed alliances with minorities in other units and campaigned in favor of national or at least regional integrity.[17]

This segmentary structure prevailing under Kasavubu was replaced by one that restored the integrity of the national government, when Mobutu ordered that all offices at levels formerly filled by Europeans be filled by persons native to other regions than those in which they served. This measure prevented such personnel from using local administrative machinery for individual or factional political ends. At the same time, the independent political structure already mentioned, whose chief feature was the MPR, took over from the administrative structure of the state the functions of political control that it had exercised in colonial times. A fuller account of these changes would of course have to give prominence to the changing functions of the army in relation to the government.

The third process involves changes in the scope of the state. Besides changing the structure of its internal affairs, the republic took over from Belgium the management of its own external affairs. Besides defense and diplomacy in general, these affairs included primarily the regulation of trade. From the days of Henry Morton Stanley, Belgian Congo was in essence an administrative apparatus to manage the export of raw materials; in this function it extended and rationalized the role of a large number of indigenous states, of which the most important were situated for centuries past on the Atlantic coast and in Katanga.[18] After independence, there was a question of whether the rights formerly exercised by Belgium would devolve upon the Democratic Republic of Congo or separately upon its constituent parts, which would thereby become independent states themselves, each with its unique set of relations with other states. This issue coalesced with the political competition between administrative segments, a rivalry that would have taken place anyway but inevitably drew upon the major economic resources. From the theoretical point of view it is important to note that the various factions whose action bore upon the corporate constitution of the state themselves extended far beyond its borders to include not only various groups of Congolese but also several foreign governments and a variety of political and economic interests overseas, differentially allied with the indigenous groups in structures that, although they possessed rudimentary internal organization, lacked the identity, perpetuity, and closure proper to corporations. The best known was the "Katanga lobby," supported by Belgian and other foreign mining interests patronizing Moise Tshombe, governor of Katanga province, in which are situated the copper mines that provide most of the state's income. Activities of the lobby ranged from a propaganda office in New York, staffed by Belgians, to the provision of a force of white mercenaries in Katanga whose ferocity soon became internationally notorious. The American government, on the other hand, more or less clandestinely supported a group of political leaders in Leopoldville (Kinshasa), known as the Binza group after the suburbs in which they lived; this group, which included Mobutu, then army chief, arranged in cooperation with Tshombe the deposition and eventual murder of Patrice Lumumba, the first prime minister. Meanwhile the Russians, who apparently had been supporting Lumumba, were forced to close their embassy.[19]

After the resolution of the Katanga secession question, the republic found that it had not after all acquired autonomy in the regulation of its own external affairs which, with respect to economic matters at least, remained largely in Belgian hands. Mobutu has since assumed this authority, although the extent to which any industrially backward country can be independent remains obscure, both historically and theoretically. The major mining companies were nationalized, and in 1974 all foreign businesses were expropriated except those that had entered into contractual relations with the government itself.

There remained the problem of the churches. In 1972 all indigenous churches except the Kimbanguist (EJCSK) were forbidden, together with most foreign denominations. In 1974 and 1975 the remaining churches, notably the Catholic, were progressively stripped of their public functions, including religious education in schools and universities; seminaries were closed and public displays of religious symbols forbidden. The theory and practice of Mobutuism became the religion of the state.[20] Accordingly there remained no legitimate administrative framework for potential opposition except the government itself, its agencies, the MPR, and the army.

The fourth process is elimination of pluralism. Despite the accession of Congolese to managerial roles upon independence, Congo remained a plural society, divided into customary (African) and bureaucratic (European) institutional sectors. I have already indicated that in the public domain the customary sector had been considerably diminished, most public functions being assumed by corporations of bureaucratic type. There remained the political function of matrilineal descent groups regulating their own boundaries and internal structures, and also regulating access to land for subsistence agriculture. The relatively important private aspects of customary institutions included the production, distribution, and consumption of food, largely dependent on female labor; in religion, magic, and healing; and lastly, marriage, household organization, and the filiation of children. Disputes about descent, land, and divorce, together with minor matters of public order, were handled by specialized courts administering the customary law appropriate to each locality.

In the bureaucratic sector, now populated largely by Africans, provision existed in statutory law for the regulation of domesticity in the European manner, but in fact most Congolese chose to remain subject to customary law in this respect.

Besides these organizational differences, the two sectors differed in culture, the European sector being marked by such items as the three-piece suit, the brass band, the French language, and the Christian name.

In recent years, Mobutu has taken important steps to eliminate pluralism. His campaign for cultural authenticity, introducing into the bureaucratic sector the loose jacket without tie (called abascos or "down with suits"), the long drum for ceremonial salutes, the libation to the dead, African personal names, and increasing use of Lingala as the national language, have been well publicized. Less well publicized but more important are the codification of customary law, which when completed will remove its administration from the control of local elders; the denial of all suits about descent and land in the customary courts, which will entail the disappearance of the descent groups; and the nationalization of land, which was deliberately intended to make it available to the bureaucratic class as a resource for industrial and commercial food production. As noted above, all but one of the independent churches that sprang up before and after national independence, most of them deeply rooted in the customary institutional sector, have been proscribed. On the other hand, magic has been given a new respectability as authentic African culture. In the remaining area of institutional contrast, which is domesticity, it seems likely that a homogenized African form will become standard-ized through the pressure of both the law and the industrial economy. Government spokesmen have insisted on the importance for social welfare, in a rapidly industrializing society, of a provision that wives and children, not lineage members, inherit a dead man's property.

These developments, if thoroughly institutionalized, should also go far toward breaking down the boundaries between different indigenous societies now incorporated in the state as categories regulated by different bodies of "customary" law. These societies, united by language and the residues or makings of common traditions, have in the past offered factional support to leaders pitted against each other or against the central government. Mobutu's policy here has been to reduce public investment in the territories of the more powerful groups and to build up the resources (and the loyalty) of those less favored in the past. This process is known to the BaKongo as "mibandakanisation" or "debakongolisation."

CONCLUSIONS

I have deliberately chosen to review political materials already well known, for the most part, in order to show that within the single perspective and vocabulary of corporation theory it is possible to describe an acephalous, lineage-based society, a colony, and an

emergent capitalist state, together with the processes of their transformation. In this perspective the state is a type of maximally inclusive corporation with a territorial base. The relations of a corporation
to its external environment include not only acts of aggression, such as
imperial conquest, but all processes of faction building based on complementary goals that cross, as factions usually do, the boundaries of
the administrative unit whose policies or constitution are at stake.

Such factors operate at every level in politics and are not
peculiar to the state in its ancient or modern forms. In a survey as
rapid as this it has not been necessary to inquire into the opinions
of the population at large. It is clear that the majority of Congolese,
perhaps all Congolese, favored independence, and that the most
effective leaders, such as Kasavubu, depended heavily on popular
support manifested in riots and systematic passive noncooperation
with the colonial government. What the majority understood by
"independence" is another matter altogether, [21] and it is clear that
the specific direction of political developments, from the constitution
of the colony to its reorganization as an independent republic, owed
little to the specific content of popular sentiment.

NOTES

1. M. G. Smith, Corporations and Society (London: Duckworth,
1974).
2. D. E. Brown, "Corporations and Social Classification,"
Current Anthropology 15, no. 1 (1974): 29-52.
3. C. N. Parkinson, Parkinson's Law (Boston: Houghton Mifflin,
1957).
4. M. G. Smith, The Plural Society in the British West Indies
(Berkeley: University of California Press, 1965); L. Kuper and
M. G. Smith, Pluralism in Africa (Berkeley: University of California
Press, 1969).
5. The chief metaphysical element in the theory of corporations
is the assertion that ideological and economic systems are dependent
upon the political structure, wherefore a political approach is superior
in explanatory power to an economic or ideological approach. (Smith,
Corporations and Society, p. 218.) Whether this is true or not, the
theory of corporations is compatible with, and complementary to,
structural analyses of both economics and ideology.
6. M. J Swartz, V. W. Turner, and A. Tuden, eds., Political Anthropology (Chicago: Aldine, 1966), p. 28.
7. A strong tendency in social anthropology of recent years
has been to apply the term "corporation" only to conglomerates capable

of coordinated movement, including factions, whether actually corporate or not (presumptively perpetual, etc.). This tendency represents a reaction against the political anthropology of A. R. Radcliffe-Brown which exaggerated the stability of corporations and their importance as the only alternative to disorder, and a return to the utilitarianism of B. Malinowski. See A. Cohen, "Political Anthropology: The Analysis of the Symbolism of Power Relations," Man 4, no. 2 (1969): 215-35.

8. M. G. Smith, Government in Zazzau (London: Oxford University Press, 1960); "A Structural Approach to the Study of Political Change," chapter 6 in Smith, Corporations and Society.

9. Smith, Corporations and Society, p. 269.

10. W. MacGaffey, Custom and Government in the Lower Congo (Los Angeles: University of California Press, 1970).

11. M. Soret, Les Kongos Nord-Occidentaux (Paris: Institut International Africain, 1959).

12. Smith, Corporations and Society, p. 187.

13. C. Young, Politics in the Congo (Princeton, N J.: Princeton University Press, 1965).

14. J. Gérard-Libois and B. Venhaegan, Congo 1960, vol. 1 (Brussels: Les Dossiers du CRISP, n.d.).

15. Young, Politics in the Congo, chapter 11.

16. W. MacGaffey, "The View from Matadi," Africa Report 16, no. 1 (1971): 18-20.

17. L. Monnier, Ethnie et Intégration régionale: le Kongo Central 1962-1965 (Paris: EDICEF, 1971); J.-C. Willame, Patrimonialism and Political Change (Stanford, Calif.: Stanford University Press, 1972).

18. J. Vansina, Kingdoms of the Savanna (Madison: University of Wisconsin Press, 1966); The Tio Kingdom of the Middle Congo, 1880-1892 (London: Oxford University Press, 1973).

19. C. C. O'Brien, To Katanga and Back (New York: Grosset, 1966).

20. "Mobutu's Messianism Threatens Churches," Washington Star, March 22, 1975.

21. R. C. Fox, W. de Craemer, and J. M. Ribeaucourt, "La deuxième independence," Études Congolaises 8, no. 1 (1965): 1-35; W. MacGaffey, "The West in Congolese Experience," in P. D. Curtin, ed., Africa and the West (Madison: University of Wisconsin Press, 1972).

5

IDEOLOGY AND INTEGRATION:
MARXISM IN YUGOSLAVIA
Lyman H. Legters

INTEGRATION AND IDEOLOGY

It may probably be taken for granted that any government will seek some type and degree of integration in the society over which it presides. Even alien rule of the more purely exploitative sort has a certain stake in maintaining an efficient and peaceable web of internal relationships in a subject society for the sake of a smoother execution of its extractive goals. And any indigenous regime that is at least mildly rational will place a still higher value upon the network of internal relationships, essentially allegiances, that represent social and/or national integration (for a surplus of integrative over disintegrative factors conditioning the developmental tendencies in a given society).

Irrespective of the style of rule that is operating, a government's success in fostering integration depends of course on much more than its intentions. A society may move toward greater integration under a regime that is seemingly oblivious to the importance of integration; and it may, conversely, disintegrate despite a government's best efforts. Just what integration will look like in a particular society depends largely, I suspect, on the nature of the primary obstacles to a firmer and more reliable network of internal allegiances. How to measure it is even trickier—unless one is impressed by the numerical incidence of certain kinds of social transactions or by the puffery of official rhetoric. No matter what methodological guide these choose, close students of a particular society are generally able to discern the direction in which it is moving, whether its internal allegiances are thickening or weakening around the salient obstacles to integration in that society. Because the issue is not merely one of policy, they may not be able to prescribe ways of achieving integration—just as governments may not—but recognition of the process when it is occurring is ordinarily not that difficult.

Integrative intentions and policies usually are surrounded by ideological supports that function a little like a cheering section: they assume the value of, proclaim the desirability of, and exaggerate the probability of victory in the struggle for integration. Now it is probably not harmful to group all such efforts and their ideological supports under the heading of national integration. But so long as governments, irrespective of style of rule or ideological profession, are about as predictable in the pursuit of integration as are mothers in defense of their young, then the modifier "national" does not add very much. And the resulting "discovery" that nationalism always reasserts itself is a particularly unhelpful kind of reductionism.

What is of greater interest, it seems to me, is the relationship between the urge toward integration and the kinds of ideological supports invoked in its behalf. My concern is to distinguish ideologies not with respect to content but with respect to source and a quality that I shall refer to as elasticity, in the peculiarly suitable context of postwar Eastern Europe and, more precisely, in the ambiguous and exceptional instance of Yugoslavia. For Yugoslavia, as its federal system already announces, possesses an especially intransigent set of ethnic barriers to integration and was, at the same time, the first East European state to recapture effective sovereignty. Finally, as a socialist society it tends to make more explicit provision for the role of ideology in public affairs than do the assorted democrats and liberals who typically form governments in West European states. This combination of circumstances renders Yugoslavia a suitable illustration of the distinction I wish to emphasize.

The customary view of ideology, or at any rate the view that seems to prevail among most European and American scholars, holds that it is best understood as a post hoc justification for values, policies, or courses of action determined by more fundamental considerations. This stance, superficially—and also, one supposes, unwittingly—akin to the Marxian view, is often described as pragmatic. Upholders of that viewpoint refuse to attach overmuch importance to the ideological pronouncements of others and seem generally to assume that they themselves are blessedly free of ideological blinders. Within this customary outlook there is room for a fair amount of dispute about the degree of weight to be assigned to ideology in societies that profess to be guided by one or another of them. But most such discussions range between the belief that ideologies are employed in the main as opportunistic camouflage for national interest and the acknowledgment that ideological spokesmen may be misled—deflected from reality—by the bodies of thought they espouse. In any event, ideology comes out of these discussions a highly malleable or manipulable factor in any given system, one that is not likely to disclose the deeper explanations of policies and policy decisions.

The great elasticity thus assigned to ideology removes it from the class of explanatory factors that resist rapid modification. Climatic conditions, literacy levels, resource bases, the composition of a population by age or technical training, the quality of soil—all these and others of similar inelasticity, although alterable, do not lend themselves to sudden manipulation in the way that ideology supposedly does. A national policy or program may rest on the perception that literacy levels must be raised or that soil quality must be improved through the use of fertilizer or that climatic limitations have to be counterbalanced by a particular trading pattern. But the policy or program has no hope of efficacy if it does not also presuppose a considerable elapse of time before such inelastic factors can be modified or circumvented. But an ideology, or some portion of it, can allegedly be revamped overnight if circumstances require it.

It is worth noting that it was precisely in this sense that classical Marxism exempted itself from the label of ideology. Marx's theory constituted an unmasking of the systemic features of capitalism as one crucial stage of historical social organization. By uncovering the most basic features of the system, his work counted as theory in contrast to the ideologies which, by the falseness of the consciousness on which they rested, served to justify and in part therefore to obscure rather than to explain. Marx went on to map out a "scientific" (in his somewhat special usage) program for changing the system that he had unmasked, but this was the dynamic aspect of theory itself—the sense in which theory was different from mere philosophy—and not a shift from theory to ideology. Later generations of Marxists relented on this point and came to speak of the Marxist revolutionary program as an ideology, but this was a relaxation that Marx's own usage did not countenance. The reasons for this shift in nomenclature need not detain us here, where the point is that Marx lent his authority to the view that ideology does not figure among the most basic features underlying any system.[1]

Nevertheless, I intend to argue that there are circumstances— neither rare nor particularly obscure—in which an ideology may be exactly as inelastic or nonmalleable as soil quality or the literacy level of a population. Examples, while not abundant perhaps, are easy enough to find. One might think of the somewhat uneven efforts of the Holy Alliance to enforce a conservative, restorationist state of affairs in post-Napoleonic Europe. That program certainly included an ideological ingredient, along with an apparent disposition to exercise force majeure in its behalf. And, being out of reach of those who might be coerced in that manner, the ideology of the Holy Alliance became, for its potential victims, an effective given, a nonmalleable feature of the reigning system. In the Spanish colonial empire one could find numerous instances in which Catholic doctrine figured in a similar way: imposed from without and carrying with it at least a negative version of the enforcement threat—deprivation of desired status or emolument—the acceptance, nominally at least, of the reigning ideology was a conditio sine qua non for the enjoyment of human standing.

A small, weak state may find itself in a condition of ideological subordination vis-a-vis a powerful neighbor. Although Finland has not been required to profess the positive elements of the ideology reigning nearby (and has even been free to deal with its own Communist Party in its own way), one can hardly imagine Finnish membership in NATO or adherence to the ideological component of international anticommunism. And this ideological component of international teristic of the country's location, must then count, however weakly, as a manifestation of the inelastic dimension of ideology. Foreign aid and technical assistance, to take a different kind of example, have commonly been accompanied by ideological expectations. Recipients of aid from the more affluent countries usually sense the ideological precondition, namely an endorsement (which may be intellectually nominal but must be politically effective) of the values inhering in the capitalist orders whence the aid comes, or the acceptance of the status quo in international politics. Aid from socialist countries commonly has a corresponding set of strings attached.[2]

Although the constraints may be mainly negative and the required professions nominal, they are nonetheless functions of one or another ideology seeking to extend its sway. And as long as these ideological demands are out of reach of the perimeter where sanctions may be applied for purposes of enforcing them (as long, that is, as they are unilaterally imposed without the prior consent or substantive contribution of the perimeter's inhabitants), they are as inelastic as soil fertility, as nonmalleable as annual rainfall.

THE SOVIET UNION AND YUGOSLAVIA

The particular case that concerns us here is the imposition of the Soviet version of Marxism in Eastern Europe after World War II. It is of course ironic that we should now be speaking of Marxism not only as an ideology but also as an inelastic type of ideology. Marx had thought of his work as theoretical, not ideological, and envisaged the utilization of his theory as a guide to revolutionary action. Lenin's

insistence on precisely that aspect of theory supplies a second level
of irony, for his epigones accomplished both the degree of dogmatiza-
tion that makes it possible to speak of Marxism-Leninism as an ideology in the Marxian sense and the further sacralization that made
Marxism-Leninism an enforceable item of export to the outer edges
of the Soviet sphere in Eastern Europe. If it is difficult to imagine
Marx accepting Soviet scholasticism as a legitimate outcome of his
theory, it is virtually impossible to conceive of Marx, with all his
sense for the particularities of social development and change, finding
any kinship between his own theory of revolutionary action and a set
of precepts exported abroad and enforceable there by the successors
of the Soviet revolutionary party in power. Yet that is what happened
in Eastern Europe when the region was encompassed within a realm
dominated by Soviet power and regulated according to a frozen
Stalinist dogma still bearing Marx's name.

As Soviet dominance became a fact of life for East Europeans
in the years from 1945 to 1948, no one in the area had any illusions
that simple subservience would be enough. The reigning orthodoxy
required positive endorsement. The "national interest" of the Soviet
Union should not necessarily have required more than certain kinds
of performance on the part of subject governments and populations.
Or if it did, then it implied a redefinition of national interest to
include ideological orthodoxy. Soviet interest, traditionally understood, might have demanded reparations, certain terms and patterns
of trade, guarantees of security, even—if we apply more ancient
understandings of the rights of conquerors—the right to enslave the
"liberated" populations. But there was no comparable warrant for
inflicting the Soviet model so pervasively throughout the area—in
agriculture, industrial organization, education and research, indeed
in every branch of public and some aspects of private life. Something
had been added, a sense of mission had been grafted onto the traditional perception of national interest, and it was no longer sufficient
to rule. Emulation also was required. This was ideology, manipulable
enough at the center to be sure, operating as an inelastic factor, a
very condition of existence, at the outer edge of expansion. The
cliched (but true) observation that this ideology lent itself very neatly
to serving all the conventional items in the inventory of Soviet national
interest is no reason to ignore the origins in ideology of the highly
specific and comprehensive demand for emulation.[3]

It would be tempting to dwell here on the ironic twist involved
when a body of social theory, conceived as a thoroughly rational
means of persuasion (coercion reserved of course for the class
enemy), is turned into a prescription, a frozen orthodoxy, that
serves primarily as an instrument of coercion—and not even against
a class enemy. But our subject is national integration, and it is in

this connection that Yugoslavia is so interesting because of the various guises in which Marxism has subsisted in that country since World War II.

It is a commonplace, but a very important one, that Yugoslavia, alone among the postwar client states of the Soviet Union in Eastern Europe, not only achieved its own liberation (the functional equivalent of revolution) but did so in spite of a fairly negative quantum of Soviet assistance.[4] Its internal cohesion for many years thereafter was served primarily by the mystique of partisan warfare against an external enemy. The wartime campaign against the German invader (and his alleged domestic collaborators) was far more effective cement for binding together the South Slavic ethnic variety, and thus a more pertinent expression of the Yugoslav idea, than anything to be found in officially sanctioned Marxism-Leninism. The partisan leaders, who were also the official postwar leaders of Yugoslavia, had, to be sure, imbibed the usual Marxism-Leninism under Comintern tutelage in the interwar period. In Yugoslavia Stalin initially enjoyed, for this reason, the consent of the government if not the consent of the governed. Tito and his lieutenants were almost poignant in their early attempts to fill their own ingrained loyalty to the revolutionary homeland with a content that could be serviceable, or even palatable, as they proceeded toward the social transformation of their own country. Djilas and others have recorded the agony it cost the Yugoslav leaders to attenuate and finally sever their ties of allegiance.[5]

The Yugoslav leadership stood in essentially the same relationship to its citizenry that the victorious Bolshevik leadership had occupied after 1917. Instead of the revolutionary fervor that supplied the Bolshevik leadership with time and opportunity to commence a revolutionary program, Tito and his party had the unifying force of the partisan movement securing for them the at least provisional tolerance of the Yugoslav citizenry as they began the transformation of their society. But where the Bolsheviks had endured the terrible loneliness of consolidating their revolution in a world that failed to produce reinforcing upheavals in more advanced countries, the Yugoslav leaders suffered the unduly obtrusive companionship of the Soviet model, a body of expectation that had to appear to the Yugoslavs—given their implied subservience to it—as a setback or even a reversal of the independent revolutionary course on which they had embarked. This ideological schema, inelastic as it operated on Yugoslavs and other East Europeans because it was beyond their capacity to modify or adjust to their own needs as they understood them, was undoubtedly a reflection of Soviet intention to achieve, on Soviet terms, another species of integration—economic as well as political—at the supranational level. Perhaps, although not necessarily, this bloc integration was viewed as requiring deemphasis of integration of the constituent

societies. More likely, regional integration was simply given higher
priority, with national or societal integration assumed as a byproduct
of the application of the Soviet model.[6] That is a subtle but, for the
Yugoslavs, crucial difference. Agreeable as the tenets of Marxism-
Leninism may have been to Tito and his associates in abstract form,
the actualities of Soviet prescription were soon perceived as a
hindrance to their national integrative mission, especially in the
economic realm.

This is not to say that any "imported" or received ideology
designed for the purposes of supranational integration will of necessity
operate against national integration. The idea of a European community has often proved quite compatible with integrative strivings and
needs in the constituent nation-states of that community. In Eastern
Europe, too, Soviet power standing behind client governments imposed
as a function of the expansion of that Soviet power was often decisive
in gaining those governments the time needed to commence an approach
to national integration. Putting it differently, in countries where no
indigenous movement had taken power in the wake of German defeat,
the governments in power could use the fabric of supranational integration within the Soviet bloc as a surrogate for popular support until
they were in a position to inaugurate the only national integration
acceptable to them—one occurring under their own direction. For
those governments and parties, Soviet tutelage was thus quite compatible with their own aspirations at the national level. Only Yugoslavia was in a markedly different situation in the years right after
the war; and only Yugoslavia challenged the Soviet model in those
early postwar years as being unsuited to its own need for the ideological integuments of national integration.

Integration I take to be a process characterized by an increasingly intense pattern of allegiance binding citizenry and state together,
the efficacy of which is measured by a general willingness to suspend,
wholly or in part, both individual and local or regional interests for
the sake of the whole society. Yugoslavia in this connection has had
a special position in Eastern Europe on at least two counts: its ethnic
diversity and traditions of ethnic particularism have been more varie-
gated, if not more intense, than those threatening the unity of any
other East European state; and from war's end to 1948 it was, and
seemed to itself to be, much more advanced than its East European
neighbors along a self-determined path of social transformation.

Thus, while Yugoslav leaders were not noticeably more or less
dedicated to Marxist-Leninist orthodoxy than were the leaders of
other states in the region, Tito and his lieutenants had a different
relationship with the citizenry and a different basis for mutual
allegiance. Yugoslavia had already arrived at a point that its neighbors would reach much later: ripeness for the integration of the

national society that was to serve as the "container" for development in the direction of socialism. (It is hard now to remember the expectation, common at least among outside observers at the time, that satellite status would be likely to culminate in absorption into the Soviet Union. Only for Yugoslavia did this outcome appear far-fetched.[7])

As noted before, the received orthodoxy itself seemed an appropriate guide to the transformation of Yugoslavia. Only the features of that ideology that gave it an inelastic quality—that it was imposed in a potentially enforceable form from without and that it was rigidified in terms of non-Yugoslav experience—rendered it unserviceable for the national integration that was on the same agenda with the transition to socialism. In this, to repeat once again, Yugoslavia more resembled the Soviet Union of 1917 than it did its contemporary East European neighbors. It should not of course be supposed that the urge toward ideological self-determination itself occasioned Yugoslavia's break with the Soviet Union. Ideology was only one of the many realms in which Yugoslav leaders would not accept the subservient status assigned by Moscow. But the break did open the way, quite gradually in fact, for the development of more distinctively Yugoslav versions of Marxism.[8]

There is a double layer of irony of course in the twin facts that Marxism did provide intellectual or theoretical resources for the task facing Yugoslavia and that the Yugoslavs, in developing the distinctive variants of their own Marxism after 1948, did not rediscover the special strains of Marxism most suited to their condition. Marxists had always recognized, in the first place, that national units would serve as arenas for initial revolutionary overthrows of the existing order; the resulting emphasis on varied paths leading toward revolution and socialism was a recurrent theme even after the Russian Revolution, for example, in the Comintern debates of the interwar period precisely when Soviet hegemony over the world revolutionary movement was being asserted. But that was not an accent that Stalinist Russia was interested in emphasizing after 1945 in Eastern Europe; it became a feature of Soviet ideological profession only with the maturing of its East European alliance in recent years—too belatedly to be of service in Yugoslavia (and too weakly to save the reform movement in Czechoslovakia).

More particularly, Marxism of the Second International stage had developed an at least embryonic theory fitted to revolutionary movements (and even regimes) in multinational settings. The Austro-Marxists and the Russian Social Democrats were, naturally enough, the principal authors of an application of Marxism to ethnically diverse and divided status. The Austro-Marxists, and notably Otto Bauer,[9] responded to the immediate problem of party organization and the

prospective problem of organizing a socialist state in the multinational
Habsburg domain by proposing a cultural autonomy for ethnically self-
conscious groups that would leave their identity intact while freeing
the political and economic realm for socialist initiative. In Russia it
was Josef Stalin, charged with solving the nationality problem for the
Social Democrats, who coupled the principle of self-determination
with a prospect of cultural autonomy.[10] The test came of course in
the Soviet Union and, while self-determination fared badly in the
aftermath of revolution, the Bolshevik regime introduced—and in large
measure still practices—a policy of encouraging the cultural dimension of ethnic particularism, withholding at the same time any substantial devolutionary or federal bestowal of power in the political
realm. What the multinational actualities of the Russian and the
Austro-Hungarian empires grafted onto received Marxian theory,
then, was an incipient provision for cultural autonomy (practiced in
the Soviet Union) and local decision making (in both Bauer and Stalin
but not implemented in the only locale that could have done so) that
was coherent with both revolutionary striving and transitional
socialism.

A combination of Marxism and federalism would be hard to
document from the writings of Marx and Engels themselves, since
their revolutionary strategy was radically centralizing in tendency.
But the corpus of Marxist thought did contain this wholly legitimate
extension into the problems of multinational political configurations.
Perhaps because the analogical threat to a unified bloc was disquieting,
this way of coping with ethnic diversity and assertiveness was not a
matter the Stalinist leadership of the postwar period was anxious to
emphasize in exercising its East European hegemony. And the problems peculiar to the union of South Slavic peoples known as Yugoslavia
were insulated from a Marxian message of great pertinence.[11]

So the tension between the ideological needs of a consciously
independent Yugoslavia and the fact that Soviet ideology was being
imposed helped to precipitate the break of 1948, after which the
Yugoslav leaders and theoreticians had to develop their own versions
of Marxism to replace the dogma that Stalin had visited upon them.
In one sense it made comparatively little difference what replacement
they devised. The crucial step was already taken when the imposed
ideology was discarded. Whatever they chose as their own version
of Marxism, even a revived Stalinism, would be their own and hence
within the reach of modification, manipulable as ideologies are supposed to be and thus no longer inelastic.[12] Nevertheless, it is interesting to examine the characteristic features of Yugoslav Marxism
against the background of a national integration that has been halting
at best and remains precarious.

YUGOSLAV MARXISM AND INTEGRATION

The four most distinctive products of Marxian thought in Yugoslavia since 1948 have been a foreign policy of nonalignment seeking
to bind together nations of the so-called third world to create an independent force in world politics; a dissenting voice, best known in the
West from the writings of Milovan Djilas, that criticized mainly the
domestic order of Yugoslavia from the standpoint of socialism; a
group of academic philosophers associated with the journal Praxis
rediscovering and reinterpreting original Marxism; and a principle
of domestic economic and political organization usually called workers
self-management, a constitutionally prescribed (and therewith also
circumscribed) neosyndicalism.

The first of these, although it is probably the most visible element of what is called Titoism, stands in no necessary relationship
to Marxism or socialism. Yugoslav foreign policy could as well have
been fashioned by leaders who do not regard themselves as Marxists
at all. Precipitated by Yugoslavia's precarious position between the
two great power blocs after 1948, the principle of nonalignment
appealed as readily to similarly situated non-Marxist governments
as to certain socialists. Its importance domestically, as an instrument of integration or intensified internal allegiances, lay in the
pride that an independent and even daring position in world politics—
defiance of the Soviet Union—could arouse in the citizenry. Thus, a
so-called Titoist foreign policy owed little or nothing to the prevailing
version of Marxian ideology, and likewise contributed little or nothing
to a distinctively socialist approach to external relations except in
the largely fortuitous sense of redefining relations among socialist
states. But it did, as an extension of the partisan mystique of independence, play a significant role as an integrative mechanism within
the country.[13]

The internal dissent associated with the name Djilas has been
recorded in the name of democratic socialism but has so far produced
little echo inside Yugoslavia. Many of those who are predisposed to
Djilas's message recall his own record as a party official and dis-
count the critique as a very belated discovery on his part. Marxists
have reason to fear that the tardily apprehended democratic require-
ment may, in the hands of Djilas, issue in a nondescript social
democracy devoid of theoretical significance. Although it is not far-
fetched to think that Yugoslav youth may one day discover Djilas's
message and learn to value the heroic stance that he has taken, at
present his audience is almost exclusively Western. Because it is
unnoticed in Yugoslavia, this quasi-Marxian dissenting voice has

considerably less to do with the problem of national integration than
does the policy of nonalignment.[14]

The Praxis group of Marxist philosophers represents a powerful and important voice from within the most serious tradition of
Marxist thought and one that has generated great resonance throughout
Eastern Europe, not just in Yugoslavia. Whereas the official Marxism
of the regime derives from the Soviet doctrinal tradition, the Marxism
of Praxis connects up with the finest intellectual tradition of West and
Central European Marxism, seeking to recapture and adapt to contemporary actualities the central messages of Marx's own theory.
Understandably, however, these Praxis philosophers developed a
vision of what their own society should become and sought to propagate it, sometimes in affirmative proposals and sometimes in critiques
of existing conditions.

There is no doubt that these Marxists exercised some influence
on the official spokesmen for the regime; this can be shown conclu-
sively by the extent to which official spokesmen adopted Praxis
terminology and modes of expression. But there is also a depress-
ingly close correlation between the periodic suppressions of the
journal and the forays of its authors into debate on contemporary
issues of Yugoslav public affairs. This suggests the crucial limitation
on their impact, their ability to effectuate their Marxian vision in
their own country. The recent discontinuation of Praxis and the provisional success of the campaign to oust the Belgrade professors
have imparted a further layer of significance to this native strain of
sophisticated and utterly serious Marxist thought, but this tends to
link the phenomenon of Praxis more with Djilas (despite the intellectual
dissonances) than with any distinctively Yugoslav thrust toward national
integration. The Praxis version of Yugoslav Marxism, an ineradicable
intellectual contribution, remains esoteric for society at large, and
suppression gives it a kind of social significance it would not have
wished for itself.[15]

The fourth distinctive element of the uneven collection that we
are calling Yugoslav Marxism has a more decided bearing on the
problem of integrating the nation. There are several ways of looking
at workers' self-management. Marxists can debate its legitimacy,
some questioning it as cryptosyndicalism and a threat to party direction of social development, others favoring it as a genuinely Marxian
device for civic training and an overdue reemphasis of the self-
emancipating accent in Marx's concept of proletarian revolution.
Social scientists can study its workings and conclude, more often
than not, that its practice falls considerably short of the claims made
for it; although a number of the sterner Yugoslav critics of self-
management in practice remain hopeful about its ultimate promise.

Virtually all observers agree, however, that Yugoslavia is committed, constitutionally and in the minds of the country's leadership, to the maintenance of the forms of self-management. However imperfect its workings, and however often it may be circumvented by centrally determined directives, it remains in place as a democratic and participatory challenge to leaders and populace alike. With its stress on local control and workplace decision making, it also helps to preserve the authentically federal and decentralizing accent in the Yugoslav system against periodic resurgences of the centralizing countertendency. Finally, whatever variety of factors contributed to the Yugoslav "invention" of self-management as its distinctive socialist form, it is not too much to suggest—on the basis of its timing and the absence of acceptable external models—that it appeared as a replacement for the obsolescent mystique of partisan resistance. As that integrative device or quasi-ideology began to lose its appeal, especially among young people who had not participated in the wartime struggle, self-management assumed increasing prominence, not only as a principle of socialist organization of production but also as a distinctly Yugoslav contribution to the multiform problems of transitional socialism.[16]

The last two points are the crucial ones with respect to integration. Workers' self-management has certainly not overcome the country's ethnic divisiveness and separatist tendencies. Neither did the partisan mystique. But both have had some efficacy as cement for a precariously balanced federation of peoples. The federal principle has been essential in avoiding a fatal clash of nationalities; it is an integrative device that does not demand too much. Self-management is not only consistent with and reinforcing of federalism. It is also the Yugoslav choice to replace the alien ideological intrusion of the Soviet model.* The fact that it is a self-determined ideological support for the system and thus within reach of Yugoslavs to alter or abrogate is no guarantee that it will not either stagnate or be over-

---

*The term "Soviet model" implies a comprehensive demand for emulation, but I have used it somewhat loosely in relation to Yugoslavia. Although it may be said to derive from the well-established tenet of primary loyalty to the Soviet homeland of the revolution, the demand for emulation was quite muted in the years before the Yugoslav break with the Cominform. The less comprehensive demands of that era focused more on acceptance of Stalin's spokesmanship in international and regional affairs, but that was enough to offend the independent spirit flourishing in Yugoslavia. It is only accurate to acknowledge, however, that Yugoslavia was never subject to the fully developed Soviet model.

whelmed by centrifugal forces. It remains, however, in this time of uncertainty in Yugoslavia the strongest integrative bond available in the ideological realm.

The indispensable quality that self-management displays, reverting now to the earlier stage of my argument, is not its specific ideological content. It is rather that it was chosen (or reinvented) within Yugoslavia and owed nothing to the tutelary power from whose suffocating presence Tito and most Yugoslavs wished to escape. Again, there is no necessary or perpetual antagonism between the self-determined quality of self-management and the inevitable constraints of membership in some international alliance or bloc. Still less is there any conflict between self-management as a prescription for the entire country, as an ideologically informed principle regulating (and perhaps also unifying) the whole society, and the measure of local autonomy that makes Yugoslav federalism viable in the face of ethnic particularism.

Indeed, the lesson that Yugoslav experience holds may be exactly in this parallelism wherein self-determination—the quality I have labeled elasticity when referring to ideology—is an unavoidable prerequisite to integration, locally and supranationally as well as nationally. The lesson would be a trivial one but for the continuing temptations offered on all these levels by relationships of domination.

NOTES

1. It does not follow of course that the Marxian conception of ideology resembles in other respects the view described above as pragmatic. I have dealt with the Marxian view at greater length in "Marx, Marxism, and Religion," Forschungen zur osteuropaeischen Geschichte 20 (1973): 35-39. For fuller accounts see George Lichtheim, The Concept of Ideology and Other Essays (New York: Vintage, 1967); Theodor Geiger, Ideologie und Wahrheit (Neuwied and Berlin: Luchterhand, 1968); John Plamenatz, Ideology (New York: Praeger, 1970). For an attempt to explain the manner in which Marxism came to be identified by its exponents as an ideology, see Herbert Marcuse, Soviet Marxism (New York: Vintage, 1961), p. 111.

2. This is a comparatively weak statement of the argument advanced by, among others, Teresa Hayter, Aid as Imperialism (Baltimore: Penguin, 1971). Marxists have always been alive to the instrumental features of economic and technical aid, and some of them are coming to acknowledge the similarities between socialist and capitalist forms of assistance.

3. The literature on postwar Soviet extension of hegemony in Eastern Europe is of course vast. Much of it is flawed, however, by the determination of self-styled "realists" to subsume ideological factors under national interest. It is part of my argument, to be sure, that Soviet ideology is, like any other, malleable at the center, but that does not preclude viewing it as having independent weight and standing in a dialectical relationship to perceptions of national interest.

4. One can debate the net worth of the Soviet Union as an ally of the Yugoslavs in World War II. Soviet forces did liberate Belgrade and confer it on Marshall Tito's partisan forces. But Soviet assistance also was withheld at crucial times. Walter R. Roberts provides a fascinating account of this particular tangle of wartime diplomacy in Tito, Mihailović, and the Allies, 1941-1945 (New Brunswick, N.J.: Rutgers University Press, 1973). The important point here is that the partisans believed that they had achieved their own country's liberation, considered this as tantamount to revolution, and knew that they were unique in this respect in Eastern Europe.

5. In this connection see especially Adam Ulam, Titoism and the Cominform (Cambridge, Mass.: Harvard University Press, 1952) and Milovan Djilas, Conversations with Stalin (New York: Harcourt, Brace and World, 1962). Earlier phases of Yugoslav involvement with Marxism-Leninism are treated in Ivan Avakumovic, History of the Communist Party of Yugoslavia (Aberdeen: Aberdeen University Press, 1964).

6. For a treatment of Yugoslavia in the explicit conceptual framework of integration, see M. George Zaninovich, The Development of Socialist Yugoslavia (Baltimore: Johns Hopkins University Press, 1968). This study also gives due weight to Yugoslav federalism as a means of keeping the drive toward national unity in equilibrium with the centrifugal tendencies of ethnic particularisms.

7. This question has been reexamined lately in a set of case studies: Thomas Hammon, ed., The Anatomy of Communist Takeovers (New Haven, Conn.: Yale University Press, 1975).

8. Two important books on these and related matters are Paul Shoup, Communism and the Yugoslav National Question (New York: Columbia University Press, 1968) and George W. Hoffman and Fred Warner Neal, Yugoslavia and the New Communism (New York: Twentieth Century Fund, 1962).

9. Especially his Die Nationalitätenfrage und die Sozialdemokratie (Vienna: Wiener Volksbuchhandlung, 1924).

10. Marxism and the National Question (1913) in Works, vol. 2 (Moscow, 1953).

11. It could be argued that Yugoslav federalism was precisely a reinvention of the multinational arrangements adumbrated in Bauer and Stalin and, moreover, a more forthright application of such

teachings than had ever before occurred. I would not quarrel with such a characterization, but it would seem that the federal system in fact owes more to the evolution of the South Slavic (Yugoslav) idea than to any conscious revival of the aforementioned strains in Marxian thought.

12. This leaves out of account the fact that an officially propagated ideology may be "inelastic" in the eyes of citizens who have no choice or voice in the matter, even when that ideology has been freely chosen by the regime. But that is the issue of democracy within socialism, a matter of profound concern to contemporary Marxist thinkers but not the point at issue here.

13. See Alvin Z. Rubinstein, Yugoslavia and the Non-Aligned World (Princeton, N.J.: Princeton University Press, 1970).

14. The various elements of Djilas's outlook are mixed in sometimes curious ways throughout his extensive publications. The daring that precipitated his removal from official inner circles is best glimpsed perhaps in The New Class (New York: Frederick A. Praeger, 1957); his somewhat odd understanding of Marxism is found most abundantly in The Unperfect Society (New York: Harcourt, Brace and World, 1969); his autobiography, beginning with Memoir of a Revolutionary (New York: Harcourt Brace Jovanovich, 1973), will doubtless shed additional light on all facets of his outlook.

15. The best introduction to this style of Marxism is to be found in the pages of Praxis, the international edition for those not conversant with Serbo-Croatian, and in the increasingly numerous English translations of such leading philosophers as Petrović, Marković, and Stojanović.

16. The literature of self-management is already extensive in English, not to mention Serbo-Croatian. A good introduction and an extensive bibliography are found in Howard M. Wachtel, Workers' Management and Workers' Wages in Yugoslavia (Ithaca, N.Y.: Cornell University Press, 1973).

CHAPTER

6

THE GERMAN DEMOCRATIC
REPUBLIC AND SOCIALIST
INTEGRATION

Arthur M. Hanhardt, Jr.
William Sharp

Since the end of World War II the political units that succeeded
Nazi Germany have had to deal with three questions relative to integration. The first was: Can "Germany" be reunited as a nation-state
similar at least in geography to pre-1939 or 1937 Germany? This
aspect of the "German question" remains unanswered. Reunification
and its attendant problems of reintegration is not one of the political
realities of the past three decades, nor is it likely to become a real
problem until there is a major shift in the European power balance.
Indeed, whatever else the 1975 Conference on Security and Cooperation in Europe accomplished, it did serve to reemphasize the permanence of two German states.

That German reunification has not been realized has not, of
course, prevented a great accumulation of rhetoric, legal studies,
and policy statements aimed at effecting reunification and keeping the
issue alive in domestic and international politics. What has at times
amounted to a German obsession with reunification has, until recently,
tended to obscure the two other questions relating to integration in
postwar Germany: How have the "parts" of Germany become internally
integrated as truncated political units? And, how and to what extent
have these units been integrated into the international blocs to which
they were consigned as an outcome of World War II in Europe?

The term integration will be used in two differing senses here.
First, we shall speak of the internal cohesiveness of a political unit.
Integration in this sense has to do with the legitimacy of the state,
the acceptance of authority by the citizenry, and the very idea of
citizenship itself. Second, we refer to international integration as
an aspect of the interaction among nation-states. The literature of
international relations contains a large body of writing and research

revolving about questions having to do with how states can overcome the divisiveness of sovereignty in order to effectively deal with larger questions of economics, security and, ultimately, human survival. The aspect of international integration concerning us here will be the extent to which national political units accept the authority of international or supranational organizations.

An important aspect of international integration is the extent to which national political units accept the authority of international or supranational organizations and models. That is to say that national integration cannot be considered apart from the international systems of which the national units are elements. Internal integration can be decisively affected in terms of its possibilities and accomplishments by the international environment.

As our title indicates, we shall concentrate here on the German Democratic Republic (GDR). Relatively less attention has been accorded the GDR than the ideologically and economically more compatible Federal Republic of Germany (FRG). Accordingly, there is a larger and relatively more accessible literature on the FRG than on the GDR. The reasons for this state of affairs go beyond matters of economy and ideology. Access to the GDR has been limited for U.S. citizens and will undoubtedly remain so even following the establishment of diplomatic relations in 1974. Both authors have visited the GDR and this essay will reflect some of our observations as we examine internal and international integration in the case of the GDR.[*]

INTERNAL INTEGRATION

Problems relating to the internal integration of nation-states most often have their origins in ethnic, religious, racial, or geographical diversity within a political unit. The GDR has none of these problems. There is only one ethnic minority in the GDR, the Sorbs. Concentrated in the area around Bautzen and Hoyerswerda near the Czech border, the Sorbs, who maintain a linguistic and cultural identity, are declining in numbers and were never of any political importance.[1]

---

[*] The senior author wishes to express his thanks to the International Research and Exchanges Board (IREX) for making possible a visit to the GDR in 1974. William Sharp participated in the internship program of the Conference Group on German Politics in 1974. The views expressed here are those of the authors.

Large and strong religious groups actively opposed to communism have not been a factor in the GDR as they have, for example, in
neighboring Poland. The area that became the GDR was traditionally
Protestant. An active policy of accommodation between the state,
and both Protestants and Catholics, symbolized politically by the
Christian Democratic Union (CDU), has been accompanied by successful efforts to isolate the religious leadership of the GDR and thus
reduce its effectiveness. Because the GDR recognizes no responsibilities for the persecution of the Jews during the Third Reich, there
has been little inclination for Jews to return to the GDR as there has
been in the FRG. Religious Gleichschaltung (political coordination)
has been an accomplished fact in the GDR for over a decade.

No racial minorities exist in the GDR and regional diversity is
minimal. There are, to be sure, jokes about Saxons and their distinctive dialect, but these stories lost what political relevance they
had when Walter Ulbricht (a Saxonian) passed from the scene.

There is another aspect of this homogeneity among the people
of the GDR that is politically important. A good many of the people
who found themselves living in the Soviet zone of occupation at the
end of the war left the area. Outward migration continued after the
institution of the GDR until the sector boundaries in Berlin were
sealed on August 13, 1961. Although it cannot be presumed that all
of the over three million people who left the GDR were political
opponents of the state, it is clear that a good many who were not in
accord with the regime departed, thereby reducing the number of
real and potential dissidents.

Relative homogeneity does not automatically equate with integration. The fact that the sources of common internal conflicts are
not present does not indicate that the legitimacy of the state is
accepted by the people. The question about internal integration is
essentially whether or not the citizenry identifies with the state as a
legitimate authority. Stated another way, Is there a national consciousness in the GDR?

This question of a developing national consciousness in the GDR
has been the subject of lively debate in the FRG. There are many in
the FRG who do not accord the GDR any legitimacy whatsoever. Since
this has been the position of the West German government until quite
recently, there are many in the FRG (and not only those who fled the
GDR) who refuse to recognize anything legitimate about the communist state to the east.

This rigid rejection of GDR legitimacy has been challenged by
the research of Peter Christian Ludz, Gebhard Schweigler, and
Arthur Hanhardt.[2] Ludz has written about "state consciousness"
among the citizenry in the GDR. According to this position the German nation is still the common object of identification and self-

definition for those living in East and West Germany. However, there
are two German states and at this level there is a growing identification of the people in the GDR with their state, which has scored im-
pressive accomplishments in production, technology, and public
welfare.

Schweigler's research led him somewhat further in the direction
of finding an emergent national consciousness in both the FRG and the
GDR. While Schweigler's analyses of survey research data support
his conclusions for the FRG, he must recognize that "on the grounds
of the bad data-base it is not possible in the case of the GDR to sub-
stantiate that . . . supports for the national system of the GDR are
shared by a majority of the people, in spite of occasional impression-
istic indicators of that possibility."[3] Schweigler's data base was
made up largely of surveys done among people who had gone from the
GDR to the FRG. As he recognized, these data and the impressions
of even the best experts are not entirely satisfactory.

Hanhardt has attempted to approach an aspect of the national
consciousness question by examining the processes of political socialization through education and other social institutions. The thesis of
this work is that, the closer the GDR comes toward realizing its
stated goal of inculcating its citizenry with the values of the socialist
personality, the closer it will have come to establishing its legitimacy
through a collective consciousness. Difficulties in establishing or
refuting this thesis begin with the official definition of the socialist
personality, which "is the embodiment of the unity of the theoretical
and the practical. It is characterized by the inseparable unity of the
scientific world view of dialectical materialism, socialist morality,
and social-political action in the construction and strengthening of
socialist society."[4] Even though that definition is vague, it has been
reinforced in recent and binding policy statements made by the GDR
leadership. Clearly a commitment of considerable proportions has
been made to achieving the socialist personality. What have been
the results?

Assessment of the results of the socialization process in the
GDR can perhaps best be attempted in the area of education. The
socialist personality, with its loyalty to the GDR, has been an
important goal of the educational system since the postwar reforms
and has been the subject of a number of empirical research projects,
some of which we shall now examine.

The development of the GDR educational system can only be
sketched here.[5] Radical reforms of the 1945-49 period readied the
educational system for the transition to the polytechnical school,
which came about in 1958 and 1959. This was a pivotal change in the
system and moved it toward closer integration with the economic
system. It was a conscious attempt to implement a unification of

theory and practice, along with other precepts of the socialist personality. In tune with dialectical materialism and the Marxist image of
man, the changes were aimed at "training . . . children to love work
and the working man."[6] In the words of the law establishing the polytechnical schools:

> Polytechnical training and education is fundamental and a
> component of instruction in all school grades. Relative
> to the children's age, instruction will be combined with
> socially useful activity, or related to productive labor.
> Central to polytechnical instruction in the lower grades
> will be industrial arts and from the seventh grade on,
> instruction in socialist production.[7]

By the mid-1960s, following the introduction of the New Economic System in the GDR, enough experience had been gathered in
the polytechnical schools to revise the program. The 1965 Law on the
Integrated Socialist Educational System stated that "the goal of the
integrated socialist educational system is a high level of education
for all the people; the education and training of well-rounded and
harmonious socialist personalities who, while consciously structuring
society, lead a fulfilled, happy, and dignified life."[8] With this law
and the later introduction of new lesson plans in Staatsbuergerkunde
(civics), greater emphasis was placed on social studies in the curriculum and concern with the inculcation of the socialist personality
was intensified. This emphasis emerges clearly from a survey of
curricular changes introduced between 1966 and 1972. During this
period about 38 percent of the instructional time in the polytechnical
school was taken up with social studies, German, and art, while
11.4 percent was devoted to polytechnical instruction and 32.1 percent
to mathematics and natural sciences. The balance of the curriculum
consisted of foreign languages (10.8 percent) and physical education
(7.6 percent).[9]

Along with the curricular changes of the second half of the
1960s came a great effort to study the problems of youth in the GDR.
During this time there also appeared a journal titled Jugendforschung
(Research on youth) published by Professor Walter Friedrich's
Central Institute for Research on Youth in Leipzig.[10] The theoretical
and empirical studies appearing in Jugendforschung provide valuable
insights into the socialization process in the GDR.

How effective has the ten-year polytechnical school been in
shaping the character of pupils to conform to the mold of the socialist
personality? Some approximations of the state of the socialist personality can be made from the results of research done in the GDR by
social psychologists, educationalists, and other social scientists.

These studies, in addition to personal observations made in the GDR, should facilitate an assessment of the impact of education in the development of socialist personalities.

Certainly one of the basic aspects of the socialist personality is an active interest in politics. Although interest and knowledge are not in themselves indicators of commitment or of any particular internalization of values and norms, they are an essential element if the program of political education is to have an impact. Walter Friedrich has emphasized the importance of group factors in sparking political interest. Teacher competence, quality of the class collective, and group norms are among the factors Friedrich has discussed.[11]

A study by Mueller and Schedlich shows the kind of variation in political interest that can be found among schools and classes in the GDR.[12] Among the questions asked of students in the extended high school (which leads directly to university matriculation) one inquired: "Do you follow political events with (a) great interest, (b) middling interest, (c) weak interest, or (d) virtually no interest?" The results (in percent) were as follows:[13]

	Great interest	Middling interest	Weak interest	Virtually no interest
Eighth grade, A-type	61	35	4	0
Eighth grade, B-type	22	45	11	22
Twelfth grade, A-type	70	26	4	0
Twelfth grade, B-type	18	73	9	0

The table is interesting for at least two reasons. First is the difference in type of school and the corresponding interest in political events. The A-type school is the modern language and the B-type the mathematical-natural science extended high school, which prepares the best students for higher education. Among the natural science students there is clearly less interest in political events than among their modern language colleagues. This could indicate either that the quality of ideological education is lower than in the B-type school or that interest in political events is not encouraged by the curriculum. A second point of interest is the variation in interest shown by a comparison of the eighth grade responses to those of the twelfth. While the A-type shows an increase in interest, the B-type schools show a slight decline in interest in political events among those in the high-interest category.

Research by Werner Hennig further substantiates the relative lack of importance of politics in the hierarchy of interests of the young. Interest in politics was found to be of only medium importance among 11 to 18-year-olds, named by only 5 to 6 percent of those interviewed. In general, politics was found to be outside young people's main constellation of interests.[14]

It is hard to be conclusive in speculating on the reasons for these results, partly because there is no indication of the sizes of the samples or their distributions. However, the table does indicate that there are significant variations in the extent to which students exhibit interest in political events in the GDR. This would further imply that there is some distance to go before the socialist personality is achieved. Such a conclusion is made more tenable by research carried out under the auspices of the Central Institute for Research on Youth in Leipzig, which found an $r = .5$ correlation between interest in politics and pride in GDR citizenship among pupils.[15] If the extent of interest, and by implication pride in citizenship, is actually reduced in the high interest category at the culmination of the educational process for individuals in the natural sciences—precisely the class of students that, given the tenets of dialectical materialism and the precepts of the socialist personality, should exhibit the most marked increase—then it is difficult to avoid concluding that: (1) not only is the educational process failing to adequately develop socialist personalities but (2) it is actually moving away from the achievement of that goal.

Another table, reporting the findings of Friedrich's research on GDR youth, taps the content of political education. In a survey of 12 and 14-year-old pupils, Friedrich sought to determine how well those interviewed understood the Marxist-Leninist conception of freedom as "understanding the necessary" (Freiheit ist Einsicht in die Notwendigkeit). The following table shows (in percent) the results:[16]

	12-year-olds	14-year-olds
Freedom is understanding the necessary	0	0
Analogous response	58	40
Freedom is personal freedom	28	50
Unclear or indefinite response	14	10

The first response is the one taught in school. It would be the answer that the socialist personality would give to the question, What is freedom? Of primary interest, for present purposes, is the increase in those defining freedom as "personal freedom" in the older age group, since the expected direction of change would be toward the formally desired response. This suggests that in the mid-1960s there was a considerable amount left to be done in achieving one of the formal aspects of the socialist personality. Once again, it must be noted that the trend is apparently moving away from the stated goals of the educational system in the GDR.

Another noteworthy aspect of the socialization process in the GDR has to do with the self-image of youths and their images of others. If socialization according to the desires of the political leadership is actually taking place, then the expectation would be that East German students would see themselves as resembling the images of the citizens of other socialist countries. This expectation was borne out in a study by Ulrike Siegel, who examined the national images of 431 students in the Leipzig area using a technique similar to that of Buchanan and Cantril in their UNESCO study of international stereotypes.[17] By having students apply a list of characteristics (hardworking, aggressive, intelligent) to the populations of various nations, Siegel found that the profile of the GDR self-image correlated highly with the profile of the students' image of the Soviets and the Cubans ($r = 0.945$ in each case). At the same time the students' image of the FRG correlated strongly with that of the United States ($r = 0.912$). The correlation between the GDR and the FRG images was $r = 0.768$. To the extent that these findings indicate growing distinctions and demarcations, this can be taken as an indicator of a reorientation in line with the ideological goal of "socialist solidarity," an international aspect of the socialist personality.

Clearly the socialization process has a long way to go, but it is important to remember that the internalization of goals, values, and attitudes is only part of the picture. State policies are of great importance in generating integrative support for the GDR. This is especially the case when an assessment of the total population is attempted.

In the absence of public opinion polls (which are often problematical even if available), informed opinion must be called upon to make estimates. Honecker's programs and policies have found widespread support in the GDR since 1971 and have contributed to the consolidation and stability of the system and the control of the Socialist Unity Party (SED) over state and society.

Soon after Honecker's succession, it became clear that he felt that Ulbricht's ideological course had strayed too far from Marxist-Leninist principles, especially when it came to the leading role of the working class. The restoration of the preeminence of the working class became a leading theme of the Eighth Congress of the SED, held in June 1971. There followed programs to place limits on the top end of the income scale, to improve workers' incomes and benefits, to ease the chronically desperate housing situation with the construction of new units and the rehabilitation of old ones, to involve workers in administrative decision making, and, perhaps most important, to improve the assortment and quality of consumer goods.

The foregoing programs had been promised before in the GDR, but looking over the performance record of the years 1971-75, concrete gains can be seen in the areas mentioned above. Wages in selected industries have risen (although the rate of increase in disposable income appears to have slowed in 1974). Benefits for workers have improved, most recently with the decision to add three days of vacation per year (for a total of 18 days). A decrease in the cost of women's wear became effective in 1974, and higher pay for apprentices is planned. Construction of new housing units and the renovation of substandard units is ahead of plan schedule with 57,000 units reported in the first half of 1974 (according to the Politburo report at the twelfth meeting of the SED Central Committee in July 1974). Finally, although even the most casual visitor to the GDR can detect yawning gaps and incredibly high prices, the variety and quality of consumer goods have steadily improved in recent years. Washing machine, refrigerator, radio, and TV production all showed significant increases in 1974.

This support has both a positive-active component and a passive aspect. Taking the latter first, wide sectors of the GDR population have been effectively depoliticized. Much of the participation in politics in the GDR is acclamation and does not involve decision making. At best the citizen might contribute ideas and suggestions for the better realization and implementation of decisions taken by the SED leadership. Public discussions preceded the final drafts of major legislation such as the Jugendgesetz ("law on youth") and open dissent was expressed by Christian Democratic Union delegates to the Volkskammer when that legislative body voted upon an abortion statute in April 1972. We also are aware of the great amount of work done in legislative committees at all levels and the occasional Buergerinitiative. Yet few of these examples involve decision making input outside the SED or without its prior approval.

The GDR citizens not involved in the SED (which has a current membership, including candidates, of 1,954,130 out of a population estimated at 17,011,343 in 1972) recognize this situation and turn off to politics beyond the minimum needed to maintain standing as a good citizen. The thus depoliticized do not comprise an opposition group or even a very critical one. Improved consumption and social security keep them in place and at least minimally satisfied even as many watch West German television and perhaps yearn for the better life "over there."

The positive-active component of support for the GDR involves those who are satisfied with the political roles they can and do occupy as active citizens, party members (either of the SED or block parties), or members of the state apparatus. The size of this sector of the population is difficult to estimate, given widespread overlapping

memberships. The total is nonetheless bound to be a significant portion of the GDR population. This group is disproportionately young
compared to the overall population. The youthfulness of the activist
sector of the GDR population is in part the result of a quarter-century
of education and indoctrination through the schools and other agencies
of political socialization discussed above.

INTERNATIONAL INTEGRATION

International integration must begin with an examination of the
concept of "socialist internationalism," which means the acceptance
of the leading role of the USSR in the socialist community. Hermann
Axen has quoted Erich Honecker to the effect that:

> the attitude to the Soviet Union and the CPSU "has been,
> is, and always will be, the main touchstone of fidelity to
> Marxism-Leninism and proletarian internationalism,"
> that the guidelines of the CPSU's Twenty-fourth Congress
> are "of universal significance," and that the SED will
> "assimilate the vast theoretical and practical experience
> of the Soviet Union and apply it in adaptation to our con-
> crete conditions."[18]

The history of the Council for Mutual Economic Assistance
(CMEA) could be viewed as a struggle between the Soviet Union
(backed by the GDR), which has desired to speed up socialist inte-
ration by means of centralized directives and supranational planning
bodies, and most other East European nations, especially Romania,
which have resisted any encroachment on national economic autonomy
and have encouraged decentralization—decision making and cooperation at lower levels of production.

Khrushchev's failure to dictate production specialization through
Soviet domination of supranational CMEA planning bodies has resulted
in the acceptance of the principles of national sovereignty and volun-
tarism in CMEA decision making. This has meant that the approach
to integration has been incremental; in recent years the watchwords
of CMEA communiques have been "intensification and perfection" of
cooperative economic ventures, which, as many have written, means
no major qualitative changes have taken place.

Presently, aside from development of multilateral cooperation
in production areas of machine building, the food industry, agriculture, and energy, the main new CMEA activity has focused on coordination of national five-year plans for the 1976-80 period. This should

simplify problems encountered in planning of cooperative production, as well as in concluding trade agreements among CMEA countries.

The role of the GDR in the CMEA is significant. Politically, it acts as the USSR's junior partner, supporting Soviet positions on a high degree of central planning and systems standardization.[19] Economically, the GDR is the second power of the CMEA: it has the largest per capita GNP of all CMEA nations, is the USSR's number one trading partner and everyone else's (in the CMEA) second largest trading partner behind the USSR.

This relationship of the GDR and other CMEA nations to the USSR is largely determined by their heavy reliance on the Soviet Union for minerals and energy resources.[20] In turn, the GDR supplies the USSR mostly with finished products such as machinery and scientific equipment. The status of the GDR as a resource-poor country will continue to be a decisive factor in the future direction of GDR-CMEA integration; conversely, energy resources can be seen as the Soviet Union's most significant economic and political lever in CMEA decision making.

A second GDR economic problem is a population decrease and consequent manpower shortage; although the government has undertaken some cooperative ventures to alleviate the problem, many economic difficulties have resulted; we will discuss them later.

Another significant factor in the GDR's economic relationships with other countries involves its special ties with the FRG, whereby trade between the two is considered intra-German trade. Thus the GDR has regular trade links with European Community countries not enjoyed by other CMEA nations.

Having briefly discussed the nature of the CMEA and the GDR's position in it, we will now view some trend indicators of GDR integration in the CMEA, discuss some problems that have arisen and, finally, suggest some directions that integration in the CMEA will take.

Although, as mentioned, the rhetoric of the GDR elite suggests an increasingly close working relationship with the USSR, trade data since the advent of the Honecker era in 1971 show primarily a rapid expansion of GDR trade with the West, a leveling off of GDR-CMEA trade, and a discernible growth decrease in GDR-USSR trade. The following table illustrates this by showing average annual growth of trade with the GDR (in percent):[21]

	1960–65	1965–70	1970–73
USSR	6.7	9.3	6.5
CMEA	7.4	11.1	10.8
Industrialized capitalist nations	7.4	16.1	18.1

Another view is as follows, showing GDR trade with selected entities as a percent of total trade: [22]

	1960	1965	1970	1973
All CMEA	67.6	69.4	67.3	66.0
USSR	42.8	42.8	39.1	34.6
Industrialized capitalist nations	21.1	21.7	24.4	27.9

In the foregoing table it is interesting to note that the Soviet Union's share of the GDR within the CMEA has steadily decreased. Whereas the Soviet share was nearly two-thirds of the total in 1960, this had declined to just over half in 1973. The growth of GDR trade with capitalist industrialized nations is explained in part by monetary inflation. In any case, the trade growth of the GDR appears to be coming from elsewhere than the USSR.

There are other indications of closer economic cooperation with CMEA nations. For example, the following table shows percentage growth rates in GDR trade with Poland:[23]

	1969-70	1970-71	1971-72
(GDR) Exports	+26.3	+14.9	+18.8
(GDR) Imports	+12.3	+ 3.7	+21.1

Additionally, although GDR-CMEA trade has changed little in proportional terms, the percentages of specialized and cooperatively produced products in GDR trade rose from 1 percent in 1970 to 17 percent in 1974.[24] Specialization of products traded with the Soviet Union grew even more rapidly, from 0.7 percent to 27 percent during the same period.[25]

Travel to other socialist nations recently given special encouragement in the GDR, is increasing rapidly.[26] Travel to the GDR, especially from Poland, also has expanded greatly. If this social and cultural exchange was intended to increase socialist brotherhood among peoples of CMEA nations, there is evidence it has been counterproductive, at least in the GDR: the thousands of Poles who visited the GDR emptied the stores of some consumer goods, thus causing unameliorable supply shortages in the rather inflexible GDR economy. Such events did little to promote international goodwill. The GDR government responded by placing a 200 Mark limit on the amount of goods that foreigners could export, but supply problems remained.

Another interesting although unrelated indicator is the level of mail traffic. While international correspondence (West and East combined) has steadily increased or remained the same in most CMEA countries, there has been a noticeable drop in the GDR. The following figures show international mail traffic of selected countries (in hundred thousands):[27]

	1968	1970	1972
GDR	196	871	706
Hungary	118	121	136
Romania	61	56	77

The GDR figures might well be explained by efforts, mentioned above, to shield the GDR from international inputs that might disturb progress toward internal integration. Correspondence and contact with West Germans by either direct contact or mail has been systematically discouraged. (The alternative explanation that decreasing correspondence might be the result of increasing personal contacts since travel to the GDR has become easier does not necessarily hold, since travel arrangements frequently require additional communication.)

As mentioned earlier, CMEA integration seems to be increasing only incrementally. One reason for this has been the practice of voluntary cooperation in the CMEA, probably the only practice that would allow the governing elites in those countries to maintain a measure of popular support. However, since USSR and GDR positions on CMEA matters appear nearly identical, the question of voluntary participation is moot. The degree of agreement between the two countries has, however, been responsible for the high amount of bi-lateral economic and cultural agreements between the GDR and USSR.

Incremental integration can be seen in the relatively small growth of intra-CMEA trade compared with trade growth between Western Countries: from 1963 to 1972, intra-CMEA trade grew only 11 percent as opposed to 28 percent in the EEC.[28] The reasons for this incremental growth can be viewed in light of CMEA integration problems.

First, As Kleer writes, levels of economic development and significantly, systems of economic management vary substantially within the CMEA.[29] Cooperative economic ventures become difficult where there are no parallel management organizations; for example, a country with a centrally focused, "command-directive" system of economic management may find it a complex task to cooperate in production with a country whose production and investment

decision making is more decentralized. Kleer concluded from his
data on consistency of annual growth rates, capital intensity coefficients,
and export and import elasticity that in the years 1960 to 1970 there
was no substantial improvement in the standardization of economic
systems or in the open character of the economies. He points to
CMEA's strategy of bringing the various systems closer together
as significant to imporving these areas.

Second, the lack of convertible currency among CMEA countries
has long been a barrier to intra-CMEA trade and has usually required
trade agreements to be based on the barter system. Some steps have
been taken to create an international investment bank within the CMEA
community but there has been little effect on trade volume.

Third, another problem in CMEA integration is the persistent
variety of products and machinery in CMEA countries. A CMEA
Commission for Standardization exists, but in view of the principle
of voluntary cooperation, standardization can be expected to be a
very long-term process.

Fourth, cooperative sharing of labor resources has been
considered another facet of socialist integration, and one that
greatly interests the GDR, whose decreasing population has caused
a chronic manpower shortage. The GDR has taken steps to import
workers in recent years. There are complex economic problems
associated with collaboration in manpower resources, such as
determining each country's share of the surplus product of workers.[30]
Also, workers must be housed, a problem in the GDR where the
housing shortage is acute.

The twenty-eighth regular session of the CMEA in June 1974
was marked by a Soviet proposal to speed up the integration process.
This met predictable resistance on the part of most other CMEA
countries, which feared a loss of national sovereignty. The result
was a communique that announced the "further intensification and
perfection of the cooperation and development of socialist economic
integration," which meant no major change. Although socialist
integration will continue on a incremental basis in the future, there
will be systemic developments, such as dependence on Soviet raw
materials, that may hasten the pace of integration.

Socialist economic integration will necessitate a standardization
of legal systems in the CMEA countries as well as the further development of socialist international law.[31] Such a gradual systemic change
will probably be paralleled by an increasing similarity of economic
systems in CMEA countries. The GDR and USSR agree on these aims.

Trade with the West, consistent with the present Soviet
attitude toward détente, will continue to increase. The GDR is actively
promoting what it terms "socialist license trade," which is aimed at
Western markets. Although there was a free exchange of technological

advancements prior to 1968, recent CMEA expansion of trade with
the West has made the marketing mechanism of license trade
economically desirable. Presently 40 percent of GDR trade with the
FRG is on the basis of licenses, while only 10 percent involves
cooperative production. [32]Although we cannot see how license
trade is necessarily an integral part of socialist integration
(free exchanges of advancement, as existing prior to 1968, would seem
to be ideologically more consistent), it has encouraged a great number
of bilateral agreements between the GDR and USSR, which seem to
agree on joint projects most readily of all CMEA nations.

Finally, the GDR's population growth problems will present
it with a dilemma. Clearly, with a stagnant population the GDR
cannot continue to expand its trade with the West while maintaining
its prominent position in the CMEA. The increasing demand for
consumer goods, presently obtained most economically from Western
markets, must somehow be balanced with GDR energy and manpower
needs.

CONCLUSIONS

Internal and international integration are closely iterrelated
in the case of GDR. Internally the two factors most important to
integration are the move toward the inculcation of socialist norms
in support of the regime and the satisfaction of the consumer and
welfare needs of the population. The education system of the GDR has
had mixed results in achieving fundamental allegiance among the
young. Since social science results that reflect critically on
ideological goals are not available, we can only make estimates.
Along with the ideologically committed are the many opportunists,
hangers-on, and indifferent who moot the question of internal
integration as a supportive factor as long as their consumer and welfare needs are met. Following the Eighth Party Congress of the SED
in 1971 strenuous efforts were undertaken to improve housing conditions and the quality and range of consumer goods available in GDR.
These efforts aimed at achieving internal socialist integration are
complicated by factors emanating from the international environment
of the GDR.

Among the external factors affecting internal GDR integration
are the West, the relationship between the GDR and the USSR, and the
place of the GDR within the CMEA.

The presence to the west of capitalist systems presents a
disturbing source of inputs for the GDR. Visitors and media from
the FRG intrude values that are counter to those of the integrated
socialist personality, which, naturally, stresses the ideals of

socialism. Attempts to shield the GDR from Western influences have had only partial success.

The satisfaction of needs related to the GDR economy are in large measure conditioned by the relationship between the GDR and the USSR. The Soviet Union is the principal supplier of raw materials to the GDR. The dependence relationship here ought not be understressed, for the GDR is relatively powerless in affecting the price structure of raw materials and, therefore, of the consumer products and housing that must be provided to maintain citizen support.

The data examined suggest that the GDR might be attempting to lessen dependence on the USSR by expanding its trade with other members of the CMEA. How far this diversification can go cannot yet be determined, but leverage gained through better relations within the CMEA could only benefit the GDR. Distinct limits are set by the Soviet domination of CMEA, but even the USSR cannot control everything. In any case a better international environment among socialist states could only help socialist integration within the GDR.

The Ninth Party Congress of the SED will meet in 1976 in a new and imposing party headquarters in Berlin. One of the prominent matters for discussion then will doubtlessly be the squeeze felt in the GDR among the internal and external factors impinging upon socialist integration: rising citizen expectations (goaded by contracts with the West), the effects of capitalist inflation, the leverage of Soviet raw materials, and small increments in improved trade relations among CMEA members.

NOTES

1. A. M. Hanhardt, Jr., The German Democratic Republic (Baltimore: Johns Hopkins University Press, 1968), pp. 9-12.

2. P. C. Ludz, "Zum Begriff der 'Nation' in der Sicht der SED," Deutschland Archiv 5, no. 1 (1972): 33-45; Gebhard Schweigler, National bewusstsein in der BRD und DDR (Dusseldorf: Bertelsmann Universitaetsverlag, 1973); A.M. Hanhardt, Jr., "Political Socialization in Divided Germany," Journal of International Affairs 27, no 2 (1973): 187-203.

3. Schweigler, National bewusstsein, p. 101.

4. Georg Mende, ed., Ueber die Entwicklung sozialistischer Persoenlickeiten (Berlin: Deutscher Verlag der Wissenschaften, 1960), pp. 96-97.

5. For a fuller treatment from the GDR perspective, see K.-H Guenther and G. Uhlig, Geschichte der Schule in der DDR 1945 bis 1968 (Berlin: Volk und Wissen, 1969).

6. <u>Protokoll der Verhandlugen des V. Parteitages der SED</u> (Berlin: Bietz Verlag, 1959), vol. 2, 1395.

7. "Gesetz ueber die sozialistische Entwicklung des Schulwesen in der DDR vom. 2. Dezember 1959," in Leonhard Froese, ed., <u>Bildungspolitik und Bildungsreform</u> (Munich: Wilhelm Goldmann Verlag, 1969), p. 164.

8. "Gesetz ueber das einheitliche sozialistische Bildungssysten in <u>Das System der sozialistischen Gesellschafts- und Staatsordnung in der DDR: Dokumente</u> (Berlin: Staatsverlag, 1969), p. 446.

9. E. Drefenstedt and G. Neuner, <u>Lehrplanwerk und Unterrichtsgestaltung</u> (Berlin: Volk und Wissen, 1969), pp. 150-51.

10. See W. Friedrich, "Zu Theroretischen Problemen der marxistischen Jugendforschung," <u>Jugendforschung</u>, nos. 1-2 (1967): 11-38 for a programmatic introduction to the journal.

11. Friedrich's main work is <u>Jugend Heute</u>, 2nd ed. (Berlin: Deutscher Verlag der Wissenschaften, 1967).

12. H. Mueller and H. Schedlich, "Schulklassenspeziefische Bedingungen der politischen Einstellungsbildung," <u>Paedagogik</u>, no. 1 (1966), cited by A. Kossakowski, <u>Zur Psychologie der Schuljugen</u> (Berlin: Volk und Wissen, 1969), pp. 150-51.

13. Kossakowski, <u>Zur Psychologie</u>, pp. 150-51.

14. W. Hennig, "Interessenstrukturen von Jugendlichen," <u>Jugendforschung</u>, no. 5 (1968): 19-33.

15. Kossakowski, <u>Zur Psychologie</u>, p. 164.

16. R. Maerker, <u>Jugend im anderen Teil Deutschlands</u> (Munich: Juventa, 1969), p. 76.

17. U. Siegel, "Nationale Gruppen im Urteil Jugendlicher," <u>Jugendforschung</u>, nos. 3-4 (1967): 103-24; W. Buchanan and H. Cantril, <u>How Nations See Each Other</u> (Urbana: University of Illinois Press, 1953).

18. R. F. Staar, ed., <u>Yearbook on International Communist Affairs 1973</u> (Stanford, Calif.: Hoover Institution Press, 1973), p.29.

19. W. Seiffert, O. Kampa, and L. Ruester, "Current Legal Problems of Socialist Economic Integration," <u>Soviet and East European Foreign Trade</u> 10, no. 2 (1974): 82-98.

20. I. Kozlov, A. Lifshits, and V. Khakimov, "Collaboration of COMECON Countries in the Key Branches of Industry," <u>Problems of Economics</u>, September 1974, pp. 20-49.

21. <u>Statistisches Taschenbuch der DDR</u> (Berlin: Staatsverlag, 1974), pp. 110-11.

22. Ibid., pp. 112-13.

23. Ibid., p. 115.

24. M. Haendcke-Hoppe, "Aussenhandel und Aussenhandelsplanu in der DDR," <u>Deutschland Archiv</u> 7, no. 2 (February 1975): 155.

25. Ibid.

26.   Staar, ed., Yearbook, pp. 32-33.
27.   Department of Economic and Social Affairs, United Nations, Statistical Yearbook 1973 (United Nations: UN, 1974), p. 402.
28.   J. Kleer, "Economic Reforms in the Socialist Countries in the Sixties," Eastern European Economics, Winter 1974-75, pp. 3-30.
29.   T. Vais and L. Degtiar, "Collaboration of COMECON Countries in the Utilization of Labor Resources," Problems of Economics, June 1974, p. 31.
30.   Seiffert, Kampa, and Ruester, "Current Legal Problems," p. 99.
31.   K. Botz and P. Ploetz, "East-West Cooperation: German Experiences," Intereconomics, no. 5 (1974): 160.
32.   F. Zschering and A. Spier, "Some Problems Concerning the Current Status and Development of the International License Trade of the GDR," Soviet and East European Foreign Trade 9, no. 3 (1973): 81-83.

CHAPTER

7

ETHNICITY AND
PHILIPPINE-MALAYSIAN
RELATIONS
Lela Garner Noble

Between 1969 and 1975 two major developments affected
Philippine-Malaysian relations. The first was the growth of ASEAN
(the Association of Southeast Asian Nations) into a regional organization characterized by increasing cooperation, a growth made
possible by the "normalization" of relations between the Philippines
and Malaysia. The second development was a growing insurgency
in Muslim areas of the southern Philippines, an insurgency allegedly
encouraged by Tun Mustapha, chief minister of the Malaysian state
of Sabah.

The coincidence of these two developments suggests that the
relationship between internal integration and external relations is
complex and reciprocal. The specific argument here is that the
continuing cooperation of Malaysia and the Philippines in ASEAN and
the emergence of a separatist movement among the Philippine
ethnic minority sharing common religious bonds with the Malaysian
majority were related in such a way as to reflect a bargain, implicit
or explicit, between the policy makers of the two states. The policy
makers acted as if they had agreed that Malaysia would refrain from
supporting Philippine Muslims but would allow Tun Mustapha to
assist them; the Philippines would continue to attack the Muslim
separatist movement but would refrain from action against Sabah or
from direct public criticism of Malaysia; the Philippines would not
press its claim to Sabah but would assert its right to the waters
around the Sulu archipelago.

Succeeding sections explain how the "bargain" was arrived at, how it has worked, and what conclusions it suggests about the relationship among ethnicity, domestic integration, and international relations.

THE ORIGIN OF THE BARGAIN

The bargain appeared to be the result of almost a decade of regional friction. For Malaysia the problems were worst with Indonesia in the years 1963-66. But problems with the Philippines, primarily over the claim to Sabah, preceded, exacerbated, and out-lasted "confrontation." There were also tensions in relations with Singapore and Thailand. Throughout these experiences Malaysian security was dependent on military arrangements with Britain, New Zealand, and Australia, but by the end of the 1960s it was clear that the British military presence in the area would be reduced drastically.

The increased evidence of international vulnerability coincided with domestic strains, which culminated in the 1969 elections. In peninsular Malaysia the announcement of election results was followed by Malay-Chinese rioting, which in turn led to the postponement of elections in the Bornean states. When elections were finally held in Eastern Malaysia in 1970, Tun Mustapha delivered Sabah's votes solidly for the Alliance. Sabah thus emerged as the most stable of all states—from the standpoint of the Alliance leaders—and Tun Mustapha as the most independent of all the state leaders.[1]

Philippine policy in Southeast Asia between 1962 and 1965, the period of Macapagal's presidency, was dominated by two endeavors: the making and prosecution of the Philippine claim to Sabah and the assumption of a mediating role in the "confrontation" between Malaysia and Indonesia.[2] In both endeavors ethnic factors were of minimal importance; moreover, both were counterproductive.

After Marcos became president in 1966 the Philippines moved to reestablish relations with Malaysia and joined Malaysia, Singapore, Indonesia, and Thailand in forming ASEAN in 1967. Cooperation, however, was short-lived. It was jeopardized in 1968 by the "Corregidor incident," which presumably revealed the existence of a secret force of Muslims being trained by the Philippines to infiltrate Sabah.

Then, after Philippine legislators passed a bill asserting Philippine sovereignty over Sabah in the process of redefining Philippine boundaries, active diplomatic relations between the Philippines and Malaysia were suspended. Malaysia abrogated the antismuggling agreement it had negotiated with the Philippines despite the protests of Tun Mustapha; withdrew its embassy staff from the Philippines; demanded that the Philippines implement its announced withdrawal of its own staff; and sharply curtailed its participation in international meetings. There also were reports that Sabah, if not Malaysia, was cultivating active contacts with Muslim dissidents in the southern Philippines.

Meanwhile domestic conditions in the Philippines were worsening, and protest was becoming more widespread, better organized and coordinated, and more explicitly purposeful. Discontent was particularly strong among Muslims in Mindanao and Sulu.

The Muslims were divided by clan, language, and location, and also by the manner in which they had chosen to accommodate themselves to a national system that they perceived as being dominated by Christians. Some, particularly the Maranao in the Lanao area, perpetuated traditional patterns of clan organization and sought to avoid contact with any alien influences, including electricity, schools, and government officials. When challenged, they fought. Others opted for integration, which was defined primarily by education in a public or private university, often with financial assistance from the government's Commission on National Integration. The third option was an explicitly Islamic one and involved training in local schools, frequently ones established by Egyptian, Arabian, or Indonesian missionaries; education overseas at universities in Egypt or Arabia; and/or participation in Islamic organizations in the Philippines and outside it. Many of these Muslims were reformists in their orientation toward Philippine Islam and Muslim society. They might or might not be secessionist in relation to the Philippines, but their higher loyalties were clearly to Islam rather than to the Philippines.

The three options were not exclusive. Muslim politicians often represented a fusion of the three: they participated fully in the party alignments and pork-barrel arrangements of the national political scene, but frequently did so with a traditional clan base that they extended by Islamic symbols, benefits, and organizations. They arranged pilgrimages to Mecca, for example; sent their sons and godsons to Cairo University; had contacts with Malaysian, Egyptian Arabian, and Libyan leaders. Muslims who tried the integrationist route were sometimes frustrated and hence found common cause with traditionalists or reformers. Traditionalists frequently respected the Islamic credentials and connections of the reformers and accepted their leadership.

Whatever their orientation, the 3.5 million Philippine Muslims were subject to many of the same problems affecting other Filipinos. They also had problems relating to continuing Christian migration into Mindanao, which by the late 1960s had reached a

level the Muslims felt was threatening to their economic,
political, and cultural interests. The economic conflict centered on
the fact that Muslim land holding practices were rooted in a
relationship between datus (clan chiefs) and clansmen, not
necessarily in Philippine law. The migrating Christians tended to
assume that they were dealing with a legal situation, and usually
also that they had both the law and the governmental agencies on
their side. Since there was no agreement on legal systems or
judges, as migration increased, fighting among Christian settlers,
a largely Christian Philippine Constabulary, and Muslims increased
in frequency, intensity, and organization.

Fighting worsened in the years preceding elections because
migration also had political implications. Muslim families and groups
had frequently fought among themselves for political followings and
positions. As Christian newcomers in some provinces began to
outnumber Muslims, changes in registration patterns inevitably not
only intensified the conflict but also added new, unpredictable factors.
Christians sometimes simply voted for an "old" Muslim politician,
for at least some of the reasons Muslims did—his connections
with the Liberal or Nacionalista benefit newtork. Frequently, however,
shifts in registration produced new Christian politicians. Under these
conditions, there was seldom any reason to distinguish between
groups organized and fighting for economic reasons and those fighting
for political reasons.

The conflict appeared to be irreconcilable since both
Christians and Muslims had a tendency to identify their lifestyles as
Christian and Muslim respectively; both identified Philippine culture
as Christian; and both had a tendency to regard their own religion and
lifestyles as superior. Whether of not an "Islamic resurgence" was
inherently secessionist, in the context of generally worsening conditions
and a preceived "Christian" threat, growing Islamic self-consciousness
and contacts encouraged talk of secession. Secessionist threats and
organizations also had traditionally been part of the bargaining process
between provincial Muslim leaders and national Christian ones:
Muslim leaders did not want to secede, they wanted rewards for not
seceding. The formation of the Muslim (or Mindanao) Indepedence
Movement by Udtog Matalam, former governor of Cotabato, in 1968
appeared to fit the old model, particularly since he seemed
temporarily mollified after Marcos gave him a watch and attention;
but the movement tapped sentiments that went beyond Matalam's
intentions and control.

Thus by the end of the 1960s Marcos was confronted
domestically with clear evidence of deteriorating socioeconomic
conditions, widespread discontent, and increasingly organized and
ideological protest groups. The level of violence throughout the

country seemed to be increasing. There were reports of outside support for both the New People's Army, an avowedly Maoist revolutionary organization concentrated in Luzon, and for Muslim dissidents, concentrated in Mindanao and Sulu. There also was evidence that foreign policy, particularly policy toward the claim to Sabah, had increased the possibility that internal problems would be worsened by external ones. For Philippine as well as for Malaysian leaders, by 1969 vulnerability was dictating caution in foreign policy; therefore, the rationale for the Malaysian-Philippine "bargain" described earlier.

THE OPERATION OF THE BARGAIN

In the early 1970s the bargain was tested by the increase in the level and scope of fighting in the southern Philippines, the growing evidence of external support for the Muslim activists, and the persistence of both concern and controversy in Islamic organizations over treatment of Philippine Muslims.

In March 1970 there were reports in the Philippine press of the return to the Philippines of a number of Muslims who had been trained abroad. One report, based on information received by the commander of the Philippine Constabulary, was that 120 Muslim youths had returned after receiving training under British and British-trained officers. A second version reported the return of 3,475 Filipino Muslims trained in "Middle Eastern and nearby countries." Both versions linked the trainees with Philippine secessionist movements like the Darul Islam and Muslim (or Mindanao) Independence Movement in Cotabato, Lamalip in Lanao, the Muslim Brotherhood of Jolo, and the Green Guardes of Zamboanga and Basilan. [3] There also were news stories in May of Muslim youth meetings in which secession was discussed, usually as a last resort if demands for reform were not met by the Philippine government.

When the level of violence escalated in Mindanao in October 1970, it was more related to the 1971 elections for senatorial, provincial, and local offices than to secession. By early 1971 fighting was worst in two provinces in Mindanao where population and hence voting ratios were changing, Lanao del Norte and Cotabato del Norte. Reports identified the Muslim combatants as "blackshirts" in Cotabato and "barracudas" in Lanao del Norte. It was usually assumed that the "blackshirts" were linked with Matalam's Muslim Independence Movement and that the "barracudas" were the private army of Ali Dimaporo, a Muslim congressman identified with the Nacionalista Party. The Christians, classified ethnically as Ilongo,

were called "Ilagas":   the translation is "rats."   In Lanao the
Ilagas were allegedly led by Governor Arsenio A. Quibranza, Dimaporo's
chief rival.[4]

Muslim and Christian groups raided villages, burned houses,
and killed. There were reports that some Muslim members of the
Philippine Constabulary participated in attacks on Christians, but
it was widely assumed the Constabulary units, predominantly
Christian and headed by an Ilongo, generally intervened on behalf
of Christians. Certainly the level of violence expanded with
increases in the number of Constabulary personnel sent into the
area. Moreover, while casualty and refugee figures were high for
both Muslims and Christians, the worst incidents involved Christian
attacks on Muslims.

The first occurred in June 1971, when a group of 23 armed
Ilongos, some reportedly in Constabulary uniforms, forced about
70 Muslims into a mosque, threw a grenade at them, and shot anyone who escaped. They raided the barrio school and killed more
Muslim children.[5] The second incident occurred on November 23,
election day in Lanao del Norte. A group of 200 Muslims had been
persuaded with promises of safe conduct and Constabulary escort
to return home to vote. According to one report they were identified
as "flying voters" and not allowed to vote when they arrived. Then
on the return trip, contrary to the safe-conduct agreement, they were
stopped at an army checkpoint. The army charged that the first
shot came from the Maranaos, but army personnel had only a few
minor injuries while the Muslims were shot by army men and booed
by the Christian civilians accompanying the soldiers.[6]

The two incidents, set in the context of continual fighting,
aroused major protest from Muslim political leaders outside the
country. Colonel Moammer Kadaffi of Libya accused the Philippine
government of having a deliberate plan to exterminate Philippine
Muslims and threatened to assume responsibility for them. In an
interview with the Beirut paper Al Anwar, Rascid Lucman,
Philippine congressman from Lanao del Sur, said that Libya was
already supplying aid to the "opposition" in the Philippines.[7]
Reuters quoted Tunku Abdul Rahman, in his new role as head of the
Islamic Secretariat, as saying that the Secretariat was considering
the mosque massacre "at the request of worldwide Muslims."[8]
Claims that the Philippines was persecuting Muslims were circulated
at the United Nations. In September the Indonesian news agency
reported that Muslim leaders had made statements expressing regret
and sympathy for their Philippine borthers and appealing to the
Philippine government for a peaceful settlement.[9] In December, as
an ASEAN foreign ministers meeting was closing in Kuala Lumpur, the
Malaysian prime minister condemned the killing of Philippine Muslims.[10]

In 1972, violence spread into other areas of Mindanao, although the overall level of fighting appeared to have subsided. In June Representative Salipada Pendatum visited Middle Eastern capitals and reportedly received a promise of aid for Philippine Muslims from Sadat. Meanwhile Kadaffi reiterated charges of genocide and on June 11 explicitly offered arms and money to Philippine Muslims.[11] Marcos's reaction marked a significant shift in Philippine tactics. Earlier the Philippine response to statements by outsiders had been to declare that the situation was a purely internal dispute over land claims and that the policy and practice of the Philippine government were to have a "liberal and sympathetic attitude" toward non-Christian Filipinos. Kadaffi's statements had been branded as "mere meddling."[12] Arrangements made for Muslim ambassadors in Manila to visit the southern Philippines had appeared to be a concession.

After the statements of June, however, Marcos invited representatives of the Egyptian and Libyan governments to visit Mindanao. He acted, despite the objections of other members of Congress, on the advice of Senator Mamintal Tamano, a former head of the Commission on National Integration and one of the few Muslim senators in Philippine history. His objective was clearly to demonstrate that criticism and aid were unwarranted.

Egypt and Libya responded by sending a four-man delegation to the Phillipines on July 1-8. Marcos, who had earlier identified the problem as caused partly by a struggle for political power, partly by contention over land rights, told them that he believed communists and other elements were provoking violence. He said that dissidents seeking to "agitate and inflame Muslims against the Government and Christians in general" were responsible for the unrest and that communists had infiltrated the Ilagas.[13] The Egyptian spokesman's conclusions were that the conflict could develop into a religious war. He cited Philippine government figures of 1,600 killed, including over 800 Muslims, since early 1971, and said, "We will follow our mission by convincing our friends in the Phillipines to try to do their best to stop the massacre and establish order." A Libyan official compared the situation to pre-1948 Palestine.[14]

The Philippine government appeared satisfied with having won a reprieve from genocide charges. In any event, despite both the intensity of the violence and its gorwing international ramifications, throughout 1971 and 1972 most Filipinos considered other events to be of greater importance. The 1971 election campaign was bitterly fought, and the results were interpreted as a major loss for Marcos. Debates in the Constitutional Convention were also bitter and had pro- or anti-Marcos implications. Bombings and shootouts occured in the Manila area. Marcos attributed them to communists; his opponents charged his own men with having staged them. Floods

deluged areas of Luzon and threatened a nationwide rice crisis.
Amid the furor, relations with neighboring states remained cordial.
ASEAN continued its meetings and statements. During the floods
Tun Razak expressed sympathy and offered help.

When Marcos declared martial law in September 1972 his
early justifications emphasized the communist threat, primarily as
represented by the activities of the New People's Army. Ironically,
by October, Muslim rather than NPA-led rebellion constituted the
most significant challenge to his regime.

The first large-scale attack was on a Constabulary camp in
Marawi City, Lanao del Sur. Fighting spread through Basilan and
the Sulu Archipelago. In late February a major offensive was launched
in Cotabato. By the end of March the Muslim forces had control of
most of Basilan and Sulu and large portions of the Lanao, Zamboanga,
and Cotabato provinces. Estimates as to their numbers ranged
considerably, but there were probably about 15,000.

The forces appeared better coordinated, better led, and better
armed than those fighting earlier. In some areas they left leaflets
announcing their objectives. Aimed at least partly at reassuring
Christians, the leaflets identified the armed men as members of
the Muslim Revolutionary Forces in Mindanao. They said that
Christians had no reason to fear that they would be harmed; the
fighting was directed against the army and the Constabulary, not
the people.[15] Other reports said that the leaders called for the
ouster of all old Muslim feudal leaders and provincial officials.

A manifesto published by the underground Free Philippine
News Service contained nineteen demands. The first demands were
for the withdrawal of government troops, the disbandment of
local self-defense forces, the removal of all government officials who
were not natives of the area, and the arrest and prosecution of the
personnel guilty for the killings of innocent Muslims. Other demands,
apparently assuming that the first would not be met, dealt with
controls on the behavior of military personnel. A third group of
demands centered on recognition that the Muslim activists were not
communists but "God-fearing people"; on freedom to practice
Islamic laws and customs without restriction; and on requests that
"foreign dignitaries, especially representatives of world bodies,"
be allowed to travel freely in affected areas.[16]

What had emerged was a loosely organized movement (it was
later identified as the Moro National Liberation Front of MNLF) with
a core of young, university-trained Muslim leaders. While many of
them had links with the older generation of Muslim political leaders,
they appeared to be renouncing those links and calling for reform
within Muslim society as well as a change in the relationship to
Philippine society. Nurul Hadji Misuari, early identified as the

main leader, had been Lucman's protegé. Misuari's wife was the
niece of the wife of Salih Ututalum, one of the long-time political
contenders in Sulu. Nizam Abubaker, a son of the mayor of Jolo,
was among the rebels. Some reportedly had doctorates in Islamic
jurisprudence from Cario University. Perhaps among the top
leaders, certainly within the movement as a whole, there were
differences, particularly in defining reform and autonomy and
consequently acceptable terms of settlement.

The external contracts of the movement's leaders were not
clear. Those who were educated in Islamic universities obviously had
relationships with Muslims in other countries. News stories said
Misuari was in Libya in 1972 and had also spent time in Sabah. It
was reported that Libyan and Sabahan aid went first to Lucman, then
later directly to Misuari. Accoring to Philippine officials, captured
Muslims admitted that they received military training in Malaysia.
Libyans admitted giving aid; Malaysian officials denied it. [17]

Within the Philippines, an underground newspaper connected
with the New People's Army, the Clenched Fist, reported "NPA-MRF"
activities and identified the Muslim fighting as part of the common
struggle. The Muslim objective, the paper alleged, was from autonomous zones in areas where Muslims have 85 percent of the population. [18] Other reports quoted an unnamed radical priest as
claiming a 10 percent infiltration of the Muslim movement by the New
People's Army. [19] The term "infiltration" of course implied that
from the perspective of the Muslims the commonality of the
struggle might be less clear. While Misuari was a member of the
Kabataang Makabayan, a radical youth group frequently linked with
the New People's Army, several years ago, his friends said that
he left it because of a conviction that the Maoists in it were neither
understanding of nor sympathetic toward Muslims. Muslim
spokesmen denied that they were communists or engaged in a
struggle to overthrow the central Philippine government.

In Sulu, Cotabato, Samboanga, and Basilan, the MNLF
appeared to include most Muslim dissident groups and to secure
a degree of coordination and discipline. Many groups in Lanao appeared to remain independent, although there were reports of
Front activity there also. In particular areas Muslim seizure of
power was associated with genuine peace and order: price ceilings
set and maintained, a complete ban on liquor, troops rigidly
disciplined. In other areas, tactics resembled more closely the
old black shirt-barracuda-Sulu clan feud style.

The martial law regime's analysis of the problem distinguished
between socioeconomic and military aspects, between leaders and
followers, and between domestic and foreign ramifications. To
deal with the socioeconomic aspects, the administration proposed

expansion of airports and ports ("to encourage tourism"), new
programs to train fishermen, provisions for a limited amount of
barter trade between Sabah and Zamboanga and Jolo, an Amanah
bank (primarily to make loans to Muslims), and government chartering
of a ship for the Mecca pilgrimage (passage was free or subsidized
if guns were surrendered). It also established a number of organizations
to plan to implement the programs and announced the commitment
of significant resources. [20]

At the same time, the administration issued reminders that
no socioeconomic programs could begin until peace and order were
restored. By April 1973 half of the 62,000 men in the Philippine
Armed Forces were estimated to be in Mindanao, and the armed
forces were being expanded steadily. [21] They also were being
bolstered by deliveries of military equipment from the United
States and by purchases elsewhere. Military personnel in the
south spoke of "sanitizing" areas and "search and destroy" missions.
There were reports of planes daily strafing areas of presumed
rebel concentration. In March 1973 the government began issuing
arms to local self-defense units. The effect was to increase the
weapons available to the Ilagas and to give them paramilitary status.
Apparently Muslims were given arms only in Sulu, and there Muslim
government supporters complained that they were not given adequate
ammunition.

Marcos moved immediately to win the support—or neutralize
the opposition—of established Muslim leaders. He called about
200 of them—congressmen, delegates to the Constitutional
Convention, governors, mayors, leaders of prominent clans—to a
peace conference in early January 1973. He offered selective amnesty
for fighters who surrendered, reiterated his programs of economic
reform, and said government troops were in the southern Philippines
not to fight Muslims but to identify and segregate foreign insurgents,
"if any." He said he had information that foreign-trained and foreign-
armed troops were active in Mindanao. [22]

The datus had little influence, since martial law left them
no power and the rebels' ideology left them no authority. Other
efforts centered on extending amnesty periods and sending special
delegations to negotiate. The administration was dealing, according
to Press Secretary Francisco Tatad, with "combined elements of
outlaws, pirates and secessionists led by a young Maoist leadership."[23]

The basic scheme for undercutting the rebels, then, was
to offer them hope through promises of socioeconomic programs,
convince them through military force that they could not win on
their own terms, provide amnesty as a transition, and use mediators
to make sure they received all the messages that the government

wanted sent. For other Filipinos the government restricted
information. Press censorship was directed at minimizing the scale
of fighting, rebel successes, and government casulties; and emphasizing
the government's generosity and rebel surrenders. Those who
surrendered "returned to the folds of the law"; those who did not
were outlaws, bandits, or Maoists.

Some of these tactics and classifications had relevance for
the foreign audience of which the government was conscious. Top
government officials also deliberately refrained from naming publicly
the foreign countries they suspected of aiding the insurgents.
While Secretary of Foreign Affairs Carlos Romulo informed both
SEATO and ASEAN that the government had evidence of foreign
involvement, he did not press the issue in either case. Nor did the
government take the issue to the United Nations, as it had done
regularly with the claim to Sabah.

There were press reports in May and June 1973 that the
Philippine government either directly or through Indonesia had
proposed to the Malaysian government that it would renounce
publicly its claim to Sabah if the Malaysian government would give
assurance that Sabah would not give sanctuary to Muslim dissidents.
In response to questioning about the reports, Tun Razak, the
Malaysian prime minister, denied that the Philippine government
had made any involvement with the "insurgency problem."[24]

The government's efforts achieved some successes. By
December there were reports in the Manila papers of mass
surrenders of rebels. Government troops also reoccupied areas
in Basilan and Mindanao. The fighting remained regionalized; the
New People's Army in Luzon was surprisingly quiet. Some of the
socioeconomic programs were begun.

Equally important were some international successes. In
late 1972 and early 1973 a Libyan envoy visited capitals of states
associated with the Islamic Secretariat with a message from
Kadaffi about the situation of Philippine Muslims. Presumably
the envoy was trying to lobby for support of the proposals Libya
later made at the Islamic Foreign Minister's Conference held in
Benghazi, Libya, on March 24-26. Libya wanted all Muslim states
to condemn and sever diplomatic and economic relations with the
Philippines. The Libyan proposals lost, and the proposals passed,
"after extensive debate," were more moderate.

The conference resolved "to appeal to peace-loving states,
religious and international organizations to exert their good offices
with the Government of the Philippines to halt campaigns of violence
against the Muslim community, to ensure their safety and realize
their basic liberties." It also named a five-man team to visit the
Philippines in three months, established a voluntary fund to help

Philippine Muslims, and asked Indonesia and Malaysia to exert
their good offices within ASEAN. Saudi Arabia, Indonesia, and
Malaysia were credited with having successfully argued the
dangers of interfering in the internal affairs of a sovereign state. [25]
        In April 1973 ASEAN foreign ministers met in Pattaya, Thailand.
Press reports indicated that the foreign ministers considered it in
their mutual interest to avoid public discussion of divisive issues.
After a private meeting of the Malaysian, Indonesian, and Philippine
officials, the three refused to discuss what they had talked about. [26]
According to the final communiqué, "the ministers took note of the
presentation of facts by the Philippine Foreign Minister concerning
the Muslim minority in the Southern Philippines, especially the
efforts being exerted. . . to improve the conditions in the area."
They also noted the Philippine expression of gratitude to Malaysia
and Indonesia for their support at Benghazi. [27]
        In June a delegation from the World Islamic League went
to Mindanao and, according to the Manila Daily Express, found
proof of rapid development and heard Muslim leaders praise Marcos
for his concern. The Express quoted the head of the delegation as
saying, "Separation is absolutely out of the question and is not to
your interest." [28] Then in mid-August the Islamic foreign ministers'
delegation visited the Philippines. The Philippine news agency
quoted the delegates as saying that they were convinced that Marcos
was sincere in solving problems and that Filipino Muslims could
expect some aid but should not allow themselves to be used by
extremists or communist groups. [29]
        Finally, in November, in the aftermath of the Middle East
war and in the midst of oil shortages, Marcos publicly condemned
Israel and called for a withdrawal of Israeli forces from occupied
Arab territory. The Arab summit meeting in Algiers then decided
to spare the Philippines from further cuts in oil deliveries.
        There was, however, an illusionary quality to many of the
successes. Reoccupation of territory was as frequently a result
of rebal tactics as of military success and as frequently associated
with the deterioration of "law and order" as with its "restoration."
While one of the earliest actions of the martial law regime was to
round up guns, the net result of the government's policy of arming
civilians was to put more and probably better weaponry into the
area. Most of the people armed were avowed enemies of Muslims,
whether or not they were identified with rebel groups. The fighting
and rising fear and tensions created an enormous number of
refugees—estimates ranged from 100,000 (Marcos's figure in
August) to 980,000—and the refugee problem was further
complicated by food shortages and continuing, perhaps increasing,
Muslim distrust of government agencies. The government's programs,

then, appeared to result in more devastation, more hostility, and more guns.

The nature of the situation was most clearly revealed by the rebels' seizure of Jolo in Feburary 1974. Many of the rebels whom the Manila papers reported as having surrendered in December 1973 same from Sulu. One was identified as having been trained abroad and responsible within the MNLF for some "foreign-trained" troops. Several were hadjis, datus, and imams, titles suggesting that they might not fit the pattern of second-generation leadership. Whatever their actual positions, they were flown to Manila to meet Marcos, who briefed them on plans for the socioeconomic program, then flown back, ostensibly to woo their former followers into surrendering. Military leaders said that former rebels were taking the initiative in hunting down the "Maoists," estimated to be two or three hundred in number. 30 Some people in Jolo believed that the decision to seize Jolo was at least partially the rebels' reaction to the new role of these returnees, who were identified as Marcos's emissaries and armed with government weapons, although at least one of them was widely known as an "outlaw."

Descriptions of what happened during the seizure and subsequent fighting differed, but there seemed to be a consensus that at least half of Jolo City was destroyed; about half of the population of Jolo City fled to Sabah, Basilan, or Zamboanga; loss of life was high; and the government continued to use massive firepower against suspected rebel hideouts throughout the island. These facts, plus what the government claimed was new information about the nature and extent of foreign involvement, further jeopardized Philippine relations with Muslim countries, particularly with Malaysia. In the context of the continuing Arab oil boycott, these relations were critical.

The Philippines attempted to deal with the international ramifications in two ways. It tried to stop Malaysia from giving or permitting what it was convinced was direct and critical aid to the rebels, and it tried to stave off condemnation and consequent oil cuts. About 80 percent of Philippine oil came from Middle Eastern sources, primarily Saudi Arabia. 31

A widely distributed Associated Press dispatch quoted "authoritatively informed diplomatic sources" as saying that the Philippine government had new evidence that Malaysia had supplied training, arms, and ammunition for the rebels. Partially based on signed statements from MNLF captives, the information was that Malaysian training for Muslim guerrillas began in 1969 when five batches totaling 90 men were taken to Pulau Pangkor, off West Malaysia, or to Lahad Datu and Banguey Island, in Sabah. Nur

Misuari was among the 90 trained. Since 1972 Malaysian sources had arranged landings to deliver at least 200,000 rounds of ammunition and 5,407 weapons. Malaysian naval boats made their last known delivery on December 31, 1973. The sources also cited an intercepted letter written by Rascid Lucman on June 3, 1972; it said that Tun Mustapha provided 750,000 pesos to Misuari and to Dr. Saleh Loong, whose relatives were identified as activist leaders. The money was for recruiting 300 men.[32]

An article in the Far Eastern Economic Review written from Manila sources contained much of the same information but said that money was originally channeled through older Mindanao Muslims—including Lucman, who had an army called Ansar El Islam. Misuari and his companions, who had formed the MNLF while at Pulau Pangkor, returned to work with Lucman. A split occurred when Lucman discovered that Misuari was not exclusively loyal to him but was operating as the chairman of the MNLF and spending funds for the "Moro People's Army." Malaysian aid stopped after the split, but Misuari successfully negotiated in Sabah for its resumption. Lucman tried regaining control of the movement by emphasizing secessionist aims and "denigrating the communist character" of Misuari's organizations and goals. When he failed, Lucman laid down his arms and was granted amnesty by Marcos.[33]

Both Associated Press and Review sources said that Romulo confronted the Malaysian ambassador with the information in a private conversation. The Associated Press account reported that a Malaysian embassy official confirmed the meeting. He said that the ambassador had told Romulo that Malaysia had no knowledge of Malaysian government support for the rebels and suggested that if the Philippines had such information, it should be made public.[34] The official also said that a similar meeting had been held in Kuala Lumpur between the Philippine ambassador and the Malaysian government. The Review article cited Malaysian sources as saying that the government had asked Tun Mustapha about the charges several months ago, but that he denied all knowledge. Sabah sources, however, said that both Tun Mustapha and the equally independent governor of Indonesian Makassar had been jointly channeling aid to the rebels, and that Suharto had questioned the governor on the issue.[35]

Later reports said that Romulo refused to comment on all reports, while Major-General Fidel Ramos, the Constabulary commander, denied knowledge of them. In Kuala Lumpur, both foreign ministry officials and Philippine diplomats disclaimed knowledge of Malaysian-trained Muslims fighting in the Philippines. Tun Razak, in response to a question in Parliament, said that 22,000 refugees from the Philippines had been given shelter on humanitarian grounds. Malaysia regarded the secessionist movement essentially

as an internal affair and consequently adhered structly to a noninter-
ference policy but had expressed concern over the Muslim's plight
to Marcos and asked that he find a peaceful and just solution to the
problem.[36]

Whatever the exact nature of the information and direct
exchanges between Philippine and Malaysian officials, Indonesia
increasingly emerged as a mediator. Marcos reportedly used a
visit between his and Suharto's wives to send word to Suharto that
he discounted reports that the rebels had received help and training
from the Malaysian peninsula but did believe that Sabah was providing
and/or relaying from Libya arms and other aid. He wanted Suharto
to persuade Tun Razak to curtail Tun Mustapha's activities, as well
as to help improve the generally deteriorating relations between
Malaysia and the Philippines.[37] Suharto and Tun Razak met in Penang
on May 3; then Suharto and Marcos met in Sulawesi in late May.
At the end of the Suharto-Marcos meeting the Indonesian statement
referred to participation by Muslims in the Philippine government and
reflected the Indonesian conviction that Manila should make every effort
to talk to the activists' leadership. The Philippine statements stressed
the friendly relations between the Philippines and Indonesia and the
multinational character of ASEAN. Apparently, because of
Indonesian objections, they omitted a reference in an earlier draft
to Indonesia's appreciation for Manila's efforts to uplift its Muslim
minority.[38]

Philippine policies in relation to other Muslim states involved
efforts at de-Muslimizing the rebel leadership by persistently
identifying the attackers on Jolo as "Maoist." The government also
tried to revise downward estimates of damage, particularly that caused
by government shelling. The primary target was Arnold Zeitlin,
Associated Press correspondent in the Philippines, whose reports
from Jolo had been widely circulated. A letter to the foreign ministers
of Egypt, Saudi Arabia, and Kuwait, signed by Romulo, claimed to
"clarify" the "false story" by Zeitlin, "suspected to be a Jewish
journalist," of "alleged continued killing of Muslims by Philippine
government troops." Zeitlin himself was summoned before the
Media Advisory Council to answer charges of "malicious, false and
erroneous reporting."[39]

The attack on Zeitlin was not successful, but the Maoist
identification campaign apparently helped. Whether of nor the MNLF
leaders were Maoist—and Manila presented no evidence that they
were—they were clearly radical and secessionist, and too many Muslims
states had their own counterparts to be enthusiastic about condemning
Manila. The Saudi Arabian foreign minister paid another visit to
Manila, talked with Philippine leaders, "pledged his government's
support for the Philippine Government's attempts to solve the problems,
and promised that oil would continue to flow.[40]

Manila was also anxious about the Islamic summit scheduled for Lahore, Pakistan, in February and the Islamic foreign ministers meeting scheduled for Kuala Lumpur, Malaysia, in June. The issue apparently was not discussed at Lahore, although the report from the four foreign ministers who visited the Philippines in August 1973 was circulated and a decision was made to keep it a secret.

There was, however, considerable discussion at the Kuala Lumpur meetings, despite Malaysia's position that the situation of Muslim minorities in the Philippines was best handled by ASEAN.[41] The Libyan foreign minister raised the issue in his opening speech. He characterized the misery of Philippine Muslims as no "less horrifying than that faced by the Arabs and their sacraments in Palestine" and said that the conference should consider finding a political solution for a problem that was not social but political.[42] In an interview he admitted that Libya and other states were actively aiding the fighting Philippine Muslims. He refused to name the other states, but denied that Libyan arms were being channeled through Malaysia. He also maintained that Libya would continue its support until the Philippine government negotiated a political settlement, which was possible, he thought, if Marcos would meet with the MNLF leaders. "If these people are listened to, they are reasonable enough to realize that they are part of the Philippines and will cooperate within the framework of the Government," he said. But he noted that thus far, rather than taking any practical steps to improve the solution, the Philippines had simply increased its military forces in the South.[43]

In contrast, the Indonesian opening statement reported that the Philippine government had accepted the establishment of a Muslim Welfare Agency, financed through the Islamic Secretariat in cooperation with the Philippine government, and that "the sincerity and willingness of President Marcos to work toward an integrated Philippine society in which Muslims could assume their rightful place were not to be doubted."[44] During the debate Indonesia argued that a call for a "just solution" should be moderated by the phrase "within the framework of the national sovereignty and territorial integrity of the Philippines." Malaysia reportedly wanted the phrase excised.[45]

The final communiqué contained four points. The first called on the Philippine government to stop all actions resulting in "the killing of Muslims and destruction of their properties and places of worship." The second stated the conviction of the conference:

that the socio-economic measures proposed by the Philippine Government to improve the condition of the Muslims would not by themselves solve the problem and urged the Philippine Government to find a political and

peaceful solution through negotiation with
Muslim leaders and particularly, with representatives of the Moro National Liberation
Front in order to arrive at a just solution to
the plight of the Filipino Muslims within the
framework of the national sovereignty and
territorial integrity of the Philippines.

The third appealed to "peace-loving States and religious and international
authorities, while recognizing the problem as an internal problem of
the Philippines," to use their good offices to ensure the safety and
liberties of Philippine Muslims. The final point announced a decision
to create a Filipino Muslim Welfare and Relief Agency and called
for contributions to support its operation. [46]
        After the conference two spokesmen for the MNLF in Kuala
Lumpur said they were "fully in accord" with the letter and spirit
of the communiqué, but Marcos would have to take the initiative in
starting negotiations. His failure to meet the demand for a political
solution would mean that "we will continue our struggle for liberation
until we can enjoy the blessing of national freedom and independence."
The Libyan foreign minister, another Libyan diplomat, and the
Saudi Arabian foreign minister went to Sabah, where the two Libyans
but not the Saudi Arabian, were reporting as receiving "Datukships"
from Sabah's head of state. [47]
        The Lebanese foreign minister went to Manila, where Marcos
gave him the Sultan Kuderat Award for his role in "protecting the
sovereignty and integrity of the Philippines" at the Islamic
minister's conference. Marcos also proclaimed amnesty for all
Muslim rebels, ruled out a military solution to the Muslim insurgency,
pledged increased economic aid, and promised that all Filipino
minority groups would be given "an active political voice in the
country." [48] Muslim attacks in Mindanao had been timed to coincide
with the Kuala Lumpur meetings, and intense fighting continued.
        In the following months peace moves and fighting remained
juxtaposed. When Tun Razak offered the defense portfolio to Tun
Mustapha after the September 1974 Malaysian elections, most
analysts thought that the offer represented an effort, dictated by
both internal and international considerations, to get Mustapha out
of Sabah. Tun Mustapha, however, postponed accepting the position.
In early January 1975 the Philippine government said that Hassan Al
Tohamy, the Egyptian secretary of the Islamic Conference, was in
Manila on the third shuttle of a peace effort and that Marcos had sent
a "top level delegation" to meet Al Tohomy in Jeddah, Saudi Arabia,
with the hope of having talks with Misuari and other insurgent leaders.
The talks were held and deadlocked quickly; a second round, originally

scheduled for April, was not held. The MNLF spokesmen demanded
the creation of an internally sovereign, politically autonomous Bangsa
Moro State, including all of Mindanao, the Sulu archipelago, Basilan,
and Palawan, that would have its own security force and exclusive
responsibliity for maintaining internal order and be loosely associated
with the Philippines. Marcos refused to accept these demands, and
the MNLF refused to negotiate unless he did.[49]

Instead, the Philippine government began a series of meetings
with those Muslims (presumably insurgents, past or present) willing
to attend. With government encouragement the Muslims renounced
any desire for independence or for the kind of autonomy the MNLF
was demanding. When the Islamic foreign ministers' meeting was held
in Jeddah in July, Marcos sent a message communicating this
renunciation and his own plan for "autonomy short of independence,"
the creation of regions in the southern Philippines that would be
headed by "commissioners" directly responsible to Marcos. The
Jeddah meeting, however, affirmed the "work plan" devised by its
own committee as a basis for negotiating for complete agreement
between the MNLF and the Philippine government, and hence implicitly
rejected the Marcos plan and affirmed support for the MNLF's
demands.[50]

In Sabah, meanwhile, Tun Mustapha's position was being
threatened by the formation of a new party determined to oust him
from office. The charges leveled against him publicly—extravagance,
corruption, authoritarianism, secessionist ambitions—were based on
his domestic activities, but the challenge and Mustapha's announcement that he would resign as chief minister clearly had implications
beyond Malaysia. One immediate effect was a decline in the flow of
supplies to Philippine insurgents.[51]

By August the Philippine government was able to announce the
"return" of several insurgents who had held important positions in the
MNLF and who brought many of their men with them. Still the MNLF
leadership refused Marcos's terms, and in many areas fighting
remained intense; and in some areas, particularly Lanao del Sur, it
seemed to be worsening. The use of extortion, frequently associated
with kidnapping, was clearly increasing. Government figures cited
1.5 million refugees.[52] Other reports cited increasing figures of
dead and wounded, growing polarization of the population, and
disruption of economic activities throughout large areas of Mindanao
and Sulu.

CONCLUSIONS

The argument has been that the experience of the 1960s convinced the policy makers of both Malaysia and the Philippines that their regimes were unstable and vulnerable. The vulnerability was caused in part by internal conflicts, which in both countries were related to ethnic factors. In Malaysia the cleavage between Chinese and Malays was perceived as primary, and conflicts within both the Chinese and Malay communities over radical, moderate, and conservative positions were linked to the basic conflict of Chinese-Malay relationships. There was another cleavage—ethnic as well as geographic, historical, and economic—between the peoples of mainland Malaysia and those of Sarawak and Sabah. This cleavage retained a potential for conflict and for secession. Both cleavages reinforced the political power of Tun Mustapha.

In the Philippines conflict was defined primarily in socioeconomic, political, and ideological terms. In the southern Philippines, however, conflict was particularly intense, defined in ethnic (or religious) terms, and had clear ethnic manifestations.

A second result of the 1960s was the realization that relations with neighboring states were important for other than symbolic reasons. Malaysia not only had the experience of "confrontation" with Indonesia, with its accompanying infiltration of guerrillas into the Borneo states, but also the awareness that Britain could not be counted on to subsidize a second such experience. The Philippines had had some Indonesian infiltration during the Sukarno period, and it suspected that Malaysia, or at least Sabah, had reacted to its pursuit of the claim to Sabah by supporting Muslim dissidents. The lesson, then, was that international conflict could exacerbate domestic conflict; the result was a major emphasis put on shared cooperation in ASEAN.

The most intense conflict in the two states after their reconciliation in December 1969 has been the Muslim insurgency in the Philippines. Despite Malaysia's self-conscious identification as a Muslim state, Malaysian policy in relation to the insurgency has been circumspect: It has denied giving support to the rebels, and in Islamic meetings it has generally insisted that the Philippine situation is an internal affair of the Philippines and that what international ramifications the matter had could best be handled within ASEAN. Sabah, however, has played a critical role in the insurgency, if it has done nothing more than provide a sanctuary and supply depot for the rebels. Official Philippine spokesmen have refrained from public criticism of Malaysia and also worked to maintain cooperation in ASEAN. Bilaterally, however, the two states have had significantly fewer direct contacts with each other than either has had with any other state in ASEAN. By

1974 the relationship was showing increasing signs of strain. The decline in Tun Mustapha's power in 1975 may reduce that strain, but the potential remains as long as the power balance in Sabah remains unsettled, the Philippine claim to Sabah remains unresolved, and conflict continues in the southern Philippines. The Philippine-Malaysian "bargain" makes possible cooperation; it does not guarantee amity.

Whether or not fighting continues in the southern Philippines still depends primarily on actions of the Marcos administration and of the Muslim activists. If the Marcos regime does what the Islamic foreign ministers have suggested, or simply implements fully all of its own promises, then it may succeed in stopping the insurgency. Most observers, however, doubt the capacity of the government to do so, whatever their evaluations of the sincerity of its announced intentions. Reservations center on three points: the socioeconomic proposals, political power, and implementation.

The socioeconomic proposals, critics say, have been distressingly superficial; some of them appear to have the potential of compounding problems, particularly in Mindanao. While Marcos has talked of land reform—of distributing land not only to tenants but also to nonlandholding Muslims—he has allowed foreign-backed plantations to expand their landholdings in Mindanao. Urging companies from elsewhere in the Philippines to expand into Mindanao seems less likely to increase employment, its avowed purpose, than to increase further the influx of Christians with dominating positions in the economy. Of equal importance is that the regime has shown a propensity to arrest precisely those people who have been most identified with efforts to bring about genuinely redistributive economic change: members of the Federation of Free Farmers and Catholic and Protestant clergy associated with them, for example.

Meanwhile, political power has been steadily centralized. It is focused in Marcos and his family and friends; shared with technocrats who seem to have authority within limited contexts; and supplemented by relics from or recruits into the old clientelist system, with leaders bribing or frightening followers into quiescence or participation in public meetings. In this situation it is difficult to find roles for Muslims. Some of them have been fitted into technocratic, or at least bureaucratic, slots, as indicated by announcements of Muslim appointments. The Muslim Council announced in May 1974 was composed of Muslims who were former members of Congress and the Constitutional Convention, retired ambassadors, and retired military men with at least the rank of colonel. Successful practitioners of the old-style politics, they can hardly be expected to give advice on socioeconomic change; nor can Rascid Lucman, recognized earlier as the "paramount sultan" of the 19 "Royal Houses of Mindanao and Sulu." Subdividing provinces to create new ones has primarily expanded political opportunities for army commanders, and grouping provinces into regions has apparently only added one more level of administrators directly accountable to Marcos. MNLF leaders have explicitly rejected these kinds of arrangements. It is difficult to conceive of any arrangements that will appeal to them and to Marcos, since the essence of the martial law regime is concentration of authority while the activists' minimum demands call for Muslim autonomy.

Those concerned over the capacity of the regime to implement reforms have noted that at local levels both civilian and military personnel have shown little evidence of "new society" characteristics. Government soldiers in Mindanao and Sulu have been criticized frequently for drunkenness, random firings, and looting. They may well be frightened and alienated, but they are making little contribution to justifying Muslim trust in the regime. Marcos's advisers and military commanders are themselves divided as to the relative priority to be given to purely military as compared with political and socioeconomic actions in the south. The division seems sufficient to obstruct implementation as well as formation of policy.

As for the insurgents, they appear to have several options. They can continue a strategy aimed at the formation of a Bangsa Moro State, either independent or internally sovereign but loosely associated with the Philippines. They can align with other anti-Marcos groups in the Philippines in an effort at internal revolution. Or they can stop or reduce fighting, with or without a negotiated ceasefire and/or "peace" settlement, until conditions under Marcos are clearly better or worse.

Secession would be difficult because of the adamant opposition of the Philippine government, which is based at least partially on Sulu's oil potential, and because of the unwillingness of most Muslim states to endorse this option. The kind of radical autonomy the MNLF leadership has now proposed apparently does have the backing of states affiliated with the Islamic Secretariat, but thus far, except for Sabah and Libya, their backing has been limited to conference statements, diplomacy, and the implicit threat of an oil embargo and/or a withholding of aid or investment funds. Since Christians constitute the majority of the population in the area of the proposed Bangsa Moro State, it seems likely that only a drastic shift in the kind and level of support from outside Muslim sources could persuade Marcos to concede autonomy, as the MNLF defines it. If this shift is not forthcoming, and if changes in the Sabah government mean decreased support from that source, then the MNLF is left with the prospect of a long-term war of attrition.

The second option would not necessarily involve sacrificing Muslim identity, grievances, or causes, but would emphasize grievances and objectives shared with other groups in the Philippines. The status of the National Democratic Front and the relationships

among the New People's Army and the now largely underground Federation of Free Farmers and Christians for National Liberation are
not clear at this point. There does, however, seem to be a basis for
cooperation, and continuing arrests of religious leaders may well
strengthen that basis. Needless to say, this kind of effort has as much
potential for violence as the other and considerably more potential
for hostile outside intervention. Whatever the state of détente, the
United States is more likely to provide weapons for fighting "communists" than for fighting Muslims. Current Muslim aid also might be
jeopardized. But if the Muslim leadership chooses to fight aid for
fundamental shifts in political and socioeconomic power, it may find
more allies among non-Muslim Filipines than among non-Filipino
Muslims.

Otherwise leaders have the choice of temporarily or permanently
abandoning the fight. Pressure or decreased support from Muslim
states and significant concessions from Marcos, if combined with
continuing casualties and defections, would increase the likelihood of
this possibility. Specifically, if Marcos offers concessions along the
lines of the proposals in the Kuala Lumpur communiqué, and if international Muslim leaders are involved in negotiations in a way that
convinces them of Marcos's intentions toward and capability for their
implementation, then the activists' leaders may decide to settle for
less than full autonomy.

At a more general level the data suggest other conclusions. For
Malaysia and the Philippines in the 1960s international conflict appeared
to have the potential for exacerbating domestic conflict involving ethnic groups.

This potential led the two states to policies of deliberately cultivated international cooperation. In the 1970s domestic conflict, particularly that involving Philippine Muslims, threatened to jeopardize
cooperation.

That the policies of cooperation endured suggests that between
1969 and 1975 it was more important for Philippine-Malaysian relations
that both states had plural societies and were in proximity to each
other than that the Muslims in the Philippines were a minority, in
Malaysia a majority. Put more strongly, the identity of the ethnic
groups mattered less than the fact that there were ethnic divisions.
The fact that the two states were adjacent to one another and confronted common regional problems mattered more than that they had
common populations. The decisive factor affecting Philippine-
Malaysian relations was that their leaders felt mutually vulnerable.
In both states domestic instability was accompanied by more pragmatic
foreign policies.

This is not to say that it was insignificant that the Philippine
ethnic group that organized for separatism was Muslim. Wilfred Smith

has argued that Islamic theology has distinctive political implications and has linked those implications to the insistence of twentieth-century Indian Muslims that they be given their own state.[53] Whether or not the "Islamic resurgence" attributed to the Philippines in the 1950s and 1960s had direct separatist implications, it seems clear that young Philippine Muslims who studied in schools in predominantly Muslim countries and participated in Islamic organizations became so discontented with conditions in their own country that they provided the nucleus for the separatist movement.

Certainly a common identification as Muslims, accentuated by the concentration of the Muslim population in a geographically marginal area of the country, provided the bond that linked leaders and followers. Although themselves divided into subgroups so distinct that they can be classified as ethnic entities, the Muslim identity was the critical one. Philippine Muslims felt different from "Filipinos" because "Filipinos" were Christian; they felt "Filipinos" discriminated against them because they were Muslim. Whether or not a separate state was a religious imperative, it seemed to be a logical one. In relation to the Philippine government, Muslim-ness was the ethnic identification that mattered.

Moreover, most of the external assistance to the secessionists has come from two of the most self-consciously Islamic leaders, Kadaffi and Tun Mustapha. It is possible to argue that, after Corregidor, Tun Mustapha had enough hostility toward the Philippine government and a close enough territory to provide incentive and capability for involvement in any insurgency in the Philippines, and that Kadaffi's involvements with insurgent groups have not been limited to those with Muslim participation. Still there is no evidence linking either with other insurgent groups in the Philippines, and public statements by Libyan officials admitting and advocating support have stressed Islamic bonds.

If concern rather than active support is considered, the importance of the rebels' Muslim identification is also evident. While the concern has been qualified by the activists' separatism as well as by their radicalism, it has remained strong enough to give Marcos genuine cause for anxiety. Since not simply the country's reputation but its oil supply is at stake, it is not surprising that the content of Marcos's statements about policies toward Philippine Muslims has a high degree of correspondence with the timing of Islamic conferences. Relations with Malaysia and Indonesia are important not just because of the proximity of the two countries or because of the priority given to ASEAN but because of their influence with other Islamic countries. The likelihood is high that Marcos can cope with whatever aid Libya and Sabah might give to the Muslims; he cannot survive without oil.

NOTES

1. It is significant that, while Tun Mustapha was born in a kampong in the Kudat District of Sabah, he claims paternal lineage from the sultans of Sulu, from whose claims the Philippine government derived its claim to Sabah. During World War II he made contacts with guerrilla movements through relatives in Palawan. Spotlight on Sabah (London: The Diplomatist Publications, 1972), pp. 4-5; Tun Mustapha, "Houseboy, Messenger, Clerk—and Then Came the War," Malaysian Business, October 1973, pp. 33-36.

2. There is a more detailed treatment of Philippine-Malaysian relations, 1962-69, in Lela G. Noble, "The National Interest and the National Image: Philippine Policy in Asia," Asian Survey 13, no. 6 (June 1973): 560-76.

3. Manila Bulletin, March 11, 15, 30, 1970; Manila Times, March 26 and 27, 1970.

4. New York Times, September 9, 1971.

5. Far Eastern Economic Review, July 3, 1971, p. 15.

6. Far Eastern Economic Review, December 18, 1971, p. 17.

7. Arab Report and Record, October 1-15, 1971, p. 533.

8. Asia Research Bulletin 1 (August 1-31, 1971): 270.

9. Asia Research Bulletin 1 (September 1-30, 1971): 352.

10. Far Eastern Economic Review, December 11, 1971, p. 20.

11. Arab Report and Record, June 16-30, 1972, p. 297.

12. Arab Report and Record, October 1-15, 1971, p. 533; Asia Research Bulletin 1 (October 1-31, 1971): 426.

13. Asia Research Bulletin 2 (July 1-31, 1972): 1099.

14. Asian Recorder 18 (September 16-22, 1972): 10988; Arab Report and Record, July 1-15, 1972, p. 343.

15. New York Times, March 24, 1973.

16. An Asian Theology of Liberation: The Philippines (IDOC Documentation Participation Project, the Future of the Missionary Enterprise, no. 5; New York: IDOC/North America, 1973), p. 63.

17. The contrived wording of some of the Malaysian denials suggested that the spokesmen could not or did not want to speak for Mustapha. Both the vagueness and the contradictions indicated that, whatever Mustapha was doing, he did not want to be publicly identified as giving anything other than refuge to Philippine Muslims.

18. See Clenched Fist 1 (July 31, 1973 and September 21, 1973) and 2 (January 15, 1974).

19. Asia Research Bulletin 3 (March 31, 1974): 2436.

20. The New York Times reported on May 11, 1973 that the reconstruction and development program for Mindanao was budgeted

at $135 million for three years; on September 6, 1974, it cited a figure of $63 million for four years.

21. Los Angeles Times, April 9, 1973.

22. New York Times, January 4, 1973.

23. New York Times, March 17, 1973.

24. Foreign Affairs Malaysia 6 (September 1973): 41.

25. Asia Research Bulletin 2 (March 1-31, 1973): 1699.

26. Bangkok Post, April 18, 1973.

27. Foreign Affairs Malaysia 6 (June 1973): 30-31.

28. Asia Research Bulletin 3 (August 1-31, 1973): 1918.

29. Asia Research Bulletin 3 (August 1-31, 1973): 2077.

30. Bulletin Today (Manila), December 2, 6, 11, 1973.

31. Far Eastern Economic Review, March 18, 1974, p. 23.

32. Asia Research Bulletin 3 (March 31, 1974): 2535-36; Straits Times, March 11, 1974.

33. Far Eastern Economic Review, March 25, 1974, pp. 12-13.

34. Straits Times, March 11, 1964.

35. Far Eastern Economic Review, March 25, 1974, p. 14.

36. Philippine Times (Chicago), May 15, 1974.

37. Far Eastern Economic Review, May 13, 1974, p. 10.

38. Far Eastern Economic Review, June 10, 1974, pp. 16-17.

39. Philippine Times, March 31, 1974.

40. Asia Research Bulletin 3 (March 31, 1974): 2535.

41. Far Eastern Economic Review, June 24, 1974, p. 18.

42. Malaysia, press release (PEN. 6/74/153) (Haluar), "Libyan Leader Replies to Tun Razak's Address," June 21, 1974.

43. In May Marcos announced that the manpower of the Philippine Armed Forces (AFP) would double in the next year, going from the current 100,000 to 256,000. Philippine Times, May 5, 1974. An article in the Far Eastern Economic Review on May 20, 1974, contrasted the 100,000 figure with 60,000, the AFP manpower at the time martial law was declared, and the current AFP budget of $300 million, 22 percent of the national budget, with the 1971 figure of $90 million. It said that two-thirds of the AFP's maneuver battalions were stationed in Mindanao. See also Far Eastern Economic Review, July 1, 1974, pp. 12-13; July 8, 1974, pp. 10-11; and Straits Times, June 26, 1974; New York Times, June 27, 1974.

44. Straits Times, June 24, 1974.

45. New York Times, June 27, 1974.

46. Straits Times, June 26, 1974.

47. Far Eastern Economic Review, July 8, 1974.

48. San Francisco Chronicle, June 29 and 30, 1974.

49. New York Times, March 9, 1975.

50. Far Eastern Economic Review, September 12, 1975, p. 24.

51. Far Eastern Economic Review, August 29, 1975, p. 28 ("Malaysia '75 Focus").

52. Los Angeles Times, September 28, 1975.

53. Wilfred C. Smith, Islam in Modern History (New York: The New American Library, 1957).

8

RACE, CLASS, AND
POLITICAL CONFLICT IN A
POSTCOLONIAL SOCIETY
Raymond T. Smith

Guyana, lying on the northeast shoulder of South America, is
the only hemisphere country in which the descendants of immigrants
from India constitute a majority of the population. (Prior to 1966 the
colony was named British Guiana; the name Guyana will be used here
unless the context clearly makes the old name more appropriate.)
This lends a novel aspect to the otherwise common pattern of racial
and cultural diversity that one finds in all countries of the Americas.
The past 25 years have been turbulent ones for Guyana. In 1950 it
was still a British colony but it passed quickly through the stages of
limited constitutional advance; suspension of the constitution for
alleged "communist subversion"; a split in the originally powerful
multiracial nationalist movement; partial resumption of advance
toward constitutional independence with a predominantly Indian-
supported party in office; outbreaks of killing, wounding, rape,
looting, and arson; imposition of a new electoral system successfully designed to replace the majority party by a minority coalition;
the speedy granting of independence followed soon afterward by
consolidation of power by the African-supported party; declaration
of republic status within the British Commonwealth and the establishment of a virtual one-party state.

The most frequently advanced hypothesis to account for Guyana's
troubled political history is that racial and cultural diversity weakens
commitment to national integrity and gives rise to political conflict.
I shall argue that, while Guyana's racial structure has certainly

---

Portions of this article appeared previously in Race 12, no. 197,
published by the Institute of Race Relations, London.

provided the framework within which political conflict has been
expressed, that conflict does not arise in any simple way from the
fact of racial and cultural diversity.

Guyana is a particularly valuable case for exploring the interplay between internal structural factors and the international environment, because British and U.S. influence is rapidly being replaced
by, or counterbalanced by, that of the USSR, Cuba, and China. For
25 years Guyanese politics have been dominated by two men—
Dr. Cheddi Jagan, an East Indian dental surgeon, and Forbes Burnham,
an African lawyer who is leader of the party now in power and prime
minister. The political situation has been profoundly affected not
only by the appeal of these men, each to a particular constituency,
but also by their external alliances and conflicts. It is ironic that
the present external pressures—from Cuba and the USSR in particular—are toward political reunification of Guyana under the leadership
of the man who was supported by the United States in the 1950s and
1960s to steer Guyana away from communism.

Three main sets of factors are important to an understanding
of the Guyana situation. They are: (1) the colonial history of Guyana,
its relation to the United States, to the now emergent Caribbean and
third world groupings, and to the communist blocs; (2) the structure
of the economy and the internal class system; and (3) the extent of
cultural differences, social segregation, and political polarization
between groups defined as "racial." It is impossible to deal with all
these factors in detail, but I will try to summarize each and to assess
the nature of their interaction. I begin with a discussion of race,
class, and culture before turning to an analysis of recent political
history in the context of international forces.

RACE, CLASS, AND CULTURE

Conceptions of race and racial difference constitute some of
the most persistent idea systems in the world; although these ideas
are conditioned by their social, economic, and political contexts,
they are not determined by those factors. It has been suggested by
Clifford Geertz that consciousness of race is an aspect of "primordial
identity," surfacing in the early stages of contact of previously separate "traditional" societies and becoming intensified as they are integrated into more complex, modernizing states, until eventually new
identities are substituted for them.[1] Such a view has the merit of
treating race as a cultural concept, but the notion of primordial
identity still has severe limitations as a means of understanding the
problems of ex-colonial societies. Geertz defines primordial attachment as something that

stems from the "givens"—or more precisely, as culture
is inevitably involved in such matters, the assumed
"givens"—of social existence: immediate contiguity and
kin connection mainly, but beyond them the givenness
that stems from being born into a particular religious
community, speaking a particular language, or even a
dialect of a language, and following a particular social
practice. These congruities of blood, speech, custom,
and so on, are seen to have an ineffable, and at times
overpowering, coerciveness in and of themselves. One
is bound to one's kinsmen, one's neighbour, one's fellow
believer, ipso facto; as the result not merely of personal affection, practical necessity, common interest,
or incurred obligation, but at least in part by virtue of
some unaccountable import attributed to the very tie
itself.[2]

Culture may indeed define certain ties as being primordial in
this sense, but it seems to me that to assume that these sentiments
have explanatory value in the analysis of racial conflict and racial
interaction in complex societies is to reduce the problem to one of
psychology, or social psychology at best. Geertz says, for example:

The power of the "givens" of place, blood, tongue,
looks, and way-of-life to shape an individual's notion
of who, at bottom, he is and with whom, indissolubly
he belongs, is rooted in the non-rational foundations
of personality.[3]

Concepts of racial identity and racial difference exist as part
of a system of cultural definitions that has a structure and persistence
of its own. Such concepts are used, along with other cultural concepts, in the structuring of societal interactions in specific historical
processes, and while this is no great discovery, it is at once difficult
and rewarding to keep it in mind in the analysis of culturally mediated
social behavior.*
The cultural symbols of race in Guyana are extremely complex.
Apart from the incorporation of ideas about physical appearance,
religion, food, dress, toilet habits, and even sexual mores, racial
stereotypes contain ideas about rural-urban differences, occupational

---

* It should be emphasized that Geertz himself is well aware of
this fact and his essay deals with just that system of social interactions.

specialization, differential birthrates, educational level, and living standards. This has been important in the growth of the idea that differences in political and economic interest correspond to differences in race. To what extent is this idea a reflection of reality and how does it become a guide for action?

The present population of about 750,000 is now more than 51 percent of East Indian descent; 30 percent of African descent; 5 percent American Indian; 1 percent Portuguese; 0.6 percent Chinese; 0.4 percent European other than Portuguese; and 12 percent of mixed racial origin. This population is increasing rapidly, and the East Indian population is increasing more rapidly than the rest. The rate of natural increase among Indians is 4.1 percent per annum as opposed to about 2.7 percent for other races.[4]

This contemporary population structure is the end product of a long process of immigration and absorption of new elements into an ever-changing system. The Guyanese social system is not composed of a series of static units in fixed relation to each other. Rather, it is a dynamic system in which there has been continuous movement of persons and groups both geographically and in terms of occupational mobility. The relevant geographical units are also, broadly speaking, economic units: they are sugar plantations; villages established by African slaves soon after slavery was abolished in 1838; rice-growing communities settled by ex-indentured Indians mainly after about 1890; two bauxite mining towns; and one major urban center, Georgetown. The villages and rice-growing communities were formed through the drift of population from the sugar plantations; from the villages people have flowed into Georgetown, into the mining areas of the interior, and on out to other parts of the Caribbean, to Britain, the United States, and to Canada.

The sugar plantations have changed greatly over the past hundred years, but in spite of considerable modernization of management and mechanization of operations, the system of internal stratification is still steeply pyramidal. A small group of top managers still contains a proportion of expatriates; the "junior staff" constitutes a relatively small intermediate group; but the bulk of the labor force consists of laborers engaged in the seasonal tasks of cutting and loading the sugar cane, working in the factory, and maintaining the drainage and irrigation systems.[5] Although sugar workers are now much better paid than they used to be, and considerable progress has been made in stabilizing a year-round labor force, field labor is still one of the least prestigious forms of employment. About 80 percent of workers resident on or close to the plantations are Indians and 15 percent Africans, but less than 25 percent of all Indians are now resident on sugar plantations as opposed to about 70 percent in 1891.[6]

Since there has been little or no mobility from lower to upper levels within the sugar industry, ambitious Indians—like the Africans before them—moved out before moving up in the occupational prestige hierarchy. Today this is changing rapidly and one can drive or walk through the staff housing area of most sugar estates and find Hindu ritual flags planted beside the spacious houses, still bearing names such as Winchester House, which only a few years ago were occupied exclusively by Europeans.

Although the dominant trend among both Indians and Africans was movement out of the plantations into independent villages, there were important differences in the experience of the two groups because of the timing of their shift from plantation labor.

The African villages were established in a burst of fervor at the time of emancipation and the churches were the focus of a concerted effort to "civilize" the Africans and incorporate them into colonial society.[7] Although the dominant activity in these villages was agriculture and plantation labor, these were not valued activities; the elite of the African villages has always been until recently, a group of school teachers and clergymen who dominated all village associational life including local government. It was the children of school teachers who most frequently made it up into the civil service and the professions. But even for ordinary villagers in these church-focused communities the emphasis upon literacy and schooling meant the possibility of filling vacancies in urban occupations such as nursing and the police when a demand arose. In 1946 no less than 97 percent of Africans were literate.

The general propensity of African villagers to migrate in search of work is even more noticeable today. Improved roads with excellent bus and taxi services facilitate contact between the villages and kin who are living in Georgetown or at the bauxite mining towns of Linden and Kwakwani. More young people are going to high school or trade school and looking to employment in the ever-growing government bureaucracies and government-owned enterprises. The bauxite industry is now totally nationalized and the takeover of the sugar industry has begun. The old élites of school masters and clergymen are rapidly being eclipsed by party officials and the managers of government agencies. Local government has been shifted to wider regional councils where party affiliation is a more important criterion for appointment than community ties. This is doing much to break up the local solidarity of the old African village communities even though kinship ties continue to be a strong basis for certain kinds of social solidarity.

In the Indian villages, by contrast, rice farming was the major reason for the establishment of the villages and for some it became the means of accumulating money and the basis for upward social mobility. The opening up of an overseas market for rice coincided with the period of the Indians' major move out of plantation labor, and this is a more important element in their attitude toward farming than any supposed racial or cultural characteristics. The local élite in an Indian village generally consists of the more prosperous farmers, owners of small rice mills or agricultural machinery, and shopkeepers. Not infrequently the same individual will be involved in all three activities and may also be a prominent leader in Hindu or Muslim religious activities.* Rural Indians have always thought of rice farming as a means of accumulating the money that can be the foundation for mobility through education. Since World War II primary education has become, belatedly, as important in Indian communities as it has always been in African villages.

Some years ago it seemed likely that rice farming would follow the pattern of "involution" described by Geertz for Indonesia as more and more people tried to make a living from rice on a land area that cannot easily be expanded and within a market that is limited.[8] Extensive mechanization over the past ten years has at least temporarily checked that process. Instead of an ever-increasing input of manual labor, mechanization has spread to a point where such operations as hand transplanting, hand reaping, and threshing by means of bull-treading are now obsolete in most areas. Although there are some indications that the rate of increase of the Indian population has been checked,[†] the population is certainly not declining. Indians have the same mobility aspirations as Africans, and therefore more of them are now relying on the public educational system as the direct ladder into higher-status employment rather than buying education with funds painfully accumulated through family labor on a small rice farm.

All these forces combine to require drastic revision of the accepted view of Indians as a stable rural agricultural population; they are now highly mobile into urban occupations and, largely but

---

* On the basis of recent field work I would say that this is changing rapidly. The construction of central mills and silos, capable of handling the new varieties of rice, has destroyed the position of the small millers; the spread of cooperative retail shops coupled with the more stringent application of price controls is sapping the influence of small shopkeepers. The new élites are the individuals with political influence and the ability to dispense patronage in the form of employment.

[†]I base this statement upon the slender evidence derived from a detailed restudy (after 20 years) of one Indian rice-farming community.

not entirely because of political factors, many are migrating overseas to Canada, Britain, and the United States.

The city of Georgetown is the obvious arena in which all these different forces and currents come into confrontation, and as we shall see it has been the center of political conflict.

In 1891 Georgetown's population was very different from what it is today. Whites made up 5 percent of the urban population, constituting a tightly knit oligarchy of planters, businessmen, and government officials. The racially mixed, or colored, population was no less than 27 percent, the Portuguese over 10 percent, Indians made up only 8 percent of Georgetown's population while Africans constituted 47 percent. The occupational distribution was fairly clear: the British were in command; the colored were the intermediate grade in the public service and represented in the still small professions of medicine and law; the Portuguese were shopkeepers and clerks in business houses but also had some representation in the free professions; the Africans were laborers, skilled workers, and a few were just beginning to push up into the higher civil service and professions. The Indians in Georgetown were, at that time, predominantly menial laborers apart from a very few who had made their way through shopkeeping into urban trade or through education into white-collar occupations or the professions. These latter were mainly the children of higher-status plantation workers such as interpreters and supervisors.

Today the situation is greatly changed and is still changing rapidly. The proportions of mixed, Portuguese, and whites in the urban population have dropped to 21 percent, 4 percent, and 1 percent, respectively. Africans still make up about half the urban population as before, but the proportion of Indians increased to more than 22 percent in 1960 and obviously much more than that now. Many Indians who continue to live in rural communities within commuting distance of Georgetown actually work in the city, so the Indian representation in the urban labor force is probably greater than in the urban resident population. But these changing proportions of the various races living and working in the urban area are less interesting than the shifting positions in the occupational status scale and the kinds of anxieties and jealousies this has caused.

Georgetown has always been an administrative and commercial center, and although there has been moderate development of light industry, this sector is quite small. High-status employment is to be found mainly in the professions and in the public service. Because the public service is the most immediately sensitive to public pressure, it has been the battleground on which wars for individual and group advancement were fought against what was thought to be prejudice, favoritism, or—in local terminology—"advantage." First the colored group had to fight against the British preference for bringing in Englishmen for top positions. They joined cause with Africans in the demand for Guyanization, and with the imminent granting of independence this battle was won. But soon it became apparent that Indians also were knocking at the door and a great deal of the political conflict of the 1950s and 1960s focused on the competition between Africans and Indians for plum jobs in the public service.*

In the discussion so far I have treated race as a "given"—almost as a "primordial" identity in the sense discussed by Geertz.[9] Relations between races have been seen as an aspect of the historical process of successive waves of immigration, their passage through the plantations and out into villages, the interior, and into the urban area. Although I have spoken arbitrarily of racial "groups," in practice one does not find such groups as organized and bounded entities at all. Let us now examine some of the distinctions between races in more detail before trying to determine their significance in the processes of daily life and of politics in Guyana.

If one looks at the way in which West Indians talk about, define, and manipulate racial categories, one confronts a bewildering, and apparently confused welter of opinions, terms, and emotional reactions to the very idea of race. In a study of kinship carried out in Guyana and Jamaica, interviewers asked informants to give the "race" of each relative on their genealogy.[10] In the course of coding this information it became necessary to develop more than 90 categories in order to express the diversity of terms. However, careful analysis of the categories themselves and the manner in which informants use them reduced this apparent confusion to rather simple proportions.

The key to understanding the way in which categories are culturally defined and constructed is to recognize that there are conceptually "pure" races that can be "mixed." The distinctive characteristic of "race," or of "a race," is that it is believed to be a distinct physical type, an entity symbolized by a particular kind of "blood." In Guyana these "races" constitute a finite array of ideally conceived pure types: European or white; African or black; East Indian; Chinese; Portuguese; and Amerindian. The census lists "mixed" as a racial type, but this is a bureaucratic classificatory device and not a culturally defined racial category. Any individual of mixed racial descent is theoretically capable of being described in terms of the specific proportion of each "blood"; in the event that it is impossible to trace the descent with

---

*In this respect the situation was very much like that in Belgium, Canada, Nigeria, and other places where "ethnic" conflict has been important.

that degree of precision, the uncertainty is accepted but a new racial
type is not thereby created.

The system of racial categories in Guyana is complicated by the
sequential appearance of new "races." The original schema involved
a polarity of "white" and "black," with a series of intermediate categories defined in terms of the proportion of each "blood." The introduction of other racial groups led to the production of new mixtures;
in Guyana the Hindi word dugla came to be applied to almost any mixture, frequently qualified by a racial term, as in "Chinee dugla" or
"coolie dugla." Such terms are not always complete in themselves
but lead immediately to explication in terms of racial or kinship origin.
Individuals of mixed racial origin are sometimes absorbed into one or
other of the major socially significant groups, which are then often
given a racial designation. Thus it has been common to speak of the
"colored middle class"—which contains individuals of quite diverse
racial origin—or of "African villages" in which a great deal of inter-
mixture between Africans, Europeans, Chinese, Portuguese, Amerindians, and East Indians takes place. It is important to recognize
the difference between the use of racial labels to distinguish major
social units, and the concept of race as a set of cultural categories
defined by reference to the distinctive characteristic of pure types of
"blood" and their mixture.

One other distinction should be made; in trying to understand
the meaning of racial categories it is usual to concentrate attention on
stereotypes—that is, the specific characteristics attributed to races.
However, it is clear that these attributes can vary a great deal—and
certainly they can receive differential stress—without altering the
basic structure of the category system. For example, it may be said
that blacks are lazy, sexually lax, and irresponsible, but these are
characteristics that may be attributed to poor, low-status people of
any race and are not the distinctive characteristic of being black.
The distinctive characteristic of being black is that the person is believed to have distinctly "black" inherited racial characteristics
symbolized as "blood," which may manifest itself in a wide variety
of ways. From the point of view of the individual, then, race is a
diffuse quality of being, relevant in a system of racial categorization,
in which the categories are defined by reference to the concept of
"blood." The specific attributes of a race may vary at different times,
in different places, and may change—often rather quickly. It therefore
would seem that it is the persistence of the racial categories themselves, rather than an array of stereotyped attributes that makes
"race" available as a device that may be used for the interpretation
of social life and the experience of social conflict.

In the West Indies there has always been a tendency to identify
"races" with "cultures," a tendency that began with the assumption

that black slaves were inherently incapable of becoming "civilized."
At the same time, and in direct contradiction there has been a deliberate, and largely successful, attempt to create a unitary society ,
through the establishment of common laws, an open labor market, and
a national system of compulsory education. Some cultural differences
persist (or are re-created) and serve as markers of identity. Even
small differences in culture can become the basis of deep social divisions; the danger of regression to racial violence is a real one that
has made itself manifest on numerous occasions in Guyanese history.
However, it is important to recognize that cultural differences between
racially defined groups are not a matter of the survival of cultural
forms. On the contrary, much of the cultural form is re-created as
a symbolic vehicle for the expression of deference claims on the part
of the upwardly mobile.

Certain basic facts about the cultural forms of everyday life in
Guyana should be made clear prior to any consideration of the role
of cultural differences in social and political life. All Guyanese speak
English as their mother tongue; some older East Indians may speak
Hindi or Urdu fluently, and many younger Indians pick up the rudi-
ments of the language through the schools attached to temples and
mosques and through attendance at Indian films. A few Amerindians
in the more remote areas continue to use their own languages. Some
efforts are being made to teach African languages, but there seems
to be little doubt that Guyana will remain an English-speaking enclave
on a continent where Spanish and Portuguese are dominant. Hinduism
has been reshaped into a "church" religion that can take its place
beside Christianity and Islam.[11] No demands have been made so far
about the teaching of language or history that would seriously conflict
with the policy of developing a "Guyanese" school curriculum, and
the university has not been troubled with disputes over the "racial"
content of the courses. Public holidays have long been arranged equit-
ably between Christians, Hindus, and Muslims, and the radio stations
broadcast special religious and musical programs to suit different
tastes. The difference in taste certainly exists, with Indian music and
Indian films being almost universally preferred by Indians. There is
no segregation in any phase of public life or in housing; reference to
"African" and "Indian" villages gives the impression of greater segregation than actually exists, although the periods of political violence
in the 1960s resulted in the large-scale movement of racial minorities
out of the villages in the areas of maximum conflict.

There has been much racial mixing, often as the result of
casual or nonlegal unions, but the kinship ties created by even informal
unions are clearly recognized and socially important. Intermarriage
between Indians and persons of other races is not common, but it
does occur and is not exceptionable when it does. On genealogies one

often finds racial intermarriage, and in these cases it occasions no comment even from people who will express strong racial prejudice in other contexts. At the level of everyday life, relations between Guyanese of all racial backgrounds are conditioned by personal, neighborhood, and associational rather than by racial factors, but racial concepts are an ever-present reality and they can always be invoked as an explanation of, or a tool to be used in, conflicts of all kinds.

INTERNAL POLITICS AND OUTSIDE INFLUENCE, 1953-66

Guyanese politics have always been oriented toward the outside; even when they have involved bitter struggles between contending groups within the country, outside alliances have generally been decisive. Until 1953 Guyana was governed directly by Britain. In that year a start toward self-government was made through constitutional reform and the introduction of universal adult suffrage.[12] The recommendations of the constitutional commission appointed by the Colonial Office stimulated a veritable avalanche of political aspirants, and a number of new parties mushroomed overnight to try to capture the votes of a newly enfranchised electorate. A broad-based, leftwing party under the dual leadership of Dr. Cheddi Jagan and Forbes Burnham was elected to office with a clear majority of seats on a platform that promised radical social and economic change and a rapid progression toward complete independence. After 133 days the People's Progressive Party was removed from office and the constitution suspended in order, it was officially stated by the British government, to prevent the subversion of the constitution and the establishment of a communist regime. British troops were landed to ensure that the wishes of the British government were observed.

During the campaign leading up to the election of 1953 there had been serious problems within the PPP, particularly over the question of strategy. Dr. Jagan was trained as a dentist in the United States, where he married a woman who shared his political interests and became the general secretary of the People's Progressive Party. The Jagans set the general radical tone and direction of the party through their writing in Thunder, the party news-sheet, and they became the chief symbols of "communist ideology" so far as the opposition was concerned. Dr. Jagan's main constituency was in the sugar plantations where wages and working conditions had always been productive of dissatisfaction.

When Burnham returned to Guyana from his studies at King's College, University of London, and the Inns of Court, he soon became involved in trade union organization. His power base was in Georgetown and his constituency was the African working class. However, he also had close ties to the urban middle class, and particularly to those whose Guyanese nationalism was rooted in the experience of British racial discrimination. Burnham joined with the Jagans soon after his return, determined to fashion the People's Progressive Party into the instrument for carrying Guyana into complete independence from British rule. He soon became aware that many who were prepared to support him personally were quite opposed to the Jagans. Their open espousal of the procommunist line was felt to be bad tactics at a time when the United States and Britain were becoming obsessed by the idea that international communism had to be stopped whereever it manifested itself within their sphere of influence.

After the PPP was removed from office, the rift between Burnham and the Jagans grew wider and eventually resulted in a split in the party. Two factions, led by Burnham and Jagan, each claimed to be the "true" PPP, until eventually Burnham organized a separate party, the People's National Congress, leaving Jagan as leader of the now depleted People's Progressive Party.[13]

This split in the PPP took place in 1955; the following ten years saw a bewildering series of shifts in party alliegance, creation of new parties, mergers, and further splits—all of which involved responses to events outside Guyana or to the anticipated actions of the British and U.S. governments. For example, in 1956 two of Dr. Jagan's most vocal non-Indian supporters, Martin Carter and Rory Westmaas, resigned from the party. Both had been on the extreme left of the party and both had been profoundly affected by Khrushchev's revelation of the crimes of the Stalin era, and by the suppression of the Hungarian uprising by Russian troops. However, their general disillusionment was compounded by the personal attacks launched by Dr. Jagan at the 1956 party congress, accusing them of leftwing deviationism. Even more important was their interpretation of Dr. Jagan's continued failure to come out in favor of West Indian Federation, a failure they interpreted as pandering to East Indian racial prejudice against being submerged within a predominantly African West Indian Federation.

Even more affected by what he interpreted as Dr. Jagan's increasing deference to Indian prejudices was Sydney King (who has since adopted the "African" name Eusi Kwayana); since 1956 he has acted as a political independent, as a member of Burnham's party, as an extreme African cultural nationalist, and more recently as a semirecluse in his native village of Buxton from whence he periodically delivers a vitriolic attack upon one or other actor in Caribbean events.

Dr. Jagan did indeed demonstrate a tendency to come to terms with Indian prejudices against federation and to woo East Indian conservatives into supporting his faction of the PPP, mainly because of his fear that new parties organized with the backing of the British sugar interests would erode his remaining Indian support through their strong antifederation platforms. [14] On the other side of the fence, Burnham was strengthening his support by projecting the image of a more competent administrator and a more politically moderate statesman. However, the elections of 1957, which marked a partial resumption in the progress toward self-government, revealed Burnham's narrow base of support. His faction of the PPP won only three seats, all in Georgetown, as opposed to nine won by Jagan's faction 14 were contested.

In 1959 Burnham formed a new party, the People's National Congre and then he persuaded the leaders of the old conservative middle-class United Democratic Party, which still held some African support, to merge with the PNC. Henceforth Guyanese politics would be dominated by Jagan's PPP and Burnham's PNC. Although each party made efforts, and continues to make efforts, to be a Guyanese national party with multiracial leadership, electoral support has become increasingly polarized by race with Indians voting solidly for the PPP (at least until the 1973 election) and Africans for the PNC. A third party, the United Force, led by a prominent businessman, Peter D'Aguiar, and formed in 1960, had enough support from the conservative section of the urban middle class and from the Amerindian population, which it carefully cultivated, to make it a factor in the closely balanced political situation.

With electoral support polarized in this way and with the population distribution favoring Dr. Jagan's party, the PPP won not only the 1957 election but also that of 1961. At this stage it appeared that the People's Progressive Party was destined to become the dominant party in Guyana's future, and the signs were that the British would reverse their previous stand and yield up power to Jagan as prime minister of an independent Guyana.

Numerous attempts were made to heal the rift between Jagan and Burnham and to produce some sort of coalition between the two parties. [15] After the 1961 election Burnham, at a public dinner in honor of Jagan's assumption of office as Guyana's first premier, renewed his pre-election pledge to support the demand for immediate independence. However, it was becoming increasingly evident to Burnham that he would be destined for permanent exclusion from power if race continued to be the dominant factor in electoral support in an independent Guyana, and if he were unable to use whatever power he posessed to bargain himself into a position of reasonable influence in a coalition. Every attempt at arranging a coalition foundered on the question of how much governmental power should be yielded up to the PNC, but the unknown factor in the situation was the question of how external power and influence could be manipulated to affect the internal balance of power. In the period after 1961 this factor became crucial.

The simplest explanation of Guyanese political process supposes that it is a struggle between racial groups to fill with their own members the positions left vacant by the British as they relinquish control. Guyanese themselves are inclined to explain local politics in this way, and indeed the explanation does cover some important aspects of the situation. But it does not exhaust all the relevant facts, nor does it provide the analytical categories necessary to an understanding of Guyanese social structure and politics. If the real basis of political conflict in Guyana is simple racial communalism, then the ideological posture of political parties and leaders would be of little account since it would simply be a mask behind which hides the real face of ethnic sectionalism. Yet we know that ideological posture has been of the greatest importance, especially to those who decide which Caribbean governments are "acceptable" to the interests, or the assumed interests, of the United States and other great powers.

Arthur M. Schlesinger, Jr., in A Thousand Days, tells how President Kennedy and his advisers thought about the Caribbean and Latin America and how they assessed the leaders of hemisphere countries.[16] In October 1961, almost immediately after taking office, Jagan went to Ottawa and to Washington with the primary purpose of seeking economic assistance. In Washington he did not make a very good impression, according to Schlesinger. President Kennedy had seen him interviewed on the television program "Meet the Press" and had thought him slow to denounce the USSR and evasive in disavowing communist affiliations. At a meeting with the President and his advisers, Schlesinger and George Ball, Jagan was found to be "romantic," "naive," and not subtle enough in distinguishing between the socialism of Harold Laski and the less benign variety of the editors of Monthly Review.

Burnham, then leader of the opposition, went to Washington a short time later. He made a much better impression, for of him Schlesinger writes:

> Burnham's visit left the feeling, as I reported to the
> President, that "an independent British Guiana under
> Burnham (if Burnham will commit himself to a multi-
> racial policy) would cause us many fewer problems than
> an independent British Guiana under Jagan." And the
> way was open to bring this about, because Jagan's
> parliamentary strength was larger than his popular
> strength; he had won 57% of the seats on the

basis of 42.7% of the vote. An obvious solution
would be to establish a system of proportional representation.

This, after prolonged discussion, the British
Government finally did in October 1963; and the elections
held finally at the end of 1964 produced a coalition
government under Burnham. With much unhappiness
and turbulence British Guiana seemed to have passed
safely out of the communist orbit.[17]

Schlesinger's statement not only betrays lack of real
understanding of Guyana's internal problems and a preoccupation with
preventing any spread of the Cuban experience, but it also passes
over in silence the consequences in human suffering that followed
upon the implementation of U.S. policy in relation to Jagan and
Guyana. The details of the manner in which the United States
persuaded the British government to impose proportional
representation on Guyana are not known, but we do know that it
took considerable time during which there was a concerted attempt
by opponents both within and outside Guyana to demonstrate that
Jagan could not govern the country.

During the election campaign of 1961 the United Force had
stepped up its campaign of anticommunist propaganda, and there
had been a series of visits to the country by anticommunist campaigners
from North America.* However, Jagan's first difficulties arose as
a result of his budget proposals, which were announced early in 1962.
In order to raise revenue to pay for long-awaited pay increases for
civil servants and to finance various development plans, Jagan,
following the advice of a British economist, proposed wide-ranging
new taxes including a capital gains tax, property tax, gift tax, purchase
taxes, and most controversial of all, a system of compulsory savings.
The storm center of opposition to the new budget was Georgetown and
the most vocal were the representatives of the urban middle class, led
by the merchants.

However, the widespread dissatisfaction caused by the increase
in prices that immediately followed the announcement of the budget
encouraged all of Jagan's political opponents—and most notable
Burnham—to join in the agitation. In early February demonstrations
against the People's Progressive Party were stepped up; the Civil
Service Association went on strike; Burnham joined with D'Aguiar

---

* Principal among these were Dr. Fred Schwartz and Dr.
Joosot Sluis of the Christian Anti-communist Crusade.

in breaking the emergency regulations that prohibited demonstrations and assembly in the immediate vicinity of public buildings; and finally on February 16 there was an outbreak of rioting, arson, and looting and Jagan was forced into the ignominious position of having to ask the British governor to provide British troops to restore order in his own capital city. This was the first clear indication that the People's Progressive Party was faced with the active opposition of the urban population, and particularly of the urban middle class, which dominated not only business but also the bureaucracy that was the instrument through which Jagan's government had to operate. [18]

A constitutional conference, which had been scheduled to be held in May 1962 for the purpose of arranging the form of the final granting of self-government, was postponed until October of the same year. At this conference, held in London, the strategy of demanding proportional representation so that Jagan's party could be replaced by a coalition of the People's National Congress and the United Force was the dominant issue. The conference ended in deadlock with the British government taking the position that the parties to the conference should be unanimous in their acceptance of the constitution on which independence would be based, and with the PNC and UF refusing to budge on the issue of proportional representation. The colonial secretary adjourned the conference, stating that if disagreement between the parties continued and there was any deterioration of conditions within Guyana, then the British government would have to consider imposing a solution. Although it was unclear what solution he had in mind, this was clearly an invitation to the opposition parties to continue their demonstration that there could be no political stability in Guyana so long as Jagan's party was in office. We know that the U.S. government was urging the imposition of proportional representation, but it is equally clear that the British government had not fully decided how, or even whether to do this in 1962.

During 1963 the campaign of disruption of the PPP government focused upon trade union activities, and the Central Intelligence Agency lent its support to the campaign in a way that was probably decisive for its success. [19] The event that precipitated a prolonged general strike was the introduction of a new Labor Relations Bill, which provided for secret polls to determine which union within a particular industry should be recognized as the official bargaining agent. This legislation had been a bone of contention for a very long time and had even been an issue in 1953. The reason was that the enactment of such a bill would probably result in the PPP-affiliated Guiana Agricultural Workers Union becoming the official bargaining agent in the sugar industry in place of the less militant Man Power Citizen's Association, which was led by one of Jagan's major opponents.

The bill was debated in the legislature on April 17, 1963; a general strike was declared on April 18 and lasted for almost three months. The strikers were sustained by considerable money funneled into Guyana through the International Confederation of Free Trade Unions and other sources in the United States, while at the same time the strike pushed Jagan into developing closer relations with Cuba and the USSR from which sources he obtained supplies of gasoline and flour, in particular, which was necessary to keep the country going. Violence stepped up during June with attacks upon government offices as well as scattered outbreaks of violence of a more general nature.

The conference to settle upon a constitution for an independent Guyana resumed on November 22, 1963, in London. Once again there was deadlock and this time Jagan agreed to let the British colonial secretary arbitrate. The decision that Duncan Sandys then announced contained the main provision remarked upon by Schlesinger after his meeting with Burnham in 1962—elections under a system of proportional representation to precede the granting of independence. Now in effect, the decision had been made to depose Jagan prior to granting independence.* Although the People's Progressive Party continued in office, it was gradually denuded of its powers through the action of the governor, and it now became the turn of the PPP to protest at the imminent shift in the locus of power and to try to demonstrate to the outside world that the imposition of proportional representation would lead to political instability and social unrest. During the first six months of 1964 there existed what amounted to a state of civil war, which became in effect a race war between East Indians and Africans. Much of the unrest centered upon the sugar estates where strikes and disturbances were countered by the employment of outside workers, many of them Africans. But the conflict escalated and became much more generally racial, with murder, rape, beating, and the destruction of property commonplace. The violence peaked with the infamous "Wismar riots" in May 1964, when all the Indians living in the town of Wismar across the river from the bauxite mining town of Mackenzie (now renamed Linden, one of Linden Forbes Sampson Burnham's given names) were driven out and their homes burned. Many were killed or injured and there

------

*This was not the announced reason, of course. The then secretary of state for the colonies, Duncan Sandys, expressed the view that the new electoral system would break the racial deadlock and bring new elements into politics.

was widespread rape and beating.* The violence resulted in a large-scale redistribution of population as Indian and African minorities moved out, or were driven out, of communities where they had lived peacefully for many years. A total of 176 people were killed and 920 injured during 1964; by the middle of June, 32 PPP members including the deputy premier and a number of legislators were in detention under emergency regulations enacted by the governor. In effect, PPP control was at an end.

Elections under the system of proportional representation were held in December 1964. Although the PPP obtained the highest number of votes with a total of 109,332, the PNC (with 96,567) and the United Force (with 26,612) were able to form a coalition government in which Peter D'Aguiar held the post of minister of finance. Burnham moved swiftly to secure his position and to forestall any further violence by using the emergency regulations to detain PPP leaders suspected of planning subversion of the imposed settlement. A conference held to fix a date for final independence was held in London, despite the refusal of the People's Progressive Party to participate, and on May 26, 1966, Guyana became independent with Burnham as prime minister.

This is the point in Guyanese history at which, in the complacent words of Schlesinger, "With much unhappiness and turbulence British Guiana seemed to have passed safely out of the communist orbit." The unhappiness and turbulence of the years between 1953 and 1964 were directly related to the degree of intervention in Guyanese affairs by Britain and the United States. There is no gainsaying the fact that divisive factors were present within Guyana itself, particularly the factors of race and of competition for limited opportunities for power and upward occupational mobility. However, the old People's Progressive Party represented a coalition of forces, and there was at least an even chance that its structure could have been strengthened to contain racial conflict. The issues that came to the fore during the 133 days of PPP rule in 1953 were mainly left in abeyance between 1955 and 1970; they were the issues of economic development and radical

---

*The Wismar massacre was followed some two weeks later by the explosion and sinking of a launch carrying African passengers from Georgetown to Wismar, resulting in the loss of life of about 25 persons. It has never been established, to the best of my knowledge, whether this explosion was a deliberate act of sabotage, the action of agents provocateurs, or an accident on the part of individuals transporting explosives for use elsewhere. It is characteristic of Guyana that all three theories have been, and continue to be, believed.

social change, and primarily they concerned the relation between the Guyanese government and people and the expatriate firms that controlled the major sectors of the Guyanese economy—the sugar and bauxite companies. As soon as the political situation was stabilized, by virtue of the fact that Britain and the United States threw the whole weight of their support behind Burnham and helped him to build up a strong internal security force of police and army units, these fundamental issues surfaced again.

THE POSTINDEPENDENCE PERIOD: UNITY RESTORED OR DIVISION CONSOLIDATED?

It is clear in retrospect, and it was clear at the time, that the British colonial secretary imposed the system of proportional representation in order to create a situation in which Jagan's party would be excluded from office. The electoral system became a simple one in which the whole country was treated as one constituency and each party contesting the elections was allotted a number of seats proportional to the votes it received. Although Jagan was excluded from office because of the arrangement between Burnham and D'Aguiar, the electoral lead enjoyed by the PNC-UF combination was slender. The manner in which the situation had been defined as a life-or-death struggle between the essentially racially based parties can be judged from the fact that in the 1964 elections no less than 98 percent of the eligible voters cast ballots. Since the East Indian population was already larger than all other races combined, even though the age structure of the population meant that the proportion of persons of voting age was lower than the proportion of Indians generally, it was only a matter of time before the PPP would be in a position to win a majority of seats even under the system of proportional representation. Burnham's position appeared to be less than enviable; he was dependent upon an extremely conservative party to maintain a majority in parliament, and he faced the prospect of a gradual erosion of seats if population growth followed its past trajectory and if race continued to be the major factor affecting voting behavior. His main source of strength lay in the fact that he controlled the police and the army, both of which were, and are, predominantly African, that he had the support of the urban population and of the ultimately decisive British and U.S. governments. He therefore began to consolidate his position using a number of different strategies.

The first, and essential, strategy was to make clear that he was not merely in office but that he had the power to implement decisions. Conversely, of course, it was politic for the PPP to challenge the legitimacy of the PNC dominance by fomenting civil disobedience of all kinds. However, after 1966 the combination of British and American aid in strengthening the army and the police, the implementation of the provisions of a far-ranging security act under which the government could order preventive detention and impose life imprisonment and/or flogging for the illegal possession of firearms, plus an increasing amount of economic assistance that provided employment and facilitated the improvement of such amenities as roads, drainage, and irrigation and housing, all served to make violent opposition less feasible.

Burnham's second problem was to increase his parliamentary strength and rid himself of dependence upon the casting votes of D'Aguiar's United Force. After 1966 D'Aguiar became increasingly critical of Burnham's economic and development plans and in 1967 he resigned as minister of finance. Three members of the PPP crossed the floor of the House to vote with the PNC and in 1968 the United Force abandoned support of the PNC and began to vote with the PPP on certain key issues. However, Burnham retained his majority since one UF member remained loyal to him.

The principal source of conflict between Burnham and D'Aguiar, apart from economic policy, was the forthcoming election. Burnham was planning to hold the election, obligatory by 1969, in 1968 and he had begun an extensive system of registration of voters for which he employed an American company, Shoup Registrations Systems International Inc., of West Chester, Pa., well known for its work in such places as South Vietnam. Rightly or wrongly, this company was suspect to the opposition, but even more suspect was the provision in the electoral law that provided for the registration of "overseas voters of Guyanese descent." When the election was held in December 1968 the overseas vote produced 34,329 votes for the PNC as opposed to 1,003 votes for the PPP. The People's National Congress obtained 55.8 percent of the vote and 30 seats in the National Assembly, as opposed to the People's Progressive Party's 36.5 percent and 19 seats, and the United Force's 7.4 percent and 4 seats. Quite apart from the overseas vote, the PNC obtained more votes internally than had been expected. This was widely attributed to tampering with the ballot boxes and to the improper use of proxy and postal votes, but it is also likely that some transfer of support from Jagan to Burnham was taking place.

The idea that Indian voters all support the People's Progressive Party is quite erroneous; there has always been a sizable minority of Indians who are deeply suspicious of the socialist policies of the PPP and who have always voted for apparently more conservative candidates. The United Force undoubtedly enjoyed some Indian support as did the large number of shortlived splinter parties such as the Justice Party, the Guiana United Muslim Party, and the National Labour

Front. With Burnham's increasing support from the United States and his ability to dispense patronage in the Indian areas it would have been surprising if he did not win the support of some of the more conservative Indians despite the residue of racial hatred left from the 1962-64 period. Conversely, a minority of Africans have always supported the socialist policies of the PPP and the party has consistently claimed that the number of such supporters would inevitably grow as the contradictions of the procapitalist policies of the PNC began to produce unemployment and increasing misery for the working class.

In order to implement his declared policy of healing the breach produced by the extensive violence of the early 1960s, Burnham made a number of high-level appointments of Indians in his government; he set up the office of ombudsman; and as early as 1965 he asked the International Commission of Jurists to investigate the question of racial imbalance in the public service and to make recommendations for its redress. None of these measures has destroyed the widespread feeling among Indians that they, and their interests, remain unrepresented, but they have produced a real situation in which Indians are in fact participating on a fairly extensive scale in the government, the civil service, the judiciary, and other key occupational areas. One therefore has a situation very like that in the 1940s when Guyanese were increasingly achieving high positions in the civil service but felt that the pace of their advance was slowed by British prejudice; here Indians are convinced that there is widespread discrimination against them, while at the same time they display obvious signs of increased participation.

Guyana was declared a republic within the British Commonwealth in 1970; since that time there has been a marked shift in the general direction of economic policy and political strategy on the part of the People's National Congress. The initial formulation was fairly muted. It was declared that Guyana would become "the world's first Cooperative Republic" and that henceforth the government's policy would be to encourage the growth of the cooperative sector alongside the public and the private sectors. There was clearly a racial-ideological element in this choice, since the African villages founded after emancipation were generally founded as cooperative villages. (The fact that they failed to progress until such time as they were brought under central government control seems to have been forgotten or ignored.) The choice of February 23 as the date of the declaration of the republic status was also designed to appeal to African pride, since this was the 207th anniversary of the Berbice Slave Rebellion led by a slave named Cuffy, who was declared to be the national hero. As many commentators pointed out, the gradual growth of the "cooperative" sector would not in itself reflect any transition to socialism, but seemed to be merely a means of encouraging Africans to participate more fully in entrepreneurial activities.

A major shift in the whole direction of PNC policies was signaled by the decision to nationalize the Demerara Bauxite Company Ltd. on February 23, 1971—the first anniversary of the republic of Guyana. Originally the government had intended negotiating to acquire 51 percent of the shares of the company, a subsidiary of the Aluminium Company of Canada, but when talks broke down Burnham decided to acquire total control. Since then the government also has nationalized Reynolds' Mines Ltd., an American subsidiary located at Kwakwani on the Berbice River. The bauxite industry in Guyana is now totally nationalized. In the wake of the new American policy of détente with the Soviet Union and China, Guyana has moved swiftly to establish itself as a vocal member of various third world organizations and is developing economic relations with China, the USSR, Eastern Europe, and Cuba.

These developments have been considerably accelerated since 1973 when the last elections were held. Prior to the general election of July 16, 1973, Burnham announced that his party hoped to secure more than two-thirds of the votes cast—a result that would provide a clear mandate for the People's National Congress to revise the constitution. In view of the continued identification of most Indians with the People's Progressive Party, or with the United Force, and in view of the fact that there was a growing feeling among the urban middle class that Burnham was already aggregating far too much power into his own hands, this was a bold announcement. As Janet Jagan points out in her analysis of the elections, there was the possibility that the pre-election demand for a two-thirds majority would boomerang as opponents of the PNC turned out in larger numbers, and marginal supporters decided that two-thirds would be too much.[20]

The PNC obtained 71 percent of the votes, giving the party 37 out of 53 seats, the PPP 14 seats, with two seats going to a merged Liberator Party and United Force. The PPP and the Liberator Party have so far refused to take their seats on the grounds that the elections were totally fraudulent since there was widespread tampering with the ballot boxes and widespread irregularity in voting procedures. During five months spent in Guyana in 1975 I met no one who believed that the elections of 1973 were fair; in the African villages supporters of the People's National Congress boast openly of the manner in which they were able to register multiple votes, to vote for people who had been long dead, and of how they coerced East Indians living in the community into voting for the PNC. In the Indian villages everyone has stories of how ballot boxes were removed by the army, opened, and stuffed with substitute votes. Whatever the truth of the matter, the fact is that the 1973 elections have put the PNC leaders in a position where they can claim formal legitimacy for whatever policies they wish to introduce.

Since the end of 1973 the government has consolidated its position and has moved markedly further toward greater centralization

of control of the economy at home and toward closer relations with
the communist countries abroad. Ownership of the two daily newspapers has been acquired by the government; of the two radio stations
one is still nominally privately owned but it does not carry material
critical of the government.* The People's Progressive Party continues to publish a newspaper, The Mirror, the main distribution of
which is in the rural Indian communities. However, the company has
grave difficulty in obtaining newsprint, which is controlled by the
government, and the typesetting with obsolete equipment is so bad
that the paper is often almost illegible. Burnham has announced
that the constitution is being rewritten, although there is considerable
opinion within the government that a new constitution is not really
necessary since the PNC at present operates a virtual one-party state.

In a speech delivered to a special party congress held in December
1974 Burnham declared that the decision had been made "that the
emphasis should be on mobilizing the nation in every sphere and not
merely for periodic elections and in support of specific actions and
programmes. It was also decided that the Party [meaning the People's
National Congress] should assume unapologetically its paramountcy
over the Government which is merely one of its executive arms."[21]
Although no formal constitutional instruments have been promulgated
to implement this decision, it appears that the office of the general
secretary of the PNC, a post held by Dr. Ptolemy A. Reid, has been
merged with that of the deputy prime minister and minister of national
development, posts held by the same individual. Vehicles belonging
to this ministry now have the PNC name painted in above the words
"Ministry of National Development." The government is gradually
acquiring more extensive control over the economy: by imposing
stringent import controls; by setting up more government trading
corporations (a government bookstore has just been opened and will

---

*   In a study commissioned by the Caribbean Publishing and Broad-
casting Association, Dr. Everold N. Hosein of the University of the
West Indies has expressed the opinion that Guyana does not now have
a free press. The government owns both daily newspapers and one of
the two radio stations. However, Dr. Hosein did not base his judgment
about press freedom simply on government ownership; he specifically
states that there is evidence of both overt and covert control by the
government of the statement of dissenting opinion and that this applies
to the nongovernment radio station as well as to the other press agencies. The government of Guyana has rejected the report as superficial and unprofessional and has expressed willingness to cooperate
in a more adequate study.

be the sole importer and distributor of school books); by increased
nationalization of major industries, with a start being made in the
sugar industry in early 1975 when the prime minister announced the
takeover of the Demerara Company, which operates two of the largest
sugar estates in the country. A system of national service has been
inaugurated; although it is not compulsory as yet, it has been announced
that completion of a period of national service will be a prerequisite
for entry to the University of Guyana and the Teacher's Training College. The minister of cooperatives and national mobilization, Hamilton
Green, has stated that the government intends to make parents' contributions to self-help projects (which are mainly party-initiated), rather
than academic achievement, the criteria for admission to secondary
schools.[22]

At present the majority of East Indians regard these developments
as inimical to their interests. This attitude stems partly from the fact
that the PNC is still considered an "African" party, even by the considerable number of Indians who are members of the party and who hold
office in both national and local government. At the same time it is
becoming increasingly difficult to distinguish between the declared
policies of the People's Progressive Party and those of the PNC, so
that Jagan has progressively had the ground cut from under him. Or,
to put it another way, the policies of the People's National Congress
are gradually converging upon those espoused by the PPP. Most important of all, Burnham is gradually replacing Jagan as the spokesman
for the Guyanese "masses" in communist and third world circles. In
April 1975 Burnham made a state visit to Cuba where he was given
Cuba's highest honor, the José Marti award, by Prime Minister Fidel
Castro. Shortly before this he had made a state visit to Peking, where
he was feted as an important "revolutionary leader," and to Romania
where he was similarly treated.

In June 1975 Jagan attended the Congress of Latin American and
Caribbean Communist Parties held in Havana, as a representative of
the People's Progressive Party. In his speech to the congress he
implicitly rebuked Cuba for having honored Burnham and attempted to
show that, far from developing socialism, the PNC is establishing
a system of state capitalism in which a corrupt bureaucracy, supported
by the military, is maintaining its position by repression, racial discrimination, and denial of fundamental civil rights.

However, it is widely rumored in leftwing circles in the Caribbean that the PPP delegates were urged to seek ways to work with,
rather than against, the ruling party in Guyana. Some credence was
lent to these rumors by the fact that, soon after his return to Guyana,
the two daily newspapers, the Daily Chronicle and the Guyana Graphic,
carried a photograph of Jagan and Burnham shaking hands as they met

at an open day at Kuru-kuru Cooperative College, which is one of the
major ideological showcases of the People's National Congress.*

CONCLUSIONS

It appears that the wheel has come full circle and that after 20
years Guyana may be on the brink of some kind of rapprochment between
its two major parties, major leaders, and major races. This will
indeed be a test of the shaping power of forces in the international
environment, for both parties will find it difficult to convince their
followers of the correctness of accommodation after 20 years of violent hostility. At the same time there is no doubt that a political
settlement of some kind is possible, and that there is nothing in the
so-called "cultural pluralism" of Guyana that would prevent it. What
we are seeing emerge now in Guyana is the class conflict that has
been masked by a long period of maneuvering in which the major
problem was to neutralize, or exploit, U.S. intervention.

The core of the support of the People's National Congress has
been the urban population that stood to benefit most from the expansion
of opportunity in bureaucratic complexes such as the civil service,
and the many new agencies created by the government, and who are
mainly at the middle and lower levels. This support remains firm,
but there is growing disenchantment among the working class—who
are feeling the effects of worldwide recession most acutely—and
among the old middle class that supported Burnham because of his
opposition to Jagan's socialism, and is now scandalized both by the
extension of government controls and by what it sees as Burnham's
"cult of personality." Many of the Indians who threw in their lot with
the PNC because of their opposition to socialism and their realization
of the futility of the United Force and other splinter parties also are
now alarmed at the rapid erosion of their position as businessmen.
Thus, a situation exists in which there are constant rumors of widespread opposition to Burnham and the People's National Congress,
even among people who were previously their supporters. However,
there are few signs of imminent danger to the stability of the regime.

---

*It was announced in Georgetown at the beginning of August 1975
that the People's Progressive Party would henceforth give conditional
support to the government of the People's National Congress. The
probable next step will be for the PPP to take its seats in the National
Assembly as a prelude to the formation of some sort of government
of national reconciliation.

Despite international economic conditions, Guyana has been relatively fortunate over the past few years. Following an initial dropoff in production after nationalization, the bauxite industry has recovered and prices have been good for the special refractory grade bauxite that is a Guyanese specialty. Sugar prices have been buoyant, and the government was able to cream off part of the considerable profits made possible by extremely high prices. The market for rice has been good, and the introduction of new hybrids producing high yields of white rice has enabled the rice board to obtain high prices in overseas markets. The balance of payments problem has been met by rigid controls on the exportation of funds and by a determined effort to substitute locally produced foodstuffs for imports.

Of course, the very conditions that have favored stability could produce the opposite effects; a downturn in prices for Guyana's exports could have disastrous effects. The elaborately constructed party machine with its local group organization, its paramilitary youth corps, its ideological training institutes, and its inevitable cult of personality could collapse like a house of cards, much as did Kwame Nkrumah's Convention People's Party in Ghana. Doubtless one reason why Burnham is moving into closer relations with the countries of the communist bloc is that they represent new markets to provide a hedge against wild fluctuations in prices in the West. But even more important in this respect are the commodity producers' organizations, in which Guyana is playing a leading role.

The geometry of this political economy is not markedly different from that in other West Indian territories where the major parties try to satisfy the desire for all-around increases in mobility opportunities and consumption, while attempting to retain a mass "labor" support by proclaiming socialist policies. The competition for jobs and political office that has marked the first phase of postcolonial development and has, in Guyana, been interpreted in terms of race is in reality the legacy of colonial rule and at the same time a barrier in the way of creating an integrated national society. By "an integrated national society" I do not mean a perfectly homogeneous social and cultural entity, but one in which social differentiation and cultural diversity are contained within an institutional structure providing sufficient communicative efficiency to ensure that conflict over national objectives is controlled and informed. Neither racial differences, nor cultural pluralism, nor even primordial sentiments stand in the way of Guyanese integration; it is the whole complex of factors inherited from the colonial past, including the system of concepts that asserts the existence and significance of races, and makes them available for the interpretation of social reality. One dilemma is that it is impossible to transcend the colonial past by ignoring it, but the interpretation of that past becomes at the same time the charter for the future.

The situation in Guyana has moved perceptibly toward a state of affairs in which it would be possible to create a strong central government dedicated to bringing about a basic structural transformation in the Guyana economy. That economy continues to be highly dependent upon the outside world, and it may well be that Jagan is correct in characterizing the present government as one in which national interests are subordinated to those of corrupt individuals, or of the petty bourgeoisie, or of international "imperialism." But if pressure from international communism results in a move toward the healing of the long-standing breach caused by British and U.S. action in the 1950s and 1960s, it will demonstrate once again the critical importance of the external political environment of these poor, small, and weak ex-colonial territories.

NOTES

1. C. Geertz, "The Integrative Revolution," in C. Geertz, ed., Old Societies and New States (New York: Free Press, 1963).

2. Ibid., p. 109.

3. Ibid., p. 128.

4. See G. W. Roberts, "Memorandum on the Racial Composition of British Guiana's Public Service," in Report of the British Guiana Commission of Inquiry: Racial Problems in the Public Service (Geneva: International Commission of Jurists, 1965), p. 139.

5. I have used the concepts of plantation, colonial (or creole), and modern systems as models for the exploration of the development of Guyanese society and its modes of integration and contradiction. See R. T. Smith, "Social Stratification, Cultural Pluralism and Integration in West Indian Societies," in S. Lewis and T. G. Mathews, eds., Caribbean Integration (Rio Piedras, Puerto Rico: Institute of Caribbean Studies, 1967). See also C. Jayawardena, Conflict and Solidarity in a Guianese Plantation (London: Athlone Press, 1963).

6. See E. Reubens and B. Reubens, Labour Displacement in a Labour Surplus Economy: The Sugar Industry of British Guiana (Jamaica: Institute of Social and Economic Research, 1962), for an account of the sugar industry in the 1950s.

7. See Raymond T. Smith, "Religion in the Formation of West Indian Society," in Martin Kilson and Robert Rotberg, eds., The African Diaspora: Interpretive Essays (Cambridge, Mass.: Harvard University Press, in press).

8. See Clifford Geertz, Agricultural Involution: The Processes of Ecological Change in Indonesia (Berkeley and Los Angeles: University of California Press, 1968).

9. Geertz, "The Integrative Revolution."

10. This study was financed by a grant from the National Science Foundation (GS-1709); field work was carried out in Guyana and Jamaica between 1967 and 1969 and consisted of the collection of detailed case studies focusing upon the construction of complete genealogies.

11. See Chandra Jayawardena, "Religious Belief and Social Change: Aspects of the Development of Hinduism in British Guiana," Comparative Studies in Society and History 8, no. 2 (January 1966); R. T. Smith and C. Jayawardena, "Caste and Social Status Among the Indians of Guyana," in B. M. Schwartz, ed., Caste in Overseas Indian Communities (San Francisco: Chandler, 1967).

12. See R. T. Smith, British Guiana (London: Oxford University Press, 1962), for a discussion of Guyana's constitutional and political history prior to 1953 and for a more detailed account of the political developments of the 1950s.

13. Leo Despres, in his book Cultural Pluralism and Nationalist Politics in British Guiana (Chicago: Rand McNally, 1967), puts forward the curious idea that L. F. S. Burnham was the victim of a plot that induced him to make the break with Jagan. Anyone who knew Burnham in those days (or knows him now for that matter) will realize how bizarre is such an interpretation. However, it is part of Despres's extended attempt to depict Jagan as an essentially racist leader of an Indian national party who used ideological rhetoric to rationalize policies based on Indian sectional interests. See Cheddi Jagan, The West on Trial (London: Michael Joseph, 1966), chapter 10, or L.F.S. Burnham, A Destiny to Mould (Trinidad and Jamaica: Longman Caribbean, 1970), for a different view of these events.

14. Jagan, The West on Trial, pp. 212-13.

15. The numerous attempts to achieve a coalition during the 1960s are detailed in ibid.

16. Arthur M. Schlesinger, Jr., A Thousand Days (New York: Houghton, 1965).

17. Ibid., p. 713.

18. While it would be erroneous to underestimate the extent of local opposition to Dr. Jagan and his policies, there is no doubt that rightwing elements in Guyana received considerable help from the United States—help that probably originated with the Central Intelligence Agency and was brought to bear through such organizations as the Institute for Free Labor Development and the Federation of State, County, and Municipal Employees working through the Public Services International. See Philip Agee, Inside the Company: CIA Diary (New York: Stonehill, 1975) for a discussion of the role of these organizations.

19. Although the involvement of the Central Intelligence Agency was widely suspected at the time, evidence was not forthcoming until

the revelations in 1967 of widespread penetration of student organizations, cultural bodies, and trades unions. In A History of Trade Unionism in Guyana 1900 to 1961 (Ruimveldt, Guyana: New Guyana Company, 1964), Ashton Chase provides an epilogue in which he notes that following Jagan's election in August 1961 there was "an unprecedented number of United States Trade Unionists [visiting] British Guiana stirring up opposition to the Government." He goes on to list some of the more prominent and says, "The records show that there were far more visits of US Trade Unionists to British Guiana in the 18 months following the 1961 General Elections than in the 18 years preceding the Elections. The motives behind the sudden manifestation of interest are not hard to find.

"It is known that the main purpose of these visits was organising opposition by trade unionists to the Government. The visitors also conducted courses and seminars at which the themes were invariably how to fight communism and the ways and means of opposing the Government" (pp. 290-91). He goes on to discuss the manner in which Guyanese trade unionists were given training in the United States and details the financial support funneled into Guyana to maintain the long general strike of 1963. Chase was minister of labor in the Jagan government during these years so he was familiar with the details of these happenings. By April 1967 the details of Central Intelligence Agency involvement were sufficiently known to prompt a barrage of questions in the House of Commons and the British newspaper the Sunday Times carried detailed stories relating the manner in which the trade union operation had been carried out (April 16 and 23, 1967). In response to questions in the House of Commons, Prime Minister Harold Wilson pointed out that the alleged subversion had taken place before he was in office, that he knew nothing of it, and that in any case Guyana was now an independent state for which he had no responsibility.

20. Janet Jagan, Army Intervention in the 1973 Elections in Guyana (Georgetown, Guyana: New Guyana Company, for the People's Progressive Party; PPP Education Committee Publication), pp. 7-8.

21. Declaration of Sophia: Address by Leader of the People's National Congress, Prime Minister Forbes Burnham, at a Special Congress of the People's National Congress, Pln. Sophia, Georgetown, 14th December, 1974 (Georgetown: Guyana Printers, 1975), p. 11.

22. This statement was made in the presence of the minister of education at the opening of a new school at Rosignol, a village mainly inhabited by East Indians, and it was reported in both daily newspapers. If there was any doubt about the authenticity of the report it was dispelled when the story was repeated in the PNC official weekly newspaper The New Nation, March 16, 1975, p. 2.

origins of, 173–76; Commission on National Integration, 174, 178; Constitutional Convention, 178, 181, 191; instability of regime, 190, 193; insurgents, options of, 192–93; international maneuvers over fighting, 177–78, 182–83, 184–89, 190–91; Marcos administration, ability of, to stop fighting, 191–92; Muslim discontent in, 174–76; Muslim secessionist movements, 175, 176; Philippine Constabulary, 175, 176, 177, 179; religious fighting in, 176–82, 183–85, 188, 189

PNC (see, People's National Congress)

Podgorny, Nikolai V., 114

Poland, 156, 165

Political Community and the North Atlantic Area, 22

Popular Revolutionary Movement (MPR), 132, 133, 134

Populist Party (Cyprus), 66

Portugal, 30–31

PPP (see, People's Progressive Party)

Praxis (Yugoslavia), 148, 149

Pulau Pangkor, Malaysia, 184, 185

Punjab, 108, 112; West, 92

Punjabi (language), 88

Punjabis, 88, 89, 91

Quibranza, Arsenio A., 177

Rabat, Morocco, 113

Rabushka, Alvin, and Kenneth A. Shepsle, 15

Rahman, Tanku Abdul, 177

Ramos, Major-General Fidel, 185

Razak, Tun, 179, 182, 185, 186, 188

Reid, Dr. Ptolemy A., 220

Rosenau, James N., 24

Reston, James, 30–31

Reuters, 177

Riggs, Fred, 24

Romania, 163, 166, 221

Romulo, Carlos, 182, 185, 186

Rosberg, Carl G., 12

Russett, Bruce, 6

Russia (see, Soviet Union)

Russian empire, 147

Russian Revolution, 146

Sabah (state), 172, 173, 174, 176, 180, 181, 182, 184, 185, 186, 188, 189, 190, 191, 192, 194

Sadat, Anwar, 178

Sampson, Nicos, 48

Sandys, Duncan, 214, 216

Sarawak, 190

Saudi Arabia, 183, 184, 186

Sayeed, Khalid Bin, 106

Schedlich, H. (see, Mueller, H., and H. Schedlich)

Scheut Fathers, 131

Schlesinger, Arthur M., Jr., 211–12, 214, 215

Schweigler, Gebhard, 156, 157

Scotland, 17

SEATO, 102, 109, 182

security community, 3

SED (see, Socialist Unity Party)

Shatt-al-Arab, 31

Shepsle, Kenneth A. (see, Rabushka, Alvin, and Kenneth A. Shepsle)

Shibli, 90

Shoup Registration Systems International Inc., 217

Siegel, Ulrike, 161

Sind (province), 91, 100, 112

Sindhis, 89, 91, 108

Singapore, 173

Six Points formula, 106, 107–08, 110, 112, 113

ABOUT THE EDITOR AND CONTRIBUTORS

STEPHANIE G. NEUMAN teaches International Relations on the Graduate Faculty of the New School for Social Research, and is a Research Associate at the Bureau of Applied Social Research, Columbia University. Previously she was Assistant Professor at Lehman College, and has also served on the faculty at Hunter College and Douglass College. She is Associate International Relations Editor at Intellect magazine, and is Chairperson of the Divided Nations Internet of the International Studies Association. Dr. Neuman holds a Ph.D. from New York University.

ARTHUR M. HANHARDT, JR. is Professor of Political Science at the University of Oregon. He has been Chairperson of the Research Committee on the German Democratic Republic of the Conference Group on German Politics, and has travelled several times to both the Federal Republic of Germany and the German Democratic Republic. He is the author of The German Democratic Republic, and his articles appear frequently in scholarly journals. Dr. Hanhardt earned his Ph.D. at Northwestern University.

INAYATULLAH is Development Administration Expert at the Asian Centre for Development Administration, Kuala Lumpur, Malaysia. Earlier he was Associate Professor of International Relations at the University of Islamabad, Pakistan. His most recent book, Transfer of the Western Development Model to Asia, was published in 1975. Inayatullah earned a doctoral degree at Indiana University.

LYMAN H. LEGTERS is Professor of Russian and East European Studies, Institute for Comparative and Foreign Area Studies, University of Washington. His articles appear in such periodicals as the New Republic, Saturday Review, Intellect, and the Russian Review; his books include Research in the Social Sciences and Humanities. Dr. Legters studied at the Free University of Berlin, from which he received a doctoral degree.

WYATT MACGAFFEY is Professor of Anthropology at Haverford College. He is the author of Custom and Government in the Lower Congo, and is a frequent contributor to numerous journals of African studies. Dr. MacGaffey earned his Ph.D. at the University of California, Los Angeles.

LELA GARNER NOBLE is Professor of Political Science at San Jose State University. Her articles have appeared in Asian Survey and the Silliman Journal (Philippines). Dr. Noble holds M.A. M.A.L.D., and Ph.D. degrees from the Fletcher School of Law and Diplomacy, Tufts University.

ADAMANTIA POLLIS is Associate Professor of Political Science on the Graduate Faculty of the New School for Social Research. She has taught at Hunter College, the University of Oklahoma, and the University of Maryland (overseas), and was Visiting Professor at the University of Essex in England. She earned her doctorate at Johns Hopkins University.

WILLIAM SHARP completed his undergraduate work at the University of Oregon. In 1974 he was an Intern of the Conference Group on German Politics in Berlin. He is currently studying at the University of Oregon Law School.

RAYMOND T. SMITH is Professor of Anthropology and Chairperson of the Department of Anthropology at the University of Chicago. He has been Professor of Sociology at the University of Ghana, Professor of Anthropology at the University of the West Indies, and Visiting Professor at the University of California, Berkeley, and at McGill University in Montreal. Dr. Smith is the author of several books including British Guiana, and has published numerous articles that examine society and culture in the West Indies. He holds a doctoral degree from Cambridge University, England.

THE INFLUENCE OF EAST EUROPE AND THE
SOVIET WEST ON THE USSR
> edited by Roman Szporluk

THE POLITICS OF DIVISION, PARTITION,
AND UNIFICATION
> edited by Ray E. Johnston

SOUTH ASIAN CRISIS: INDIA, PAKISTAN,
AND BANGLA DESH: A Political and Historical
Analysis of the 1971 War
> Robert Jackson

THE SOVIET WEST: Interplay Between
Nationality and Social Organization
> edited by Ralph S. Clem